Head Dress of the British Heavy Cavalry

Head Dress of the British Heavy Cavalry

Dragoon Guards, Household and Yeomanry Cavalry 1842-1934

David JJ Rowe

Schiffer Military History
Atglen, PA

Dedicated to the Memory of
the late Anna Pollak O.B.E.
Mezzo-Soprano of Sadler's Wells Opera

Book design by Robert Biondi.

Library of Congress Catalog Number: 99-62260.

Printed in China.
ISBN: 0-7643-0957-9

We are interested in hearing from authors with book ideas on related topics.

Published by Schiffer Publishing Ltd.
4880 Lower Valley Road
Atglen, PA 19310 USA
Phone: (610) 593-1777
FAX: (610) 593-2002
E-mail: Schifferbk@aol.com.
Visit our web site at: www.schifferbooks.com
Please write for a free catalog.
This book may be purchased from the publisher.
Please include $3.95 postage.
Try your bookstore first.

In Europe, Schiffer books are distributed by:
Bushwood Books
6 Marksbury Ave.
Kew Gardens
Surrey TW9 4JF
England
Phone: 44 (0)208 392-8585
FAX: 44 (0)208 392-9876
E-mail: Bushwd@aol.com.
Free postage in the UK. Europe: air mail at cost.
Try your bookstore first.

Contents

Foreword

By William Y. Carman F.S.A., F.R.HIST.S. F.C.M.C.H. (USA), former Deputy Director of the National Army Museum at the Royal Military Academy, Sandhurst and in Chelsea, London.

Those who have already read any of the articles written by the author will appreciate the depth of his research as well as the coverage of past writing on metal cavalry helmets, this book being a conception of detail often neglected in the past. I know of no one else who has applied himself so firmly to the intricacies of the evolving types of head-dresses and the varied sources of information and recording, which are made so clear to all.

Owning, as he does, many of the actual helmets, he has been able hands-on to examine the smallest particular of manufacturing, which, plus the additional information gathered on helmets in private possession has enabled him to assemble valuable classifications.

He includes the minutia needed to understand the variations chosen by the regiment to display its own speciality which soon points out how a helmet could be faked or just have fittings added to present a complete helmet.

The quotations from official documents show the author's persistent pursuit for genuine facts to demonstrate how reliable the result is with no concession to vague dating or confusion of basic facts.

The wide sphere of sources which the author has used show that little has been elusive and the result is a major work that is not easy to improve. However, as in all specialist subjects, there is not always a final word, especially in the yeomanry field where an unknown item of head-dress may appear, either because the yeomanry units lacks records, or they have not been published.

However, I am sure that all who read this book will have learned much, and will have enjoyed the ease of understanding many traditional methods of production where many of the skills have disappeared never to return.

Acknowledgements

My thanks go to the late Anna Pollak O.B.E. who over many years encouraged me to 'put pen to paper' and to record and share the knowledge acquired over many years relating to cavalry helmets. Thanks to Malcolm Fisher, of Regimentals, London for 'finding' me a publisher, to W.Y. (Bill) Carman F.S.A.,F.R.HIST.S. for kindly agreeing to write the foreword for this book, and for permitting me to quote from the many books written by him, to Ron Harris for also allowing me to quote extracts from his many publications. To Major Paddy Kirsting, Curator of the Household Cavalry Museum for allowing me to closely examine helmets in the museum's collection, to Geoff Frost M.AMS for reading every chapter and checking the details with a fine tooth comb, for taking the photographs of the 1842 Royal Horse Guards officers pattern helmet and for permitting the use of the photograph of the Hertfordshire Yeomanry helmet and others in his collection, and to my good friend, the late John Collins formerly of the 5th Royal Inniskilling Dragoon Guards.

I also express my thanks to the following for their assistance. Peter D. Athawes, R.Q.M.C. Les Atkinson of the Blues and Royals, the late Leslie Barlow, Michael Blacklock, J.M. Brereton, M.D. Brittain, Brian Daly, Major David Ellis of 251 Squadron, The Royal Signals, Phil Greenaway, Philip J. Haythornthwaite, Captain G.W. Howson, The Life Guards, Hugh King P.AMS, W. Lambert Esq, Roy Manser, R.J. Marrion Esq, Sergeant Sam McKee R.E.M.E., P.J.R. Mileham, Frank Mitchell, John and Boris Mollo, Bill Mortimer, Christopher Rothero, J.D. Sainsbury, R.J. Smith, Robert Twedwen, J.N.P. Watson, formerly of the Royal Horse Guards, Ray Westlake, F. Wilkinson Esq, Major Roy Wilson, Mrs Hermione Wynn, secretary to Colonel Sir Mike Ansell, formerly of the 5th Royal Inniskilling Dragoon Guards, and to Mr T. Hodgson, the Curator of the Hollytrees Museum, Colchester.

Finally I express my appreciation to the staff of the following establishments and publications, and to the members of the societies listed, for their assistance in one form or other. Essex County Libraries Services, Hampshire County Libraries, the Prince Consort's Library, Aldershot, Adam & Charles Black (Publishers), Aldershot Military Museum, Almark Publishing Co Ltd, Band International Magazine, Her Majesty's Stationery Office, Military Modelling Magazine, Regiment Magazine, The Guards Magazine,The Household Cavalry Regiment and Regimental Museum, Soldier Magazine, Blunderbuss Antiques, Bosleys Military Auctioneers and Valuers, Christies South Kensington Limited, Military Antiques (Islington), Phillips Auctioneers, Spinks Auctioneers, Tradition (London), Wallis and Wallis of Lewes, Sussex, and to The Aldershot Militaria Society, The Crown Imperial Society, and last but not least The Society for Army Historical Research.

List of Plates

1

Introduction

Having first become interested some twenty-seven years ago in the metal full dress helmets worn by cavalry regiments of the British Army both regular and yeomanry during the period c. 1842 to 1922 inclusive, I have over the years amassed a considerable amount of both photographic and written material on this subject. I was however continually disappointed to find that there was an almost total lack of reference books on this specialised subject available to the serious collector of head-dress. There are of course a few notable exceptions, two most informative of which being the books by the noted author W.Y. Carman on both the regular and yeomanry cavalry head-dress, and R.H. Rankin's excellent book entitled *'A Pictorial History of Military Head -Dress 1660-1914*, which whilst covering most types of military head-dress, both british and continental, due to its vast scope, only briefly covers the metal helmet worn by the cavalry regiments of the British Army.

The only other source of reference known to the author are the *'Dress Regulations for the Army for 1846 and for 1900 and 1934'*, originally published by the Adjutant-Generals Office and the War Office respectively, these publications being on sale several years ago as a reprinted books. Regrettably these official publications give very little instructive information on the metal cavalry helmet, there being only a brief description of the officers full dress helmet in the 1846 version. However for the 1900 publication there was additional information on the various pattern of helmet plate worn by each regiment, accompanied by an illustration depicting an example of a Life Guards officers helmet and similar illustration of a 3rd Dragoon Guards officers helmet. The Dress Regulations of 1934 also gave information of the pattern of helmet plates worn, but regrettably there were no illustrations as such.

Over the years several articles have been published in various British militaria journals and magazines concerning British cavalry helmets, however, they all either covered the generally known patterns and therefore did not go into any great detail, or if covering the 1871 pattern officers helmet, quoted verbatim to the descriptions as given in the Dress Regulations *of 1900 and 1934. Additionally* these articles failed to explore the possibility of the existence of other examples of helmet plates, this being a subject that has not been omitted in this book

Whilst the distinctive devices on both the officers and the other ranks full dress helmet plate, and in some instances the plume colour, are unique to individual regiments, and therefore are of some assistance in identifying a particular helmet, there are other less obvious means of identification. Very little for example has been written or recorded of the fittings to the officers pattern helmet, such as the chinchain, ear rosettes, plume holder and the actual plume rosette which in my research has been identified as tending to differ in pattern for several of the regiments concerned and can therefore be used as an aid to identification.

With the current and foreseeable shortage of good condition, undamaged helmets available for purchase by the collector and the limited availability of head-dress from either arms fairs, auction sales or specialist militaria dealers, and with prices for helmets in any condition continually rising, a prospective buyer needs to feel reasonably confident that the helmet under consideration for purchase is 'all belonging' and that it has not been fitted with associated parts sometime during its life, albeit that the replacement parts may have come from another helmet.

It is possible and indeed likely, that on helmets currently and in the future to be offered for sale that there may be associated fittings or even reproduced parts, which not originally belonging to the helmet have a tendency to reduce its collectable appeal and its saleable value. These parts might include such fittings as the ear rosettes, the chinchain or more likely the plume, all of which over the years have been expertly reproduced. In consideration of the above and for the purposes of this book, I have therefore separated the composite parts of the helmet into named component categories to assist the identification of the correct pattern fittings most likely to be seen on an officers and an other ranks helmet of the regular cavalry and the yeomanry cavalry regiments of the British Army.

• • •

Before concluding this chapter, I wish to state that I do not consider myself to be an 'expert' on British metal cavalry helmets, but merely a knowledgeable student of this most interesting item of military head-dress. That said, whilst it has been a 'labour of love' to write this book, and every effort has been made to include information on all the known patterns of British metal cavalry helmets of the period 1842 to 1934, I acknowledge that it is possible that there exists a variation of any of the helmets described in this book, of which the author has no knowledge. Indeed, such an example may well exist within the private collection of a reader of this book, the owner being unaware that within their collection is an previously unrecorded and unique example of a particular item helmet. Should this prove to be the case, then I sincerely hope that the collector concerned will make known the particulars of the item of head-dress, anonymously or otherwise, in order that the relevant details may be recorded and made available to present and future collectors.

2

Purchase and Supply of the Helmet

Officers

Collectors of militaria will I am sure already be aware that during the period with which this book is concerned a commissioned officer was responsible for the ordering and purchase of his own accoutrements, helmet, sword and uniform. These items were obtained from the outfitter or military tailor appointed to the particular regiment in which the officer was to serve, who maintained pattern books showing the relevant uniform details.

Alas a great many of these fine establishments have over the years either merged or ceased trading altogether, many of whom at one time had premises in Aldershot, the '**Home of the British Army**', whilst many more had premises in London. The following is a brief list of some of the better known outfitters/tailors with the title of the regiment's they are known to have supplied being given alongside each 'outfitters' name:

Messrs Andrew of Pall Mall	Life Guards
Bates of Jermyn Street	7th Dragoon Guards
Hamburger and Company of Covent Garden (Makers of the 1847 pattern helmet)	Regiments of both the Dragoon Gds & Dragoons
Hawkes and Company of Piccadilly	2nd Life Guards, 4th (Royal Irish) Dragoon Guards, Norfolk Yeomanry, and the Montgomeryshire Yeomanry Cavalry
Jenner & Co, 56 Conduit Street	The Essex Yeomanry
Sandilands of 12 Pondwick Street	3rd Dragoon Guards

Additionally most Garrison towns such as the aforementioned Aldershot in the south, Colchester in the east, and York in the north of England also had their fair share of regimental outfitters.

As with most things in life, the more one pays, the better the quality, a good example of this being a helmet in the private collection of an acquaintance of mine, which once belonged to an officer who in c. 1872 transferred from a 'light cavalry' regiment to one of the Dragoon Guards Regiments. His helmet, which would normally have been of copper and brass covered in gilt, actually consisted of the skull, plume mount, and helmet plate etc being of hall marked solid silver, which was then gilded to give it a gold colour in order to conform with the relevant Dress Regulations.

At the turn of the nineteenth century for an officer in one of Queen Victoria's elite regiments of cavalry, the cost of providing a complete uniform, including helmet, sword, and saddlery was to say the least most expensive. Few, if any Victorian cavalry officers could afford to live on their army pay, however as a great many of them came from either titled, or well to do English 'country seat' families this financial outlay was probably not a great hardship.

A prime example of the 'officer class' in the cavalry just prior to the turn of the nineteenth century, is exemplified by the following named officers who were serving in the three Household Cavalry Regiments in 1897 (1).

1st Life Guards	
Lieutenant Colonel	Sir S.M. Lockhart Bt, M.V.O
Captain	Hon C.E. Bingham
Captain	**H.S.H. Prince Adolphous A.A.E.G.P.L.L. of Teck. K.C.V.O.**
2nd Lieutenant	Hon R.M. Hall
2nd Life Guards	
Lieutenant Colonel	The Earl of Dundonald C.B. M.V.O.
Captain	The Earl of Longford
Lieutenant	**Hon M. Bowes-Lyon**
Lieutenant	Sir E.P. Stacey Bt
Royal Horse Guards	
Major	Lord G. Binning
Captain	Viscount A.J.C. Sudley
Lieutenant	Viscount H.W. Chrichton
2nd Lieutenant	Duke of Roxburghe
2nd Lieutenant	Viscount C.S.H. Castlereagh

Of particular interest are the following details taken from a copy invoice dated 1903 that was submitted by Messrs Hawkes and Company, Helmet, Army Cap and Accoutrement makers of 14 Piccadilly, London, to an officer serving in the 2nd Life Guards. The invoice reveals that the cost of his helmet and **plume was £12.0.0., his full dress tunic** was £19.19.0, his wire cord aiguillette's with case cost £13.0.0, his front and back cuirasses were £18.18.0 and his sword cost £6.0.0., making a total of £69.17.0 for these few items of uniform alone (2). Hardly a small outlay when one ponders what the average income of a working class labourer might have been at the beginning of the twentieth century. N.B. In 1896 the approximate annual cost of clothing a rank and file member of the Life Guards was £7.6s.0d.

It is also of interest that directly after the Second World War, the then Secretary of State for England, Lord Shinwell was reported as "being *delighted with the proposal that the Household Cavalry should once more adopt full dress for ceremonial occasions".* The problem however was the supply of officers full dress uniforms which had always been their private property. Lord Shinwell agreed to a small committee being formed, under the Chairmanship of the Marquess of Cambridge, a former officer in the 1st Life Guards, to purchase items of full dress uniforms from past serving officers. In view of the likely cost of a complete full dress uniform, including horse furniture etc at this period of time, it is hardly surprising that such a major problem arose and that decisive action was needed in order that once again the Household Cavalry Regiments could be seen in their full splendour on the streets of London.

Warrant Officers

Warrant Officers in the Household Cavalry were, and still are issued with their full dress helmets, which closely resemble the commissioned officer's pattern, the most noticeable difference being in the plume domes which are of the other ranks pattern in white metal, unlike the officers which are of gilt metal and differ between each regiment.

Dress Regulation for the other ranks uniforms were not produced and there seems to be no uniformity with regards to the full dress helmet and uniform worn by Warrant Officers, such as the Regimental Sergeant Major, and the Bandmaster in the British Cavalry of the Line, the quality of their uniform appearing to vary from regiment to regiment.

There exists a most interesting photograph of the R.S.M. of the 4th Dragoon Guards in full dress c. 1881 in which it can clearly be seen that his tunic is of N.C.O.'s quality, albeit with slightly more gold braid to the collar of his tunic, whilst his helmet is most definitely of officers pattern. Conversely there is a photograph of R.S.M. Barry of the King's Dragoon Guards c. 1897 which shows him holding his helmet which is of other ranks pattern, whilst the lace to his collar is not unlike that on a junior officers tunic. And to confuse the matter further there is a photograph of the Bandmaster of the 3rd Carabiniers (Prince of Wales's Dragoon Guards) taken c. 1927 which shows him holding what is clearly an officers pattern helmet and wearing a tunic of officers quality. N.B. In a photograph c. 1899 of the Regimental Sergeant Major of the 9th (Queen's Royal) Lancers it can clearly be seen that he is wearing the officers swan feathers plume in place of a horsehair one in his chapka (lance cap). Additionally his tunic is close to being of officers quality, as is his waist girdle.

With regard to the above subject I have it on good authority that during late 'Victorian' period and the 'Edwardian' era and possibly even later, that when a Regimental Sergeant Major was newly appointed, the officers of his regiment contributed financially towards the cost of his full dress uniform, which would also of course include his helmet, and if this explanation is borne of truth it would help explain much of the 'mix and match' of the Warrant Officers uniform as described above.

Other Ranks

Accoutrements, uniform, sword, saddlery and of course the head-dress was issued to the rank and file soldier. As of 1848 these issue items were divided into clothing, necessaries and accoutrements, being governed by the Royal Warrant and Regulations Regarding Army Services, which specified the articles to be provided, and how often. For the heavy cavalry, the metal helmet complete with plume was at this period to be replaced once every four years.

It is possible for a collector to come across a helmet that has an issue mark on the brass rim of the rear peak. e.g. 1DG 9941432 indicating that the helmet was issued to a soldier serving in the 1st (King's) Dragoon Guards. It is not unusual for a helmet to have the issue mark of one regiment, whilst bearing the helmet plate of another regiment, however this does not necessarily indicate that the helmet has been 'made up' of assorted contemporary parts. This helmet plate/issue mark difference might have occurred when a regiment that was below strength received a draft of men from a similar regiment, the drafted men taking their head-dress with them, where upon arrival it was then only necessary for the plate of the new regiment to be fitted to their helmets.

An excellent example of a soldier moving from one regiment to another occurred during the long military career of one John Cusack M.M., who joined the 2nd Dragoons (Royal Scots Greys) in 1908, was posted to the 1st (Royal) Dragoons in 1909/10, and was in 1917 posted again, this time to the 6th (Inniskilling) Dragoons, this being the regiment he was serving with when being awarded the Military Medal during the First World War. At the cessation of hostilities he continued to serve as a professional soldier and in 1919 was again posted to another regiment, this time to the Mounted Military Police.

3

Component Parts that Make Up the Helmet

For ease of reference and identification the helmet has been broken down into its component parts, and throughout this book the following is the sequence in which each item of head-dress will be described. As with any manufactured item there will always be slight variations in design, dimensions and quality, and the fact that there might exist a helmet where the colour of the head lining, or the chinchain backing differs slightly from the colour described in this book does not in any way indicate the item concerned is 'wrong', but more probably that the difference is simply a manufacturers variation. N.B. It is not intended however to imply, that the order in which the component parts are listed below, would have been the sequence of assembly used by a helmet manufacturer.

1. The Skull
2. The Plume Holder
3. The Headband and Lining
4. The Helmet Plate
5. The Ear Rosettes
6. The Chinchain
7. The Plume
8. The Plume Rosette

In addition to giving a full description of the make-up of the helmet for each of the regular cavalry regiments, I have included information regarding the amalgamation of the regiments, concerned, their changes of title, regimental personalities, and other information that I hope will be of relevance to both the collectors of cavalry head-dress and to readers interested in the regiments covered by this book.

4

Regiments: The Household Cavalry

The Household Cavalry Regiment can through various changes of titles (see Appendix 2) trace its ancestry back to the gentlemen cavaliers who followed King Charles II into exile and were with him at his Restoration in 1660, these troops eventually becoming the Life Guards. The Royal Horse Guards (now the Blues and Royals) can trace their history back to the same period, being the descendants of troops of parliamentary cavalry who upon their disbandment took up service with King Charles II.

A Brief Description of some of the Major Items of The Last Pattern of Officers Full Dress Uniform.

Aiguillettes

First worn c. 1829, the name is French and means needles, this referring to the trophy tags (points) which hang at the end of the shoulder cords, which are made of 15 ligne plaited Gold Wire Basket Cord. N.B. The aiguillettes of Warrant Officers are made of 11 ligne plaited Gold Oris Basket Cord (12).

Boots

The high 'wing' tipped boots worn since 1812 are known as jack boots because the leather was "jacked" or stiffened (4A). These days the boots are made from calf leather and dressed hide, with the uppers, welts, seats, and heels all being hand sewn. For the Life Guards the spurs, chains, and buckles are made of nickel, with the straps being of light hide, however in the Blues and Royals whilst the spurs are of nickel, the chains and buckles are made of brass (12).

Breeches

Also known as pantaloons, they were originally buff and were coloured with ochre. The pantaloons were changed to white in 1812 for all three Household Cavalry regiments (4A), and are made from buckskin.

Cartouche Belt and Box

There are two differing patterns of cartouche belt, the one known as the 'Gold' belt being of gold lace, and mounted on red morocco leather for the Life Guards, and on crimson morocco leather in the Royal Horse Guards, these belts being worn mainly when in mounted or dismounted review order. The other belt known as the 'White' belt is of white buff leather and is worn when in guard order, undress, and No. 1 dress. The colour of the flask cord which is held in the centre of the belt by loops, differed slightly being red for the 1st Life Guards, blue for the 2nd Life Guards, and red for the Royal Horse Guards (12).

The cartouche box was originally used to carry powder and shot in the bygone days of flintlock weapons. However with the improvements to firearms and the introduction of percussion weapons and the breech loading carbine, the cartouche box was no longer needed for its original intention, and it became a purely ornamental item. There were slight differences for each of the three regiments, with the box for the 1st Life Guards having a small gilt badge and being smaller overall than the one worn by the 2nd Life Guards, with the Royal Horse Guards having their own pattern of cartouche box, on the flap of which was the Royal Arms in dead frosted gilt.

Cuirasses

A pamphlet produced by the Household Cavalry Museum (4A) states that, *'The old cuirasses worn from 1661 to 1730 were black and not worn for ceremonial occasions, and not worn at all from 1730 to 1821'* (4a). However in his book on the dress of the Life Guards (4B), Charles Stadden a military artist and model maker noted for his accuracy to detail, illustrates two officers of the 1st Life Guards c. 1817 wearing polished steel cuirasses with a gilt ornament to the centre. Additional W.Y. Carman confirms that at the Great Review of June 1814 special cuirasses were worn by the Life Guards, and that all three Household Cavalry regiments were wearing them by 1817 (101). Polished steel cuirasses with gilt scales, straps, and buckles of regimental pattern were worn at the Coronation of King George IV in 1821, which with some alterations are very similar to those worn today. The cuirasses are lined with red morocco and edged with velvet, blue in colour for the Life Guards, and maroon for the Royal Horse Guards, with regimental pattern straps being worn with the cuirasses.

Tunic

The full dress tunic dates from 1856 being for the Life Guards of scarlet cloth with dark blue velvet to the collar and cuffs, having gold laurel, oak, and acorn leaf decoration, with laurel and oak embroidery to the rear skirts. The colours are reversed for the Royal Horse Guards, the tunic being of dark blue cloth with scarlet collar and cuffs, and having gold embroidery as for the Life Guards. Gilt button are worn by both regiments and are of regimental pattern.

Waist Belt and Sword Slings

There are two types of waist belt worn, the 'Gold' belt and the 'White' belt, each being of regimental pattern. The gold belt is of regimental pattern gold lace, whilst the white belt is of buff leather, each belt being fitted a frosted gilt belt plate, again of regimental pattern. The sword slings 'Gold' are of a slightly differing pattern for each regiment, whilst the 'White' slings are the same for both regiments (12).

Active Service

Whilst the Household Cavalry is famous throughout the world for their ceremonial duties, prior to being mechanized they were true fighting horsed cavalrymen in every sense of the word, having seen action in battles too numerous to mention. The battle honours awarded up to the outbreak of the Great War bear testimony to their great fighting abilities, and the following are the names of some of those honours: Dettingen, Peninsula, Waterloo, Tel-el-Kebir, Egypt, Relief of Kimberley, Paardberg, and South Africa 1899-1902.

Amalgamations

In 1922 the 1st Life Guards and the 2nd Life Guards were amalgamated to form the regiment known today as The Life Guards, with the Royal Horse Guards being merged with The Royal Dragoons (1st Dragoons) in 1969 to form the Blues and Royals (Royal Horse Guards & 1st Dragoons).

The Head-Dress Prior To 1842

It was not until the 12th March 1812 that a warrant was raised and the Life Guards were authorised to wear a brass helmet with a horsehair crest, the Royal Horse Guards at this time not being fully accepted as Household Cavalry, and wearing differing head-dresses (3).

Various patterns of head-dress were worn by the officers and men during the period 1812 to 1842, and for those collectors of helmets wishing to study the helmets of this period further and in greater detail, I strongly recommend the most informative book by W.Y. Carman F.S.A., F.R., Hist.S. entitled 'Head Dresses of the British Army - Cavalry.

The 1842 'Albert' Pattern Helmet

The Officers Pattern (See Fig: 1.)

The Prince Consort has been credited with the idea of the German style helmet authorised for the Household Cavalry in 1842 (4). At this period there were three regiments of Household Cavalry, these being the 1st Life Guards, the 2nd Life Guards, and the Royal Horse Guards. However it was not until 1846 that official mention of this new pattern helmet was made in a publication produced by the Adjutant-General's Office, Horse Guards, entitled 'Regulations for the Dress of General, Staff, and Regimental Officers of The Army 1846, in which the description read as follows: *Life Guards "of German silver, plume of white horsehair" and Royal Horse Guards, "of German silver, plume of red horse hair"*, hardly an enlightening description to say the least.

Eleven years later, the 1857 version of the above mentioned publication was produced, however it also gave very little additional useful information, merely describing the helmet as *being of "German silver mounted with gilt ornaments, and silver garter star in front"* I therefore hope that the detailed description of this pattern of helmet given in this chapter, will help to make up for the lack of official information, and will be of interest.

Probably the most famous officer ever to wear the 1842 pattern Household Cavalry helmet was Field Marshal Henry William Paget, 1st Marquess of Angelsey[1] K.G., G.C.B., G.C.H. who was Colonel of the Royal Horse Guards from 1842 to 1854. N.B. There is an excellent colour painting depicting the Marquis of Angelsey in full dress uniform holding his helmet, in the officers mess at Combermere Barracks, Windsor, which is reproduced in colour, full page size, in the Regiment Magazine (50).

The Skull

The early pattern skulls measured between 9" and 9 1/2" in height from the crown of the skull down to the top of the front peak, and were far more dome shaped than the later 1871 pattern skulls. Made of German silver/silver plated or in some cases of best quality white metal.

The skull consisted of a left and a right hand section joined in the centre, to which was added the front and rear peak sections. The two skull sections were soldered together to form the dome shaped skull, whilst the peaks were attached to the skull by means of small rivets, the joints being hidden from view by the gilt metal oak-leaf band that encircled the waist of the skull.

At the front of the skull was a very short 3/4" wide oak-leaf band covering the front seam joint, which extended downwards from beneath the front finial of the plume mount base (described later) terminating beneath the top of the crown that surmounted the helmet plate. It was secured by means of the stud on the underside of the band, positioned close to its top, being passed through a corresponding hole in the skull and secured by a nut. Additionally, at the bottom of this band was a hole through which passed the top stud of the helmet plate, again being secured with a nut.

At the rear of the skull was a 1" wide band of similar design to cover the rear skull joint which extended downwards from beneath the rear finial of the foliated plume mount base, and terminated beneath the edge of the rear peak binding. This band was attached to the skull by means of two short studs located at the back of the band being passed through corresponding holes in the skull and then secured as above. Around the waist of the skull was the aforementioned gilt metal floriated band being 3/4 inches in depth, which was attached by means of small rivets.

The peak edges were bound with gilt metal, with the peaks themselves being decorated with large gilt acanthus sprays, which were attached by what appear to be small rivets. These acanthus sprays, could depending on the depth of the front peak cover it entirely, albeit that on the early pattern helmets the peak was so long that it came down as far as the tip of the wearers nose. See Fig: 1A. for an illustration of the acanthus spray decoration to the rear peak. The inner section of the peaks was lined with a thin leather known as skiver, which was usually dark green in colour. N.B .*It is said that in 1856, a shorter peak was introduced, at the wish of Queen Victoria, who liked to be able to recognise the Officers of her Escort* (4).

The Plume Holder

This consisted of a gilt foliated plume socket, having seven, or more commonly eight finials, which fitted inside a shorter socket of similar pattern, but having four, multi-petalled leaf finials. The socket measured approx. 2 1/2" from the tip of the finial down to the point where it joined the gilt metal floriated base, which itself had eight multi-leafed finials. The complete plume base/socket assembly was secured to the skull by passing the three studs positioned as in north, east and west, or alternatively four studs situated at all four points of the compass. These studs, located on the underside of the plume mount base, were

Figure 1: Royal Horse Guards 1842 officers pattern. The helmet shown complete in all its splendour. Compare the front peak decoration with that of the other ranks helmet as illustrated in Fig: 2. Photo: G. Frost. Courtesy of the Household Cavalry Museum.

Figure 1a: Rear view of helmet. Note the profusion of acanthus spray decoration to the rear peak. Photo: G. Frost. Courtesy of the Household Cavalry Museum.

Figure 1b: Inside view of helmet showing the felt headband. Photo: G. Frost Courtesy of the Household Cavalry Museum.

Figure 1c: Officers 1842 pattern plume. Of particular interest is the square 'ball' located just above the threaded part of the stem base. Photo: G. Frost. Courtesy of the Household Cavalry Museum.

passed through corresponding holes in the upper part of the skull onto which was then placed a brass nut. The rear stud of the plume mount base also assisted in securing the rear oak leaf seam band to the skull, as this stud passed through a hole located at the top of the band and on through the hole a the skull. N.B. On one helmet examined by the author a thin 'home made', steel plate had been affixed to the inside of the skull at the point where the plume stem entered the helmet to give the crown of the skull additional strength. This fitment was secured in place by the studs on the plume base (4).

It is not unusual to find that some of the finials at the top of the plume socket are either bent inwards, outwards, or in some cases completely missing, as overtightening the plume retaining "fly nut" (described later) tended to pull the plume downwards into the socket bringing pressure to bear on the delicate finials, and thus causing damage to them. (See Fig: 1A.)

The Headband and Lining

With one exception, the few 1842 officers pattern helmets of the Household Cavalry examined by the author were minus their head lining. However one Life Guards helmet seen by the author had a cloth lining similar to that fitted to the later pattern helmets, and a Royal Horse Guards officers helmet also seen, had traces of a leather lining, with a red silk upper section which had a drawstring to enable the wearer to adjust the lining for a comfortable fit.

The lining was sewn onto the headband, which was of either pressed felt (See Fig: 1B.), or alternatively of hard leather, and was attached to the skull by the ear rosette socket. This socket, which was located just above the leaf and scroll band that encircle the waist of the helmet, was passed through a small hole cut into the headband, and then on through a further corresponding hole at the side of the skull, where it was secured by two small rivets with washers, the rivets passing through both the headband and the skull. It was onto this socket that the chinchain was secured, being held in place by the ear rosette.

The Helmet Plate

As mentioned earlier, the 'Dress Regulations' of 1846 and of 1857 gave very little useful descriptive information, and to be fair to whoever compiled these publications, the writer of same had no way of knowing of the wide interest that would be shown in the finite detail of these helmets, by collectors and students of military dress well over one hundred and fifty years after the original text was written.

The plate itself consisted of a wreath of laurel leaves (left) and oak leaves (right) encircling a rococo pattern shield surmounted by a large "Victorian" crown, the whole in gilt metal. Upon the shield was a silver Garter star, onto which was mounted a gilt metal oval shaped Garter, pierced with the motto "Honi Soit Qui Mal Y Pense."[2] on a blue translucent enamel ground. Within the Garter, the cross in red translucent enamel framed in gilt metal on a silver ground (See Fig: 1.). The plate/badge consisted of four separate pieces, these being as follows: the crown/wreath/rococo shield, the silver Garter star, the gilt Garter, and the back plate onto which was laid the enamel.

The helmet plate was assembled by placing the enameled back plate within the garter, which had two small lugs positioned at east and west, these lugs were then passed down through corresponding slots in both the Garter star and the rococo shield/wreath where it was secured by means of a thin brass pin which passed through a small hole at the end of each of the two lugs. The complete helmet plate was then attached to the skull of the helmet by passing the three/four studs located at the back of the rococo shield, together with a stud at the rear of the crown, through corresponding holes in the skull and by then securing them with brass nuts. N.B. It is of interest that on this pattern of helmet plate the Garter and the Star were noticeably smaller than on the later version, and that it lacked the "Collar of the Garter", which will be mentioned again later in this chapter.

The Ear Rosettes

The gilt metal ear rosettes were of a rose pattern, with a single row of seven petals, being similar in appearance to the rosettes fitted to the Dragoon Guards helmets. They had a threaded stud brazed/soldered to the inside centre of the rosette, which when screwed onto the ear rosette socket held the chinchain in place. N.B. On a helmet examined at the premises of a Sussex auction house, the ear rosette did not have the usual threaded stud, as in its place were two metal prongs which where passed through corresponding slots in the side of the skull to secure the chinchain.

The Chinchain

The chinchain was of gilt metal links sewn onto either a black leather backing, or alternatively black leather backed with black velvet. The chinchain measured some nineteen and a half inches in length, being one and a quarter inches in width, and as mentioned earlier was secured to the helmet by being attached to the ear socket lug. N.B. On the helmet seen at a Sussex salesroom as mentioned above, the loose end of the chinchain was held in place by a hook which hung down from, and was secured behind the lower petals of the ear rosette.

The Plume

The plume was white for both the 1st, and the 2nd regiment of Life Guards, and red in colour for the Royal Horse Guards, being of horsehair, or alternatively of shredded whalebone. The falling plume was bound to a cloth covered wooden circular mound which gave the plume its shape, there being a threaded stud at the top of the plume stem onto which was screwed the rosette. The falling plume measured some eighteen and a half inches from top of the plume rosette down to the bottom of the plume.

To the base of the falling hair plume was a "shaving brush" tuft of the same colour and composition as the main plume, with a brass threaded shaft at its base which terminated with a brass threaded stud onto which would be secured the plume securing "fly nut". Above the brass threaded shaft was a **brass square 'ball'**, which prevented the plume from being pulled to far down into the plume socket (See Fig: 1C.). The plume was secured to the helmet by passing the brass threaded stud down through the plume socket and base, and on through a corresponding hole in the skull of the helmet, where the plume was finally secured by the brass "fly nut" being screwed onto the threaded part of the plume stem.

The 'fly nut' consisted of a brass/steel 'circle' being approximately 1/8 inch thick and approximately 3/4 inches in diameter, with a threaded hole to the centre, and having a brass hoop measuring some 3/4 inch in height soldered to its outer edges, which was held between a finger and the thumb when being screwed onto the plume stem. N.B. The diameter of the 'circle' and height of the hoop often varied according to the manufacturer.

The Plume Rosette

The plume rosette, which was made of gilded copper or alternatively of gilded brass had a threaded socket to the centre of its underside to enable it to be screwed onto the threaded stud at the top of the plume stem. At this period in time all three regiments of the Household Cavalry had the same pattern plume rosette which was similar in design to the ear rosettes and measured some two and a quarter inches in diameter.

The Other Ranks Pattern (See Fig: 2.)

The helmet for the 'rank and file' of the three regiments was an issue item, and as such is now extremely rare and collectable. The helmet in the author's collection has the suppliers name engraved on the back peak, this being *'Andrews, 9 Pall Mall, London'* (See Fig: 4.). The helmet was similar in outward appearances to the officers helmet, however there were several major differences, these being as follows.

The Skull

On the other ranks helmet the thickness of the white metal was much greater, which whilst increasing its ability to withstand the knocks, and wear and tear occasioned by the duties of a private soldier, also increased the weight of the helmet. Also, in addition to the left and right hand sections of the skull being soldered as on the officers pattern helmet, there were two small riveted tabs on the inside of the skull, one being located near to the front plume base stud, the other close to the rear plume base stud (See Fig: 3.).

The front and rear seam bands, and also the waistband were originally probably of gilding metal, which however over a period of rigorous cleaning tended to reverted to its original brass colour. Both peaks were bound with brass, with the front peak also having a small rivet at the upper part of each side as an additional method of securing the binding to the peak itself. The decoration on the rear peak was very similar to that on the officers helmet, however on its inner side it did not have the skiver lining. On the front peak the gilding metal/brass acanthus spray decoration was much less profuse than on the officers helmet, being very similar in appearance to that on the peak of the Dragoon Guards pattern of helmet, the inner section of this peak being lined with skiver (See Fig: 2.). for peak decoration.

Figure 3: Inside view of skull, showing the front stud for the headband, and the three studs for the plume base. Author's collection. Photo:Courtesy of the National Army Museum.

Figure 4: The rear peak. Note the suppliers name of 'Andrews 9 Pall Mall London' inscribed on peak. Author's collection. Photo:Courtesy of the National Army Museum.

The Plume Holder

This fitment was very similar in appearance and dimensions to that on the officers helmet, but was of gilding metal/brass. The plume socket appears to have been brazed to the base of the plume mount, which was attached to the skull by means of three threaded studs, positioned at north, east and west. Additionally the upper inner of the skull was reinforced at the point where the plume stem passed down into the helmet.

The Headband and Lining

On the only example of this pattern of helmet examined closely by the author, the lining was absent. However there were remnants of leather still attached to the headband, and it is therefore reasonable to presume that the original head lining would have been of brown leather. The actual headband was most unusual, as in addition to the normal method of attaching it to the skull, (by means of the ear rosette lugs/rivets) there was at the inner front of the skull a short threaded stud which was passed through a corresponding hole in the front 'flap' of the headband, and then secured in place with a small brass nut. There was also a similar stud plus flap at the back of the skull, and both these fitments appeared to be contemporary and 'all belonging' (See Fig: 3.).

The Helmet Plate

It is when looking at the helmet plate that the difference between the officers pattern and that of the other ranks becomes obvious. Not for the rank and file a **fine gilt, silver and enameled plate,** instead there was a gilding metal/brass crowned wreath and shield, a silvered 'hobnailed' Garter star and a one piece die-struck Garter with motto and Cross (See Fig: 4A.). The plate/badge itself consisted of three separate pieces, these being the crowned wreath/rococo shield, the silvered Garter star, and the Garter with the motto and Cross.

The helmet plate was assembled in a similar method as for the officers plate, except that there was no enameled back plate. The helmet plate for the other ranks had three studs positioned at north, east and west, and was affixed to the helmet in the same method as on the officers helmet.

The Ear Rosettes

Measuring 2 1/4 inches in diameter, they were of similar pattern to the rosettes fitted to the officers helmet, except that they were in gilding metal/brass instead of gilt metal.

The Chinchain

The chinchain was comprised of brass links mounted on black leather, measuring twenty and a half inches in length, and one and a quarter inches in width (See Fig: 26.).

The Plume

Similar in appearance to the officers pattern, the only noticeable difference being evident once the plume was removed from the helmet. Once removed, it could be seen that in place of the square 'ball' that was positioned above the threaded stud on the officer's plume, there was a **brass ring** which held the hairs of the brush in place and prevented the plume from being pulled to far down into the plume socket. N.B. Compare the height of the brush fitted to the plume illustrated in Fig: 2. with the brush fitted to the Dragoon Guards pattern of plume as illustrated in Figs: 15 and 16.

The Plume Rosette

As per the officers pattern, but in gilding metal/brass.

Figure 2: The Life Guards 1842 other ranks pattern helmet. Note the considerable height of the horsehair plume which has been parted to show the plume's brush. Author's collection. Photo: R. Biondi.

Figure 2a: Offset view of the helmet. Note the extreme length of the front peak. Photo: R. Biondi.

Opposite, Figure 4a: Close up detail of the other ranks pattern helmet plate. Photo: R. Biondi.

Figure 4b: Side view of helmet in which can be seen the pattern of ear rosettes fitted to this helmet. Photo: R. Biondi.

Transitional Period

At an English auction house salesroom in 1970 there appeared a most unusual helmet, this being of the Royal Horse Guards, and of officers quality, with what was most certainly an 1871 pattern skull (to be described later in this chapter), complete with a contemporary "Victorian" helmet plate. What was unusual was that the plume holder was not the ball and spike pattern as would have been expected, but was the socket pattern with finials, as fitted to the earlier, 'Albert' pattern helmet, being complete with an 'Albert' pattern plume. It is possible that this helmet was not as at first might appear, a "made up" helmet, but was in fact a transitional period helmet, although my research to-date has been unable to confirm this. However in 1939, J.F.R. Winsbury in replying to questions raised in the *Journal of the Society for Army Historical Research (SFAHR)* (5) regarding the differing pattern of helmets worn in the Household Cavalry did refer to *"the possibility of there having been an intermediate pattern helmet".*

Whilst extremely rare, it is not unknown for fitments from "Albert" pattern helmets to be used on the 1871 pattern, and I have seen a copy photograph of Major General E. Harnett wearing the full dress uniform of the 7th Dragoon Guards, with his helmet on a nearby table, which is of 'Albert' pattern, but is fitted with the later 1871 pattern plume socket.

The 1871 Pattern Helmet

The Officers Pattern (See Figs: 5. and 10.)
The actual date that the three regiment's of Household Cavalry adopted the 1871 pattern helmet is given as 1883 by the Household Cavalry Museum and as c. 1879 by Captain H. Oakes-Jones in his article published in the Journal of the SFAHR (5). N.B. Whilst the second 'Albert' pattern helmet is generally described as the "1871 pattern" it is possible that this pattern of head dress was actually taken into wear by the Household Cavalry sometime prior to 1871.

It is not unreasonable to expect that with the dawn of the twentieth century, and the publication of new *Dress Regulations for the Army* in 1900, that included within this official War Office book would be a far more detailed description of the helmets worn by Her Majesties regiments of Household Cavalry. Alas this was not to be, for the *Dress Regulations 1900* merely stated ***"Helmet**-German silver with gilt ornaments", and* gave details of the plume colours, albeit that there was a nice illustration of a Life Guards officers helmet included on plate four of this book. It was not until 1973 that an informative description of the helmet was actually produced, this being given in pamphlet No. 2. of the Dress Regulations of that year, fuller details of which are given later in this chapter.

Royalty, and a great many distinguished officers have worn the 1871 pattern helmet, and below are the names of a few of the more prominent ones.

H.R.H. Albert Edward, Prince of Wales[3] (later became King Edward V11). Colonel-in-Chief of the 1st, the 2nd Life Guards, and the Royal Horse Guards 1880.
King George V Colonel-in-Chief The Household Cavalry 1910. (6).
King George VI Colonel-in-Chief The Life Guards, and The Royal Horse Guards 1936. (6).
Field Marshal His Highness Prince W.A. Edward of Saxe-Weimer K.P., G.C.B. Colonel of the 1st Life Guards 1888. (1).
H.S.H. Prince Adolphus of Teck Captain, 1st Life Guards. 1895.(6).
H.S.H. Prince Alexander of Teck Captain, Royal Horse Guards 1904, Major 2nd Life Guards 1911. (6).
Field Marshal Sir Edmund Allenby[4] G.C.B., G.C.M.G., G.C.V.O., K.C.B., C.B. Colonel of the 1st Life Guards c. 1925.
Field Marshal, Rt.Hon Viscount Sir Garnet J. Wolseley[5] K.P., G.C.B., G.C.M.G., Colonel of the Royal Horse Guards 1895.
Lieutenant C.G. Bowes-Lyon[6] 2nd Life Guards c. 1882.
Lieutenant Colonel Frederick Gustavus Burnaby[7] Royal Horse Guards 1885.

When describing a feature/fitment of the 1871 pattern helmet, for both the officers and other ranks, I have used the term 'was', however the word 'is' also applies as the helmets worn by the regiments today have changed very little since first being adopted.

The Skull
Of German silver, with the front and rear peaks edged with gilt metal, the inside of both peaks lined with green skiver, although it is also possible to find officer's helmets with the rear peak unlined. The skull itself was made of two sections, left and right, being soldered together, with the front peak being attached by means of small rivets. The construction of this skull differed from the earlier pattern in that the rear peak was a part of each of the two main sections, and not a separate piece as on the 'Albert' pattern helmet.

The front seam joint was hidden from view by the helmet plate, whilst the rear seam joint was covered by a gilt metal escallop-shell pattern band which extended downwards from beneath the rear point of the plume holders star shaped base, to terminate beneath the edge of the rear peak binding. The band was secured in place by being soldered to the skull at the top of the band, and by means of two small brass studs soldered to the reverse of the band, these studs passing through corresponding holes in the skull, the upper stud being secured with a nut, the lower stud which was located towards the centre of the rear peak having a small brass circular 'nut'. N.B. It is not unknown to find an officers helmet having a narrow strip of metal running east to west across the upper section of the inside of the skull, or a helmet having this fitment, with an additional, even narrower metal strip running north to south, also on the inside of the skull.

Having observed this structural addition on a helmet in a private collection, and on another helmet at the Household Cavalry Museum, I am of the opinion that this unofficial modification intended to reinforce the skull, was privately commissioned and carried out at the officers own expense.

With regard to the rear seam covering there were two slightly differing pattern of rear seam band, both being approximately one inch wide and of escallop-shell pattern in gilt metal, the later version being a sealed pattern of 1897 for the Royal Horse Guards helmet, although in is not unknown for all three regiments to be fitted with either pattern of rear seam band. At the front of the waist a gilt metal laurel-leaf band to the left hand side of the waist of the skull, with a gilt metal oak-leaf band on the right, (when viewed from the front) both bands being secured to the skull by bend over tabs. N.B. Some officers pattern helmets had an alternative pattern waist fitting, which was a one inch wide oak-leaf band on both sides of the front of the skull. Neither pattern of band encircled the complete waist of the skull as was the case with the 'Albert' pattern helmet.

The Plume Holder (See Fig: 5B.)
This fitment consisted of a silvered four-sided fluted stem above a gilt bulbous shaped ball, which was mounted upon a gilt eight-pointed star, hereafter referred to as the plume holder. This fitment was attached to the skull by means

Figure 5: Royal Horse Guards. A late, King George VI example of an officers helmet, complete with yak hair plume having the pattern of rosette with the 'proud' centre. Author's collection. Photo: R. Biondi.

Figure 5a: Side view of helmet. Compare the length of the front peak with that of the helmet illustrated in Fig: 2A. Photo: R. Biondi.

Figure 5b: Rear view of the helmet with the plume removed to show the rear seam band. Photo: R. Biondi.

of four studs located on the underside of the star shaped base, and positioned at north, south, east and west. The studs were passed down through matching holes in the skull and then secured with brass nuts and washers, and as on the earlier pattern helmet the north (back) stud also passed through a slot in the rear seam band to assist in securing this fitment.

The stem of the plume socket had a 'key' located above the thread at its base, which was passed down through a hole in the centre of the star shaped base, this having a slot to accommodate the aforementioned key, then on through a hole in the crown of the skull. Onto this stem was then placed a steel ventilated collet, which was attached to the skull by means of the studs of the star shaped base that were in the north and south positions. Finally a brass circular 'nut' was placed onto the threaded section of the plume socket stem completing the assembly. This pattern of plume holder which could be disassembled, consisted of five separate pieces, these being, the silvered socket, the gilt ball, the gilt star shaped base, the collet, and the circular 'nut'.

On a post 1945 pattern helmet seen in a private collection, the construction of the plume holder differed in that the socket, ball, and base fitment although being three separate components, could not be disassembled. The plume mount also differed, in that the four base studs were situated in the north-west, south-east, south-west, and north-west positions, and onto these studs was placed a large circular metal ventilated collet, which was secured to the skull by brass nuts and washers. Additionally there was no requirement for a brass circular 'nut' on this fitment.

The Headband and Lining

Both the headband and the ear rosette socket were similar to that of the 'Albert' pattern helmet, as was the method of attaching same to the skull. For the Life Guards the lining was usually of beige quilted cloth/silk, although grey silk, leather, and leather with a silk upper section were also used. A post 1902 helmet of the 2nd Life Guards seen by the author had a **dark brown** quilted head lining.

Of the Royal Horse Guards helmets I have examined, most tended to have chamois leather linings, (See Fig: 5C.) although red leather, padded cloth/silk, and leather with silk were also fitted to these helmets. The lining which was sewn onto the headband was fitted with either one, or two drawstrings to permit adjustment for a comfortable fit.

The Helmet Plate

Although similar in outward appearance to the 'Albert' pattern helmet plate, this later version differed in several respects, and I therefore give a full description of the helmet plate as described in the *Dress Regulations for The Army 1900,* under the heading *'On Full Dress Head-Dress'*, followed by the authors description with the additions/changes made to the plate being shown in bold type:

> *1st Life Guards: 'Within a wreath of oak leaves and laurel, on a frosted gilt centre surmounted by a crown, the Star of the Order of the Garter. Around the centre, the Collar of the Order, with the George upon the lower edges of the stems of the wreath. The colours of the Garter cross, and the field are carried out in enamel. The Star in silver, the remainder gilt'.*
>
> *2nd Life Guards: As for the 1st Life Guards, except that the field of the cross is in silver. Royal Horse Guards: The Star of the Order of the Garter'*

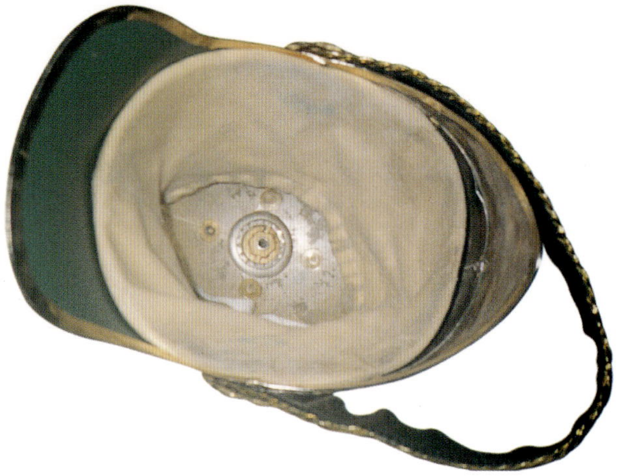

Figure 5c: Inside view of an Household Cavalry officers helmet in which can be seen the chamois leather head lining, and the collet of the plume holder base. Author's collection. Photo: Author.

With regard to the '**field carried out in enamel'** referred to above, as quoted in the above Dress Regulations, the author has never seen, nor knows of any collector, who has seen an actual example of a helmet plate with the field of the cross in enamel. I would suggest that to enamel something in silver, always assuming that this is possible, is a waste of effort, for surely silver needs no 'enhancement', and I suspect that this particular reference is in fact an error.

Author's description: A gilt plate, surmounted by a 'Victorian' crown and surrounded by a wreath, of laurel leaves to the left, (when facing the helmet) with oak leaves to the right. N.B. Two different pattern Victorian' crowns were used, one being a large crown with a **double arch** each side of the orb, mostly found on the Life Guards helmets, the other being a smaller crown with single arches, found mainly on the Royal Horse Guards helmets, although it is possible to find either pattern of crown on a helmet of any of the Household Cavalry regiments. At the bottom of the wreath where the oak and laurel leaves meet, **'The George'**, in gilt metal, this being the figure of St. George on horseback, slaying a dragon. Above The George and within the wreath of laurel and oak leaves, the **'Collar of the Order of the Garter'**, consisting of a collar of eleven pierced hoops which join with the base of the crown on its left and right hand side. To the centre of the wreath a silver diamond-cut Garter star, or alternatively a silver hobnailed (beaded) Garter star. Note: The **Garter star was now considerably larger** than on the earlier pattern helmet plate. Upon the star, an oval shaped gilt metal Garter having rope pattern inner and outer edges, pierced with the 'Motto of the Order of the Garter', this being "Honi Soit Qui Mal Y Pense" backed by blue translucent enamel. To the centre of the Garter, the Cross of St. George in red translucent enamel, with the field of the Cross in silver. (See Fig: 6.)

There were at least two variations to the Cross of the Garter assembly, the difference being in that on one version the silver field of the Cross formed part of the pierced garter, whilst on the other, the Cross was part of the backing plate onto which the enamel was laid. I would however suggest that this is once again a maker's variation rather than a regimental one.

Additionally it is possible to find a helmet plate where the colour of the Garter is silver instead of gold. I suspect that this has probably occurred because the actual Garter was made from sterling silver, and that the gilt that once covered the silver has either reacted against the precious metal, or simply worn off over a period of time.

Opposite, Figure 6: Close up view of the helmet plate in which can be seen the Collar of the Order of the Garter that surrounds the star and the centre device. Author's collection. Photo: R. Biondi.

HONI SOIT QUI MAL Y PENSE

Figure 6c: Offset view of the helmet showing the ear rosette, this pattern having the 'proud' (raised) centre. Author's Collection. Photo: R. Biondi.

The helmet plate was made up of **the same number of component parts** as on the earlier 'Albert' pattern, and was assembled in a similar manner. There were five studs to the reverse of the plate, these being positioned as follows, one behind the crown, two behind the laurel leaves, and two behind the oak leaves of the wreath. In addition there were two small bend over blades (tabs) at the bottom centre of the plate, which passed through parallel slots in the skull. These slots were located one either side of the centre seam joint, and once passed through, the tabs were flattened against the inner skull.

The Ear rosettes

It was with this pattern of helmet that the ear rosettes of both the regiments of Life Guards changed. For the 1st and 2nd Life Guards the ear rosette adopted was of a multi-petalled pattern, having four inner rows of petals, measuring 2 1/4" in diameter, and being distinctive from that of the Royal Horse Guards pattern. For the 'Blues' the rosette is best described as being of a single rose having one inner row of seven flat pointed petals (See Fig: 9.). This rosette was almost identical to the one fitted to the 'Albert' pattern helmet, except that the centre of the rosette was **proud** (raised), it was however of the same dimensions as the Life Guards rosette. Both this pattern and a variation which was very similar, but **without** the proud centre and also measured 2 1/4" in diameter, are generally to be found on the helmets of the Royal Horse Guards, although it is possible to find a helmet of any one of the three regiments fitted with any of these patterns of ear rosette. At the centre of the reverse of this fitting was soldered a stud, some 13/16th of an inch long which permitted the rosette to be 'screwed' onto the ear rosette socket. N.B. For both pattern of ear rosette the highlights such as the centre and the outer petals were of burnished gilt, with the remainder of the rosette being in matt gilt.

The Chinchain

There are normally only two types of chinchain to be found fitted to Household Cavalry helmets, these being the one inch wide version, and the pattern that measured one and a quarter inches in width, graduating down to three quarter of an inch at the centre of the chain. Each version was sewn onto either a black leather backing, or mounted on black leather and backed with black velvet. The chinchain was attached to the helmet by passing the hole at each end of the chain/leather backing, over the lug of the ear rosette socket onto which was then 'screwed' the ear rosette. On the very many helmets of all three regiments that the author has examined for the Life Guards 44% of the chinchains were graduated and 25% were velvet backed, and for the Royal Horse Guards 56% were graduated and 28% velvet backed. (See Fig: 26.)

The Plume

Once again the Dress Regulations of 1900 are of very little assistance, merely stating *'White horsehair in the 1st and 2nd Life Guards, red horsehair in the Royal Horse Guards'*, there being no mention of the different pattern rosettes worn on these plumes, nor the fact that shredded whalebone was also used for the plumes in the Life Guards.

For all three regiments the complete plume was made up of a short upright 'brush' type inner plume, surmounted by a falling hair plume that was arranged to fall over a circular mould at the top of a four sided metal stem. This stem had a threaded section at the top for the rosette, with a similar threaded section at the point where the hair of the 'brush' was bound to the stem, onto which was placed a gilt screw-on ball, whilst at the bottom of the stem was a further threaded section for the 'wing' nut. The plume had a domed appearance at the top with the hair being parted down the centre, and was supposed

Figure 6b: Royal Horse Guards c. 1952. Officers pattern helmet plate disassembled for cleaning, together with the plume holder. Author's collection. Photo: Author.

Figure 7: A fine study of an officer of the Life Guards c. 1994. Of interest is the regimental method of wearing the chinchain under the lower lip. Photo: Courtesy of Brian Daly.

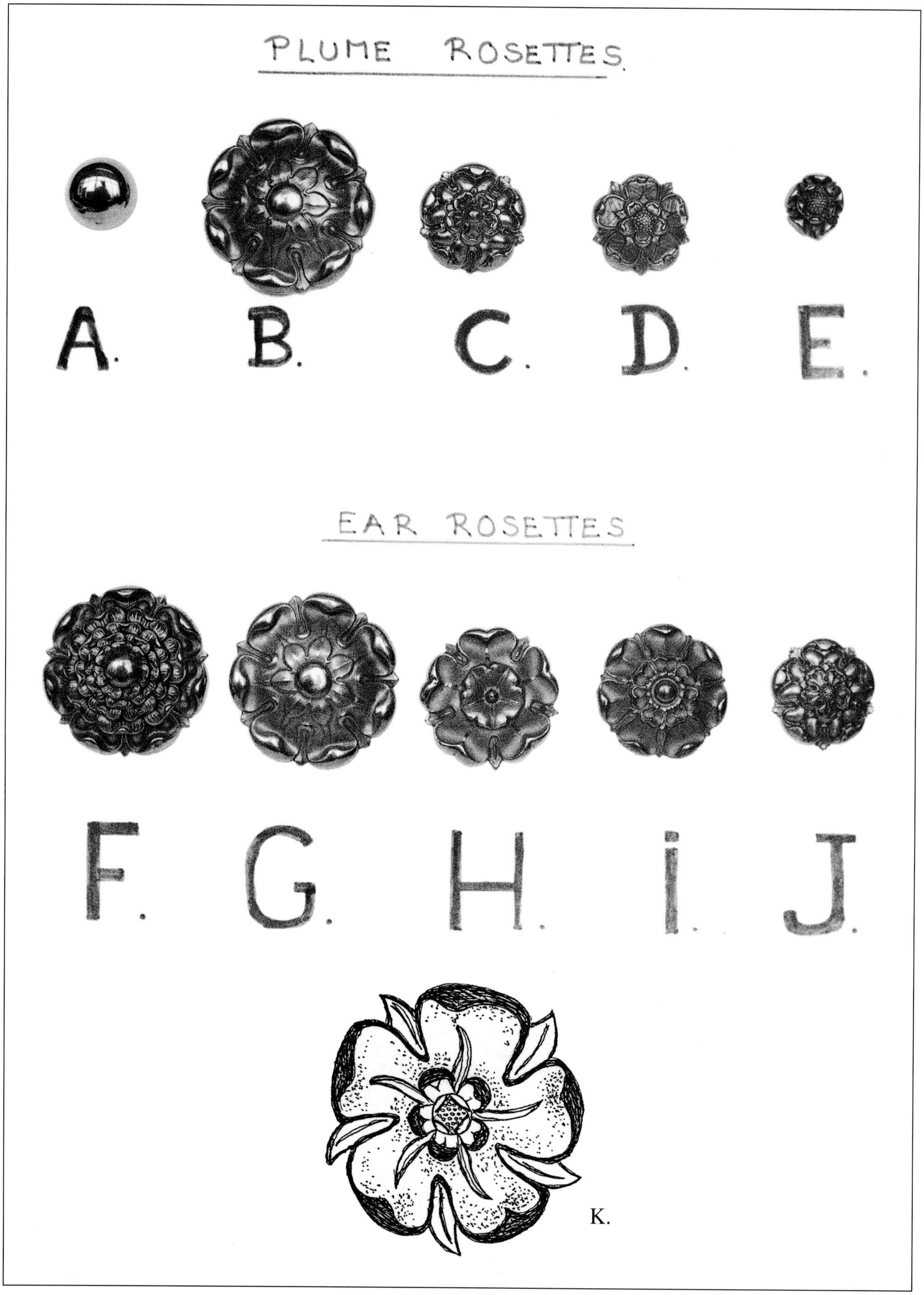

Figure 9: Various types of ear, and plume rosettes as fitted to the officers and other ranks 1847 and 1871 pattern helmet. Example "K" at bottom not to scale – other ranks pattern ear rosette as fitted to the Dragoon Guards, 1st and 6th Dragoons and certain Yeomanry regiments including the Essex Yeomanry. N.B. The pattern of ear rosette illustrated in example "I" was also produced as a plume rosette. Author.

to hang so as to be level with the bottom of the helmet at the back. However on many helmets seen by the author the plume was somewhat shorter that described above.

Whilst the aforementioned Dress Regulations quote horsehair for the Royal Horse Guards, it is also known that at certain periods in their history the officers of this regiment wore plumes of yak' hair, the hair having been taken from the under belly of a yak, and dyed red/scarlet. The Regimental Museum, in a memorandum on Household Cavalry helmets state that *'The present day pattern of state helmet was introduced in 1883', and that 'It is not known why the yak hair plume was introduced, possibly something to do with the Colonel of the Blues at that time, F.M. Lord Strathnairn, an officer who distinguished himself in the Indian Mutiny'.* What is known is that two helmets seen by the author, formerly belonging to officers who served in the regiment between the years 1889 to 1915, and 1899 to 1919 respectively, were both fitted with the yaks hair plume, with both plumes appearing to be contemporary with their helmets.

The plume was attached to the skull by passing the plume stem down the plume socket, down into the skull, where it was then secured by means of the brass, or alternatively steel 'wing' nut.

The Plume Finial/Rosette

For the Royal Horse Guards the plume rosette was similar to the ear rosette, being a single rose in gilt metal. This rosette was fitted with either a short tube soldered to the inside of the rosette, or alternatively having a cut-out section on the inside of the rosette into which was secured a small nut to enable the rosette to be screwed onto the plume stem. N.B. As with the ear rosettes, the highlights of the plume rosette were normally of burnished gilt.

For the 1st and 2nd Life Guards things are not quite so simple, as two different pattern of plume finial are known to have been used, these being a medium sized gilt metal multi-petalled rose, and a simple burnished gilt, metal hemisphere (half ball) (See Fig: 10.).

Many photographs of officers in full dress uniform taken prior to 1922 have been closely studied by the author, but are regrettably of little help as they do not show sufficient detail to identify which pattern plume finial is worn. However, it is the 'exception that proves the rule', and there exists an excellent studio photograph of H.R.H. Prince Alexander of Teck in the full dress uniform of the 2nd Life Guards c. 1914, where it can clearly be seen that the plume on his helmet is fitted with the hemisphere pattern finial (6). N.B. An officer's helmet in the authors collection has the plume stem stamped **2 LG** and is fitted with the gilt hemisphere finial, as on the Prince of Teck's helmet plume.

Many years ago, a then Research Assistant of the Department of Uniforms at the National Army Museum, Chelsea, London, kindly undertook to look into this matter on my behalf. Having examined five Life Guards officers plumes in the museums collection he forwarded his findings to me, which as shown below regrettably do not provide a finite answer:

> 1st Life Guards c. 1900 with hemisphere finial.
> 1st Life Guards c. 1910 with rose finial.
> 2nd Life Guards c. 1879 with rose finial.
> 2nd Life Guards c. 1920 with hemisphere finial.
> The Life Guards c. 1936 with hemisphere finial. (8).

Although we may one day receive further information to show precisely at what period each regiment may have worn a particular pattern of finial, it is possible that we may never really know the answer to this question.

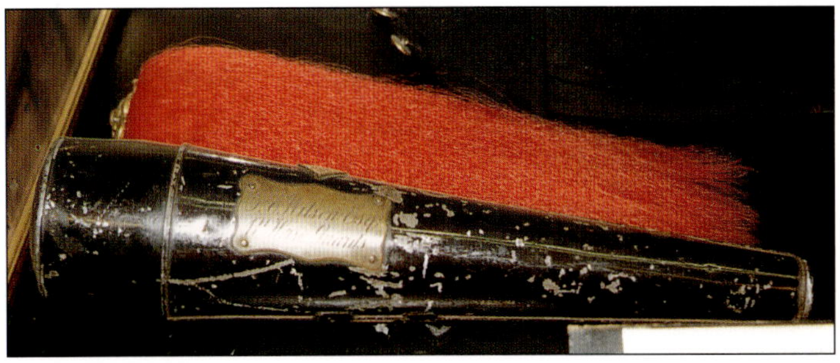

Figure 8: Victorian officers plume tin of the Royal Horse Guards named to G.C. Wilson. Compare the shape of this tin with the one illustrated in Fig: 62. N.B.G.C. Wilson. Captain: 21st November 1894. Photo: G. Frost. Courtesy of the Household Cavalry Museum.

Regimental Staff Officers

'The *Dress Regulations 1900'* state that 'the Adjutant and Riding-Master wear the uniform of their rank', and this would of course include the full dress helmet with plume.

The regulations continue by stating that 'The Medical Officers, the Veterinary Officer, and the Quarter-master wear the uniform of other Officers of corresponding rank, with the following exceptions:'

> '**Cocked Hat** (Instead of the Helmet for Medical Officers and Veterinary Officers). As described in paragraph 7; the Medical Officers with gold lace loop, tassels, and plume of black cock's-tail feathers; the Veterinary Officers plume is of red swan feathers. ***The cuirass is not worn'.***

Paragraph seven as referred to above, describes the Cocked Hat as follows: 'Cocked-hats will be of black silk. Dimensions for medium size: The left side of 6 1/4 inches high, the right side 5 3/4 inches; each corner 4 3/8 inches long. On the right side, a black silk cockade with a loop fastened by a button; at each corner a bullion tassel, consisting (except where otherwise stated) of nine gold bullions and eleven crimson bullions under them, 1 3/4 inches long, exclusive of the head; midway between the loop and tassel, front and back, a band of 1 3/4 inch black braid of oak-leaf pattern'. N.B. This pattern was sealed on 29.11.1898.

The official description of the cocked hat as given above omits certain relevant details and I therefore offer below the a fuller description as given in Roy Manser's excellent book on the Household Cavalry (12):

> 'The outer material is of black silk plush on a gossamer body. On the left side, the crown rises to approximately 6 1/4 inches, and on the right to 5 3/4 inches. The front and rear straight edged ends are each embellished with a gold bullion tassel. A black oak-leaf braid band 1 3/4 inches wide decorates the right side of the front and rear. At the centre of the right side, a gold wire corded and embroidered device is affixed, with a gilt button of regimental pattern. The hat has a white silk lining to the crown and a leather head band' (12).

The Warrant Officers Helmet

It was, and still is the practice within the Household Cavalry Regiment for Warrant Officers (see below) to wear a full dress helmet of similar pattern to that of the officers. The helmet was fitted with a plume holder which had the bulbous ball beneath the socket in **gilt,** as opposed to white metal, as on the other ranks helmet, with the helmet plate being of gilt, silver, and enamel. However, the Warrant Officers pattern plume was fitted with a **white metal hemisphere**

Figure 10: 2nd Life Guards c. 1902-1922 officers pattern. Helmet complete with horsehair plume. Compare the plumes hemisphere with the R.H.G. rosette illustrated in Fig: 5. Author's collection. Photo: R. Biondi.

Figure 10a: Offset view of helmet showing the regimental pattern ear rosettes. Photo: R. Biondi

Figure 10b: Side view of helmet. Compare the depth of the helmet plate crown with the pattern fitted to the R.H.G. helmet as illustrated in Fig: 6.

finial, as worn by the rank and file, regardless of regiment, and not, the gilt hemisphere, or rosette as fitted to the officers plume.

There are two colour illustrations of the Kettle-drummer of The Life Guards c. 1981, both mounted and dismounted, in review order, wearing the Warrant Officers pattern helmet in the *Regiment Magazine*, Issue One (49). It is possible, that at the time that these pictures were taken, the musician concerned was the most high ranking Kettle-drummer ever to have served in a British cavalry regiment.

N.B. Warrant Officer rank in the Household Cavalry includes soldiers holding the post of Regimental Corporal Major, Squadron Corporal Major, Regimental Quartermaster Corporal, and Trumpet Major (the helmet is only worn by the Warrant Officer holding this post, when in mounted, or dismounted review order). Additionally it is unique to the Household Cavalry, that the rank of sergeant does not exist within the regiment. In its place is the rank of **corporal**, hence the post of Regimental Corporal Major is the equivalent of Regimental Sergeant Major in the foot guards etc.

The Rank and File

Throughout its history there have been a great many former soldiers, who having served in the ranks of the Household Cavalry went on to achieve fame and fortune in way or another. One person who springs to mind, was once a trooper in the Royal Horse Guards, being now known as Ray Milland[8] the famous actor and film star.

The Other Ranks Helmet (See Fig: 11.)

The helmet for the other ranks closely resembled that of the officers pattern, but with several differences. Therefore, below is a full description of this pattern of helmet, with the major differences being highlighted in bold text.

The Skull

Of **white metal,** the peak edges, front waist band, and rear seam band being in **gilding metal**, with the peak, and waist leaves etc. being attached by small rivets. The front peak only was lined with skiver, with the rear seam band and the main construction of the helmet being in general, similar to that on the officers pattern helmet.

The Plume Holder

Again as for the officers pattern, except that the bulbous shaped ball beneath the white metal socket was not in gilt as on the officers helmet, but was in **white metal**, with the star shaped base being in **gilding metal**, as opposed to gilt metal. This pattern of plume holder was constructed so that it could not be **disassembled,** and was attached to the skull by means of the four brass studs located beneath the star shaped base, they being positioned at north-west, south-east, south-west, and north-east positions. These studs passed through matching holes in the skull, and then on through a metal ventilated collet, where they were secured with nuts and washers.

The Headband and Lining

The headband was as for the officers pattern, and was attached to the skull in a similar manner. The head lining, which was sewn onto the headband was of **brown leather, having eight sections** (leaves), which met at the centre of the skull, the end of each of these sections having a small, metal supported hole, through which a drawstring was passed and then tied. Additionally, on the left and the right side of the inner skull was a **brown leather strap with a buckle**, which permitted some form of adjustment to the head lining.

Figure 11: The Life Guards 1871 other ranks pattern. This example is of the Victorian era and has the helmet plate crown with the double arches. Author's collection. Photo: Author.

The Helmet Plate

As with the earlier pattern of head-dress, the helmet plate for the rank and file was much simpler than the officers version. It consisted of a plate, surmounted by a 'Victorian' crown with double arches each side of the orb, surrounded by an oak and laurel wreath, and, as on the officers plate there was 'The George', at the point where the oak and laurel leaves met, **the whole in gilding metal**.

Within the wreath was the Collar of the Garter, having eleven hoops, however unlike the officers pattern plate, **the hoops were not pierced**. Within the collar, and surmounted on the plate, was a **white metal eight-pointed rayed star,** to the centre of which was a **gilding metal die-struck** oval shaped Garter with the Motto, and the Cross of St. George. The metal Garter and the rayed star were attached to the wreath/plate by means of **four thin metal pins** on the reverse side of the Garter/Cross, they being positioned at north-west, south-east, south-west, and north-east positions.

The complete helmet plate was attached to the skull by means of **three studs**, positioned, one behind the crown, with a further stud behind each of the side wreaths. Additionally there were **four, two pronged, metal bend over blades** (tabs) located to the lower rear of the plate, one behind the lower part of the oak leaves, another behind the lower part of the laurel leaves, with a further two blades being positioned one above the other to the lower centre of the plate. These blades passed through parallel slots in the skull, where they were then bent outwards, and flattened. N.B. It is not unusual to find that on a helmet plate that has been removed from the skull of the helmet, that these blades have either been cut short, or removed completely.

The plate/badge consisted of three separate pieces, these being the Crowned wreath/plate, the Garter star, and the Garter with the Cross. N.B. During the past twenty-one years, two differing pattern helmet plates have appeared at auction salesrooms in England. They being, one that was offered for sale in a Sussex salesroom in 1978, described in the catalogue as being a ***'NCO's HP of the 2nd Life Guards, with the field of the Cross silvered', not of officers quality, GC, red enamel slightly chipped'.*** The other, which was fitted to a helmet, was offered for sale in a Kent salesroom in 1980, being described in their catalogue as a ***'NCO's helmet of the Life Guards'***, with the plate being described as a ***'three piece helmet plate with the central cross finished in red'.***

I reserve my judgment on the former plate until such time as further information comes to light, if it ever does. However, with regards to the latter plate, it is my opinion that this was in fact an officers plate, with the blue enamel missing from the Garter. This might explain why the Garter star was not referred to in the salesroom catalogue, albeit that there was an illustration of the helmet, in which it could clearly be seen that the star was of the beaded pattern, and not the rayed version normally fitted to the other ranks helmet.

The Ear Rosettes

The Life Guards, as for the officers, but being in gilding metal. However, some late Victorian pattern helmets were fitted with a rosette of the standard pattern, but which had a hook which hung down from, and was secured behind its lower outer petals, and it was onto this hook that the 'loose' end of the chinchain was attached. The rosette on the opposite side of the helmet did not have this additional fitment, and the chain was secured in the method previously described in this chapter.

Royal Horse Guards helmets were fitted with a gilding metal rosette, of single rose pattern with a **flat centre**. They did not wear the pattern of rosette with the proud (raised) centre, which it appears was exclusively used on officers helmets. All the above types of rosette had the short threaded stud to the reverse.

The Chinchain

There were two patterns of brass chinchain, one being graduated, the other not, both however were sewn onto a black leather backing.

The Plume

Life Guards, as for the officers pattern, except that the screw-on ball at the top of the stem, located immediately beneath the inner 'brush', was of **gilding metal/brass.**

Musicians of the Life Guards wear white plumes in their helmets when in review order, the Trumpeters however, wear a red plume in the above order of dress. The regimental Farriers are distinguished by the black plume fitted to their helmets.

It would appear that at this period of time, and indeed for a great many years to come, the Life Guards did not wear their plumes with the most distinctive **'onion' shape** as worn today. I will however again refer to this unique and most interesting feature later in this chapter.

The ranks and file of the Royal Horse Guards, including the farriers and musicians wear red plumes, complete with the **gilding metal/brass** screw on ball.

Plume Finial

The other rank's, of all three regiments wear a **white metal** hemisphere on top of their plumes.

N.B. whilst the overall height of the 1871 pattern helmet complete with plume is some two inches shorter in height than the equivalent 1842 'Albert' pattern helmet, a 6ft 1 inch tall trooper in his full dress uniform, and wearing his helmet complete with plume, is raised to something like 7ft 7 inches from the plume finial down to the heel of his jack-boot.[8A]

1902 and Onwards

With the death of Britain's longest reigning sovereign Queen Victoria on the 22nd January 1901 and the subsequent Coronation of King Edward VII on 6th August 1902 came a change from the Victorian crown which had depressed arches, to the Tudor (or Imperial) crown, more commonly referred to as the 'King's' crown which had raised arches.

For the three Regiments of the Household Cavalry this resulted in the Victorian crown on the helmet plate gradually being replaced by the Kings' crown (See Fig: 5.), with similar changes taking place to such items as the crown at the top of the regimental standard, on the standard bearers belt, on the cartouche pouch, the waist belt, the musicians and trumpeters state coat, the drum and trumpet banners, and the horse furniture etc.

Dress Regulations 1911

The Dress Regulations for the Army 1911 gave no change in its description of the helmet, nor in the helmet plate of the various regiments.

Amalgamation - 1922

Under Lloyd George' Government and the Geddes Axe (the system was named after its sponsor) of 1922 many of the thirty-one cavalry regiments that had fought in the First World War were amalgamated, and even the Household Cavalry was not spared in this cost cutting exercise. The First and Second regiments of Life Guards were merged (10) and given the name 'The Life Guards (1st and 2nd)'. It is said that 'On amalgamation the officer's of the Life Guards were to wear the helmet plate centre badge of the old 1st Life Guards' (3), although whether or not this in fact took place is unknown to the author. The Royal Horse Guards were however more fortunate, for their amalgamation was not to take place for a further forty-seven years.

Change of Title - 1928

It was in this year that the title of The Life Guards (1st and 2nd), changed to the more simplified 'The Life Guards' (10) and has remained thus ever since.

Marching Order - 1933

An interesting paragraph which is reproduced below appeared in an 1933 edition of the Cavalry Journal (11) relating to the Household Cavalry Regiments, their helmets, and their journey to Windsor. It read 'The practice of **wearing the full dress head-dress in marching order** is still customary in the Household Cavalry, the helmet which crumples easily if packed, being worn minus the plume with khaki when changing station by road between Knightsbridge and Windsor'. 'These two stations being the town and country homes of the Household Cavalry'. N.B. The above reference to khaki refers to the service dress uniform.

The above information relates to a period in time when one of the two regiments would be stationed at Knightsbridge Barracks (Hyde Park) in London, with the other regiment being stationed at Comberemere Barracks, Windsor. The practice of wearing the helmet on the march seems to have ceased shortly after 1933, as there is an excellent photographic illustration dated October 1935 entitled '***A scene on the Great West Road,*** the accompanying description reading as follows. 'The Life Guards on their way from Hyde Park Barracks to Combermere Barracks, pass the Blues proceeding from Windsor to London', in which all ranks, of both regiments are wearing khaki with service dress (khaki peaked) caps (10).

Dress Regulations 1934

The Dress Regulations for the Army 1934 again shows no change from the description of the helmet as given in the *Regulations of 1900*, however the helmet plate for the Royal Horse Guards, described under the heading' *On Full Dress Head-Dress* ' now reads *'As for the Life Guards, except that the field of the cross is in silver'.*

In these same regulations however, under the heading: Regimental Staff Officers , the post of **Director of Music** is now included along with the Adjutant, and Quarter-master as wearing 'the uniform of their rank', which includes the **full dress helmet**, but not the cuirass. N.B. The post of Riding-Master is for some unknown reason now omitted from this section.

Yak Hair Plume - 1952

Regarding the yak hair plume worn by officer's of the Royal Horse Guards as mentioned earlier in this chapter, the following interesting extract reproduced here as originally written, is taken from a book relating to the Household Troops that was published in 1952 (13) and reads as follows. *"Officers plumes being made of yak's hair, and as yak hair is now difficult to obtain, rumour has it that nylon may be used"*. The importance of this statement is that it appears to confirm that the yak hair plume was being worn c. 1952. Fortunately the rumoured use of nylon did not become reality.

Change of Crown - 1953

With the Coronation of Queen Elizabeth II in 1953, once again the crown on the helmet plate etc. changed, this time it was to the pattern known as the St. Edward's Crown, which remains the same to the present day.

Description of Helmet - The Ministry of Supply 1955

The following is an extract from a scarce 1955 publication by the Ministry of Supply, Directorate of Equipment and Store, relating to the full dress helmets and plumes of the Life Guards, and the Royal Horse Guards, containing some most useful detailed information, which with the exception of the stores issue number for each item, is reproduced here as it was printed:

Helmets, Household Cavalry, Bodies, Officers, Life Guards

A helmet made of best quality white metal with spike on ball of gilding metal on an eight-pointed star screwed to the skull. The skull is in two parts joined down the centre of back and front with a one inch gilt band down the centre back seam. A gilding metal gilt plate incorporating the St. Edward's Crown over a Garter Star, with enameled inset centre with laurel leaf on the right and oak leaf design on the left side, it is secured to the front centre of the helmet by plated screws, nuts and washers. The peak portion is lined with green skiver. The bottom edge of the helmet is bound with gilding metal gilt. Head leather is of tan coloured roan and it is lined with scarlet rayon. Brow is of felt and sandwiched stout buckram. Gilding metal gilt rosette 2.1/4 inches in diameter screw into the side and secure the end of the curb chain at each side. Chain is linked, 3/4 inch wide at the centre and 1.1/4 inch at the ends, 18 1/2 inches in length, and is mounted on black leather. Worn by Officers, Life Guards.

Helmets, Household Cavalry, Bodies, Officers, Royal Horse Guards

As preceding item except that the centre back band and side rosettes are of slightly different designs. Worn by Officers, Royal Horse Guards.

Helmets, Household Cavalry, Bodies, Warrant Officers

As item 1. above. Worn by Warrant Officers I and Warrant Officer II, Household Cavalry.

Helmets, Household Cavalry, Bodies, Other Ranks

As item 1.above, but plate has Garter Star in brass and is not enameled.

Helmets, Household Cavalry, Plumes, Officers, Life Guards

A white horsehair plume. The hair is arranged at the top to fall over a circular mould which fits on to a four-sided metal stem held in position by a screw on dome at the top and ball screw underneath. The hair hangs from the mould to a length of 18 inches to be level with the bottom of the helmet at the back. The plume is fitted to the helmet by passing the metal stem through the spike of the helmet and securing by a butterfly screw at the base. When worn the plume should hang parted from the centre front. Worn by Life Guards Officers (14).

Helmets, Household Cavalry, Plumes, Officers, Royal Horse Guards

A yak hair dyed scarlet plume. It is of similar construction to the previous item, but the screwed on dome at the top is of rose design resembling the rosettes worn each side of the helmet.

As will be seen from the above the Warrant Officers helmet was/is an officers pattern helmet, however it would appear that this was not always the case as a late version 'King's' crown Warrant Officers helmet examined by the author in 1972 was fitted with the other ranks leather head lining which would suggest that upon reaching Warrant Officer rank the former N.C.O. retained his other ranks pattern skull, plume, chinchain and ear rosettes, to which was fitted the officers pattern helmet plate and plume holder.

It is of interest that in the above description the skull is described as being **best quality white metal**, this being the first known official confirmation that the skulls of the officers pattern helmets were no longer of German silver. However this change appears to have taken place earlier, as the author has seen many **officers** helmets having white metal skulls and bearing the 'Kings' crown on the helmet plate.

Whilst in the above there are several important omissions, such as the colour of the enamels, 'The George', the Collar of the Order of the Garter etc., the depth of information given in this publication is without doubt a vast improvement on the *Dress Regulations for The Army published in 1900, 1911, and 1934*, and this additional information is therefore most welcome.

Royal Horse Guards Amalgamation of 1969

On the 29th March 1969 Field Marshal Sir Gerald Templar, KG, GCB, GCMG, KBE, DSO, DCL, gave a loyal address to Her Majesty the Queen upon the amalgamation of the Royal Horse Guards and the 1st The Royal Dragoons, to form the newly titled regiment The Blues and Royals (Royal Horse Guards and 1st Dragoons). N.B. F.M. Sir Gerald Templar was Colonel of the Royal Horse Guards from 1962 to 1969 and of The Blues and Royals from 1969 to 1979 (10).

Dress Regulations c. 1973

As mentioned previously in this chapter it was not until 1973 when Pamphlet No. 2. Household Division, of The Dress Regulations for Officers of the Army was published (15), that any detailed information on the full dress helmets, and uniforms for officers of the Household Cavalry became generally available. These regulations, produced by the Ministry of Defence, were obtainable from Her Majesties Stationary Office, London. N.B. It is conceivable that the Ministry of Supply publication referred to above was used as the basis of information for the *Dress Regulations 1973,* as a great deal of the text is very similar, and in some instances identical.

However there are several important changes in the more recent publication, and I have therefore included in full, and as printed, the description of the helmet and plumes as given in the Pamphlet No. 2. (1973), with the changes being given in bold text:

> *Full Dress. Mounted Review Order.*
> *Helmet. Of best quality white metal with spike on* ***base of gilt*** *metal on an eight-pointed star screwed to the skull of the helmet. The skull is in two parts joined down the centre of back and front, with a 1-in. gilt band down the centre back seam. A* ***gilt*** *plate incorporating St. Edward's crown over a Garter star, with enameled inset centre with a laurel leaf on the right and oak leaf design on the left side, is secured to the front of the helmet by plated screw, nuts and washers. The peak portion is lined with green skiver. The bottom edge of the helmet is bound with* ***gilt enamel****. Head leather is of* ***chamois****. Brow is of felt and sandwiched stone buckram. Gilt metal rosettes are of different patterns:*
>
> ***L.G. Four inner rows of petals.***
> ***R.H.G./D. One inner row of seven flat pointed petals.***

N.B. I would suggest that the reference to the bottom edge being bound in gilt enamel is a printing error.

> *Chain is linked, 3/4-in. wide at the centre and 1.1/4-in. at the ends, and is mounted on black leather. Length of the chain is:*
> *L.G.* ***6.1/2-in.***
> *R.H.G./D. 18.1/2-in.*
>
> *Plume.*
> *L.G. White horsehair. The hair is arranged at the top to fall over a circular mould which fits on to a four-sided metal stem held in position by a screw-on dome at the top and ball screw underneath.* ***Dome and ball screw are gilt.*** *The hair hangs from the mould to a length of* ***24.1/2-in.*** *to be level with the bottom of the helmet at the back. The plume is fitted to the helmet by passing the metal stem through the spike of the helmet and securing by a butterfly screw at the base.* ***It is worn with an "onion" at the top (having been tied under the dome when not worn).*** *When worn the plume should* ***be*** *parted* ***down*** *the centre front,* ***and hang just below the bottom of the helmet.***
> ***R.H.G./D. Horse hair treated to look like yak hair and dyed scarlet, of similar construction to the L.G. pattern. A gilt rosette is worn at the top of the plume. The overall length of the plume is 23-in. and it hangs straight to reach the bottom of the helmet at the back".***

Figure 12a: The Officers full dress uniform store, Knightsbridge Barracks. June 1986. Note the labels attached to many of the helmets to identify the wearer. Photo: Author. By kind permission of the Household Cavalry Regiment.

Again no mention is made of the colours of the enamels, nor the Collar of the Order, or the 'George'. Additionally no mention is made that the reason for the difference in the chinchain lengths is because in the Life Guards it is worn under the lower lip, and in the Blues and Royals (R.H.G./D.) is worn on the chin.

At last there is an official reference to a yak hair plume for the Blues and Royals, albeit that it is of 'treated' horsehair. With regards to the plume of the Life Guards, if the length quoted above is correct, and there is no reason to suppose that it is not, then its length had increased from 18 inches to 24 1/2 inches since 1955. Whilst on the subject of this plume, the **'onion' shape** at the top, is achieved, by washing the plume, and then placing it inside a cloth 'plume bag' with a suitable throng (such as a boot lace) being tied around the plume at the top to form the 'onion' shape and then being left to dry.

How the Helmet was worn in 1974

With regard to my earlier reference in this chapter relating to the 'Albert' pattern helmet having the length of its peak reduced in order that Queen Victoria could identify who was riding as her escort. Photographs taken by the author of the Blues and Royals at Hyde Park Corner, London in 1974, on their way to the Trooping the Colour Ceremony, clearly show that the helmet's of the officers were being worn **with the front peak so far forward as to completely cover the nose of the wearer,** making identification of the officer concerned almost impossible (See Fig: 12.). Quite what Queen Victoria might have thought about the above is anybody's guess. She might well however have remarked that *'We are not amused'.* N.B. The ceremony of Trooping the Colour is known within the British Army as 'The Queen's Birthday Parade', and is held on a Saturday morning early in June, to honour the Official Birthday of the Sovereign (12).

Figure 12: Mounted officer of the Blues and Royal's passing Hyde Park Corner. June 1974. Note the position of the officers helmet's peak. Author's collection. Photo: Author.

It was in this year that whilst in the course of collecting information on the other ranks and the warrant officer pattern of helmets that I visited the troopers quarters at Horse Guards, London. I was shown into the room where the troopers helmets and uniforms were laid out prior to their going on duty as either 'boxmen' (mounted sentries), or as dismounted sentries. To my utter amazement I observed that a few of the helmets in this room bore the 'Tudor' pattern crown of the late King George VI on the helmet plate, it then being at that time some twenty one years since the Coronation of Queen Elizabeth II.

The Officers Full Dress Store - Knightsbridge Barracks 1986

In June 1986 at the invitation of Captain Peck, the then Quartermaster of the Blues and Royals, I visited the officers full dress store at Knightsbridge Barracks, London. It was a most rewarding visit, and much valuable information regarding the full dress helmet currently worn by officer's was obtained. On three wide shelves were stored some thirty helmets, minus chinchains and plumes, these helmets having previously been worn by officer's of both regiments, who were currently engaged on various duties away from the mounted squadron (See Fig: 12A).

Of the thirty odd helmets that were stored on these shelves, three bore the 'King's' crown to the helmet plate, instead of the St. Edward's (ERII) pattern crown as one would have expected, with one being fitted with a **beaded** garter star, in place of the more usual diamond-cut pattern. Of the head linings fitted to these helmets, one was of leather, one of leather with a red silk upper section, and one was of similar pattern to that of the other ranks, with the remainder being of chamois leather. With one exception, all the helmets had light green skiver to the front and rear peaks, the sole exception being one having the rear peak unlined. The chinchains for these helmets where grouped together on hooks, being the none-graduated version and all having black leather backing. The ear rosettes were loosely contained in a box, in which both Blues and Royals, and The Life Guards pattern of rosettes were present. Additionally there was one helmet on a wooden stand, being of the Life Guards Regiment complete with chinchain and plume, and ready to wear.

The Merger of 1992

The Life Guards and The Blues and Royals regiments merged on the 19th October 1992 to form The Household Cavalry Regiment, each unit retaining its own identity, uniform, and traditions.

The Head-Dress worn Today

For the Household Cavalry Regiment of the present day, the aiguillettes, badges, button, epaulettes, cuirasses and helmets for both officer and troopers, are made by a Birmingham based company that was originally established over 300 years ago in London, by the name of Firmin and Sons. This *"company provides men and horses with most of the metalwork apart from the stirrups and horseshoes"*. With regard to the full dress helmet, it is of interest that *"including trimming and sewing it takes about **three-and-a-half days** to make a new helmet"*. The breastplates (cuirasses) *"start life as a 2ft square sheet of steel, they are 'bit by bit, beaten, rolled and shaped before being attached with metal fittings and studs. They are polished, copper-plated, polished again, nickel-plated and burnished to a mirror finish, and take about four days to make" (32).*

Finally with regards to the plumes of the two regiments, these are made by a company known as The Plumery, they being the sole supplier of plumes to the British Army. For the plumes of the Household Cavalry they use Chinese and Mongolian horsehair which is dyed, or bleached, woven, sewn, and mounted onto a metal stem.

When I visited The Plumery a couple of years ago I was shown by the proprietor, a yak hair plume as currently worn by the officers of the Blues and Royals. This hair, which is gathered from the under belly of the yak has a fluffy texture which is unlike the feel of horsehair which is sleek when touched. The yak hair plume does however not come cheaply, for at the time of my visit the purchase price was in excess of £100.

'Inside the Regiment' 1998

During a visit to Knightsbridge Barracks in 1998 the following interesting information was passed to me by serving members of the Household Cavalry Regiment, which whilst it may not have the approval of the officers of the regiment or the Ministry of Defence is I feel worthy of a mention.

If it Hurts, it Fits

Cavalry helmets were/are not made as fashion items and within the regiment it is advised that if the helmets becomes uncomfortable, *'do not 'lift' the helmet to ease any pressure on the wearers skull but leave it alone'*, as if lifted, when it is replaced the discomfort will be increased. It is not unknown whilst 'stationed' at Horse Guards for the wearer of a helmet that is uncomfortable to 'bang down' the helmet onto the ball that surmounts the heel post within the stables, to modify the shape of the skull for a better fit. Additionally by bending the plume socket slightly forwards, the wearer can push the helmet further back on his skull which apparently makes it more comfortable to wear. I have also been reliably informed that this modification 'carries' the plume better. N.B. The author does not recommend that a collector carry out the above modifications on helmets in their collection.

The Glint of the Sun

The troopers appeared to be 'at home' with helmets having dented skulls, as the sun tends to catch the creases/dents giving the skull extra sparkle. Additionally a dented helmet gives the wearer the appearance of being an 'old sweat' whose helmet has seen much service.

Cleaning can lead to Damage

The skull of the helmet is cleaned by the trooper rubbing 'brasso' metal polish onto the skull using his fingers. The polish is then wiped off with a clean cloth, with any surplus polish that has become dry and caked into the 'nooks and crannies' such as the waist leaves or helmet plate crown, being removed by a stiff brush that has had chalk dust sprinkled onto its bristles. It is whilst 'brushing' the helmet that accidental damage may occur, as the bristles of the brush may catch parts of the helmet plate that stand proud, such as the orb of the crown, or the oak or laurel leaves, and cause then to fracture or break off.

A possible further cause of accidental damage that may occur whilst the above 'brushing' is taking place, is to the plume mount, often referred to as the 'turret' by the troopers. This fitment is a natural 'handle' by which to hold the helmet secure whilst brushing the helmet plate, and it is not unknown for the plume socket and ball fitment to fracture and break off from the star shaped plume mount base. N.B. Once again the author does not recommend that collectors use the method described to clean a helmet, as the metal may well be fragile.

Damaged Plates - Other Ranks Helmet

Before moving on to the future of the helmet, I reproduce below an interesting additional extract from the 1955 Ministry of Supply, Directorate of Equipment and Store publication mentioned earlier, relating to damaged helmet plates:

<u>Helmets, Household Cavalry, Plates</u>

A separately demandable component item of Helmet, Household Cavalry, O.R. It is the gilding metal plate worn on the front of the helmet and is used to replace worn or damaged plates of repairable helmets by the armourer of the regiment.

Towards 2000 and Onwards

I have it on good authority that the Household Cavalry Regiment, in conjunction with the Defence Clothing and Textile Agency is investigating the possible use of a plastic based helmet skull, and a plastic based cuirass, both of which have been seen by the author. Trial pattern helmets made of polymer and then coated to give a white metal appearance have been received by the regiment where they where fitted with the plume holder, helmet plate, head harness and lining, ear rosette socket and chinchain, front waist leaves, and rear seam band by the regimental armourer. This possible move away from the metal skull has been prompted by the need for helmets to be produced more quickly by the manufacturer, that will fit the head of a trooper whose hat size falls between two recognised sizes.

However the problem experienced with the first of these polymer based skulls relates to its actual shape, for whereas the heads of most human beings fall within an accepted hat size, e.g. 6 3/4 inches, 7 inches, 7 1/8 inches etc., the actual shape of a persons skull can vary considerably. Whilst the shape of the metal skull currently in use may, by applying **gentle hand** pressure to the front/sides of the skull be slightly altered to achieved a better fit, there is no equivalent 'give' in the polymer based skulls, which may tend to fracture if similar light pressure is applied to the front/sides.

The proposed cost of a 'plastic' skull is expected to be 25% less that the current cost of a white metal skull, which will reduce the overall present day cost of £1,200 for a helmet complete with all fittings, excluding plume. N.B. this is not the first occasion that a British military head-dress has been 'reproduced' as the musicians in the band of the 17th/21st Lancers, (now part of the Royal Lancers), have been wearing a chapka (lance cap) with the body of the cap being made of fibre glass for several years.

The Regimental Museum

Visitors to London, should not miss the opportunity of watching the spectacle of the Changing of the Guard at Buckingham Palace, and the Changing of the Queen's Life Guard held on Horse Guards Parade, (this also being the location for Trooping the Colour in early June of each year). Until the early 1990s this magnificent ceremony, with its sparkling helmets, swirling plumes, highly polished cuirasses, and beautifully groomed horses took place in the courtyard of Horse Guards, however due to its popularity, the number of spectators who wished to enjoy this ceremony became to great for it to be safely held in the courtyard, and its location was therefore moved to Horse Guards.

For those visitor's, who having seen the above ceremony and now wish to see the earlier pattern full dress helmets as described previously in this chapter, they could hardly do better than to visit the Household Cavalry Museum[9], at Combermere Barracks, Windsor, Berkshire, which is but a short train journey from London.

At the museum there is a splendid collection of both officers and other ranks full dress uniforms, accoutrements, and swords, including of course the aforementioned helmets. There are uniforms dating back to the Waterloo period and beyond, and also on display is the cork artificial leg, tunic and helmet of the 1st Marquess of Angelsey referred to earlier in this chapter. On my last visit to the museum, I was informed by Major Kirsting (Rtd), the Curator of the museum, *"that the present Marquess of Angelsey"*, an author of great note, *"is a frequent visitor to the museum"*.

Also included within the many exhibits, which are all displayed to enable the visitor to fully appreciate these items from bygone days, are many helmets and uniforms relating to the former 1st The Royal Dragoons, which since the 29th March 1969 has formed part of the Blues and Royals Regiment and therefore is fully represented within the various exhibits.

There is also a souvenir shop, where visitors who wish to may purchase such items as buttons, cap badges, regimental ties, model soldiers, and military prints, to name but a few of the goodies available, which are all reasonably priced. The museum does not charge for entry and is open 10am to 1pm and 2pm to 5pm, Mondays to Fridays, but is closed at weekends and on English bank and public holidays.

NOTES

[1] The Marquess of Angelsey, formerly known as the Earl of Uxbridge commanded all the cavalry at the Battle of Waterloo in 1815. It was here that a burst of grapeshot, almost the last of the battle shattered his right leg (4).

[2] *"Honi Soit Qui Mal Y Pense"* (The motto of the Order of the Garter) translates to *'Evil to him who evil thinks'*.

[3] H.R.H. The Prince of Wales in the mounted review order of the Royal Horse Guards, appeared on the cover of the London Illustrated News of 24th July 1880 (6). The actual uniform he wore is on display in the main uniform gallery at the National Army Museum, Chelsea, London.

[4] Field Marshal Sir Edmund Allenby nicknamed "The Bull" commanded the Egyptian Expeditionary Force and was victorious over the Turkish troops at Megiddo in September 1918 (7).

[5] Field Marshal Sir Garnet J. Wolseley commanded the Gordon Relief Expedition of 1885.

[6] Claude George Bowes-Lyon K.G., K.T., G.C.V.O., T.D., LL.D., D.L., J.P. (1855-1944) later the twenty-second Lord Glamis, inherited the title Earl of Strathmore and Kinghorne. He was the father of Elizabeth Angela Marguerite Bowes-Lyon who married the Duke of York, afterwards King George VI, her present title being **Her Majesty Queen Elizabeth the Queen Mother** (94).

[7] Lt Colonel F.G. Burnaby was over 6'4" tall, with a 48 inch chest and weighed 15 stone, he must have looked truly awesome wearing full dress uniform and mounted upon his horse. He is reputed to have once wrapped a mess room poker around the neck of the Prince of Wales. He was an adventurer, hot air balloonist, politician and a writer, and died fighting the Mahdists at Abu Klea in 1885. Lieutenant Lord Binning (R.H.G.) went to the spot where Burnaby died and found a young private in the Bays (2nd Dragoon Guards) endeavouring to support Burnaby's head on his knee. The lad's grief, with tears running down his cheeks, was a touching as his simple words: ***"Oh Sir here is the bravest man in all England dying, and no one to help him"*** (10).

[8] In the late 1920s a young man of eighteen years of age, born Reginald Truscott-Jones (Ray Milland) in Neath, Wales served for a time in the ranks of the Royal Horse Guards before leaving the shores of England for a career as a film star in Hollywood. In his autobiography (9) he relates details of some incidents that occurred during his time with the regiment, including a most colourful description of how when his horse bolted he, *"finished up in the Buckingham Palace courtyard, alone and without a friend in the world"*.

[8A] According to the Regulations published 1st March 1895, the height requirements for the cavalry were to be as follows: Household Cavalry, From 5ft. 11ins. to 6ft. 1in. Heavy Cavalry, From 5ft. 8ins. to 5ft. 11ins. Medium Cavalry, From 5ft. 7ins. to 5ft. 9ins. Light Cavalry, From 5ft. 6ins. to 5ft. 8ins. (99).

[9] The Household Cavalry Museum is located at Comberemere Barracks, St. Leonards Road, Windsor, Berkshire. Telephone number: 0753-868222 ext. 203.

5

Regiments: 1st to 7th Dragoon Guards

'The Dragoon Guards are descended from the cuirassiers of the early 17th century[1], men completely covered in armour' (61), however as armour gradually disappeared they fought more frequently on horse, and upon the introduction of the light cavalry (light dragoons) who scouted, skirmished, and fought independently, the Dragoon Guards and Dragoons retained their role of heavy cavalry.

Some Brief Details of the Full Dress Uniform c. 1900.

The Tunic

With the exception of the 6th Dragoon Guards the officers wore scarlet tunics, the collar of which was in the regiments facing colour which was either in cloth, or in velvet dependent on the regiment concerned and was ornamented with gold lace and carried a regimental pattern collar badge. The shoulder cords were plaited and gold in colour, as was the Austrian knot that decorated the cuff. This knot varied in height dependent on the rank of the officer, e.g. Lieutenant, a single knot, Captain, a double knot, and Field Officer (Major and above), a triple knot, however in the 6th Dragoon Guards the cuff decoration was of special regimental pattern that differed from that of the other regiments. For the rank and file the tunic was similar but of a lesser quality, the collar of which was faced in the regimental colour being piped in yellow and carrying a collar badge, with the shoulder straps being in similar colours and carrying the regimental numeral and initials in metal. For the other ranks the much simpler pattern Austrian knot cuff decoration was of yellow braid/cord.

For all ranks of the 6th Dragoon Guards the tunic colour was blue, this dating back to 1851 when it was proposed that the regiment should be converted to the light cavalry role. The blue tunics were adopted, but the conversion order was canceled, although the regiment retained its blue tunics. For the officers the Austrian knot was in gold cord, however for the rank and file it was in white.

Trousers & Pantaloons

Of blue cloth, the officers having a single 1 3/4 inch gold lace stripe down each seam, the exception being in the 2nd Dragoon Guards who had a single stripe of white cloth, and the 6th Dragoon Guards who had double white stripes. For the rank and file the stripe was yellow cloth, except in the 2nd Dragoon Guards who wore a single buff/white stripe, and the 6th Dragoon Guards who had a double white stripe.

Shoulder Belt and Pouch

For the officers, of gold lace in the regimental pattern with a gilt metal buckle, tip, and slide also of regimental pattern. In the 6th Dragoon Guards the buckle, tip, and slide, together with the breast ornament of prickers and chains were in silver. The pouch was black leather with a silver flap usually bearing the Royal Cypher, with the rank and file having a white leather shoulder belt with a black leather pouch.

Active Service

The seven regiments of Dragoon Guards have fought as cavalrymen across the far reaching corners of the world. Their battle honours are numerous, with some of the earlier, more famous being: Abyssinia, Afghanistan 1879-80, Balaclava, Blenheim, Delhi, Egypt 1882, Lucknow, Pekin, Peninsula, Salamanca, Sevastopol, South Africa 1846-47, South Africa 1899-1902, and Waterloo to name but a few. N.B. The Albert pattern helmet was worn by the officers and men at Balaklava, Lucknow and Sevastopol.

Cavalry of the Line

The Household Cavalry were/are not "Cavalry of the Line," which was comprised of the Dragoon Guards, Dragoons, Hussars, and Lancers. The Dragoon Guards were the senior regiments of line cavalry and whilst parading with other line cavalry regiments, as might have occurred at a royal review they took precedence over the Dragoons, Hussars, and Lancers.

Head-Dress Prior to 1847

For the seven regiments of Dragoon Guards it was some time after 1812 that the cocked hat was replaced as the form of head wear worn by the men of these regiments. This new head-dress took the form of a peaked helmet of black leather, having a brass plate with a 'GR' cypher, below which was an oval plaque with the title of the regiment. The helmet was completed by having rosettes, chinscales, and a high comb upon which was a 'thistle' type brush, together with a very long black hanging horsehair mane. See: Carman page 25, plate: 9.(3). During 1818 a 'Roman' style peaked helmet having a black metal skull, with gilt leaf decoration was introduced, the head-dress having a large flat-ended rayed plate bearing the Royal Arms. The skull was surmounted by a black metal crest, topped by a large black bearskin crest, lion's head bosses and chinscales completing the helmet. (See: Carman page 27, plate: 10.(3).)

1834 saw the introduction of what has frequently been described as *'the most beautiful of all the British cavalry helmets'*. The skull and peak was of gilt metal for the officers, having a large rayed plate bearing the Hanoverian Royal Arms, with a band beneath the plate upon which was the regimental title. On top of the skull was a highly ornamented gilt metal comb to which could be attached a black fur crest, or alternatively a gilt metal finial in the shape of the forepart of a lion. Gilt Tudor rose ear rosettes, and gilt chinscales completed the head-dress. (See: Carman page 29, plate: 11 and page 31, plate: 12. (3).)

A further change occurred c. 1843 when a gilt/brass peaked helmet was taken into wear, having a rayed plate with Royal Arms with title band beneath, ear rosettes and chinscales in gilt, all of which were similar to those of the last pattern , albeit that the Royal Arms were now those of Queen Victoria. The skull of the helmet was surmounted by a highly ornamented crest into which was inserted a black horsehair mane (two feet, ten inches long) with a 'thistle' shaped hair brush to the front of the crest. (See: Carman page 33, plate: 13.(3).) This pattern of head-dress was worn for some four years until being replaced by the 'Albert' pattern helmet.

It is not hard to imagine the reaction of a newly commissioned subaltern, who in the latter part of 1846, having purchased his Cornetcy (2nd Lieutenant) at a cost of around £800, paid for his accoutrements, helmet, uniform, sword, and horse furniture, and is then informed that sometime next year a new pattern of helmet is to be introduced for wear in the regiment, which he must purchase at his own expense.

There is a good representation of many of the helmets referred to above included in a series of fifty coloured cigarette cards produced by John Player & Sons in March 1931, entitled 'Military Head-Dress'[1B] Each card carries a reasonably accurate description of the head dress on the back, although a couple of the dates given are in my opinion questionable.

The 1847 'Albert' Pattern Helmet

My research has identified two differing dates for the authorization of the 'Albert' pattern helmet. W.Y. Carman in his excellent book on cavalry head-dress (3) states that *"A Horse Guards order of 30th July 1847 authorised a new pattern helmet for Dragoon Guards and Dragoons. This became known as the 'Albert' pattern and had been inspired by the Russian and Prussian helmets recently taken into wear"*, and continues *"The new issue was not that rapid and the Illustrated London News did not herald the new arrival until 23rd October 1847"*. He further states that *"The helmets are now in course of manufacture by Messrs Hamburger And Co., of King Street, Covent Garden. The customary' period was not close at hand and it was not until 1850 that all regiments were issued with the new helmet"*.

In their book on the British Cavalry Division at Balaclava in 1854, (20) John and Boris Mollo state that *"The new metal helmet was authorised by a Circular Memorandum, dated 23 October 1849. It was similar to, but slightly simpler than the 'Albert' helmet adopted by the Household Cavalry in 1842, which was the first helmet of the* ***pickelhaube*** *style adopted by the British Army"*. Having been acquainted with Bill Carman for several years, and having met Boris Mollo on several occasions in the past, I leave it to the readers of this book to decide which of the two dates quoted by these well respected authors they accept.

There are differing contemporary views on the suitability of the 'Albert' helmet, Lieutenant Colonel John Luard in his book on military uniforms (16), published in c. 1852 wrote on this subject, an extract of which is reproduced below exactly as written. "The *helmet lately decided on for the heavy cavalry: it has two great defects. The first is the plume, which in every sense of the word as already explained, most objectionable for a horseman; the second is the peak, which coming to a point almost like the head of a salmon, is not well calculated to protect both eyes from the glare of the sun; and it is brought down in continuation of the curve of the head-piece, which brings it so near the nose, that the wearer cannot see straight before him without throwing back his head or his helmet"*.

Another contemporary view, from an officer writing from the Crimea, was more favourable, describing it thus *"The most comfortable headdress, the weight being low on the head, the peak in front is quite sufficient for the eyes and that in the rear not only keeps the neck dry, but is a great protection from a sword cut. As proof of its serviceable qualities, no Dragoon is ever seen with any other headdress on, not even a forage cap, whereas scarce a shako is now found in the army"*. (17). N.B. The shako referred to was the head-dress worn by members of the 4th, and 13th Light Dragoons during the campaign in the Crimea.

The 'Albert' pattern helmet was worn on active service (minus the plume) throughout the Crimean campaign of 1854-1855, and in The Charge of The Heavy Brigade at Balaclava on the morning of the 25th October 1854 by members of the 4th (Royal Irish) Dragoon Guards, the 5th (Princess of Wales's) Dragoon Guards, the 1st (Royal) Dragoons, and the 6th (Inniskilling) Dragoons. Also taking part in this historic charge were the 2nd (Royal North British) Dragoons, who wore their famous black bearskin in place of the metal helmet. In the latter part of this war the 1st (King's) Dragoon Guards arrived in the Crimea, and were present at the siege and capture of Sevastopol in 1855 where they also wore the 'Albert' pattern helmet.

This pattern of helmet, again minus the plume, but worn with a puggree (a scarf of thin muslin or a silk veil wound around the crown of the helmet and falling down behind as a shade) was also worn 'in action' by men of the 2nd Dragoon Guards (Queen's Bays), during the India Mutiny, including their famous charge at the Relief of Lucknow in 1857.

One of the most interesting officers to wear this pattern of helmet was Brigadier-General (later to be Lieutenant-General G.C.B.) James York Scarlett[2] who commanded the Heavy Brigade in the Crimea. He led his command of the five previously mentioned regiments, numbering rather less than 600 sabres against the Russian cavalry estimated to be between 3,000 to 4,000 strong, and after a fierce engagement put the enemy to flight. He was reported as being the first man to enter the enemy's ranks, his helmet being **'stove in'** and received five wounds, though none of a serious nature.

There is however some confusion as to which helmet Scarlett actually wore in the charge, as apparently two differing pattern of helmets exist, one being similar to the normal 'Albert' pattern, but having a flattened peak and being without a central device/badge on the helmet plate, the other being a regulation 'Albert' pattern helmet and having the central device (described later) of the 5th Dragoon Guards. In an article that appeared in the Journal of the SFAHR by Major A. McKenzie Annand (18) which was accompanied by an illustration of each of the two aforementioned helmets, he investigated this matter in an attempt to establish which helmet was actually worn in battle by General Scarlett. In the illustration of Scarlett's regulation pattern helmet it can clearly be seen that the helmet has suffered a **serious blow to the upper skull** close the crown on the helmet plate, there is however no visible evidence of any damage to the other helmet. Major McKenzie Annand mentions that there may *"some-*

where he a third, black helmet", and concludes that *"he is unable to decide just which helmet Scarlett wore at Balaclava"*. N.B. In 1934 both the helmets mentioned above, plus other military relics formerly belonging to General Scarlett were on display at Townley Hall Art Gallery and Museum, Burnley, Lancashire, and may well still be there to this day.

Another officer who took part in the Heavy Brigade charge was Major (later to be Lt General) W.C. Forrest of the 4th (Royal Irish) Dragoon Guards, and he is recorded as saying *"I got a crack on the head, but the brass pot (his helmet) stood well and my head is only slightly bruised"* (19). His helmet, but now bearing the helmet plate and plume of the 7th regiment of Dragoon Guards, who he commanded from the 30th August 1859, is on permanent display at the National Army Museum, Chelsea, London.

Dress Regulations 1855

The 1847 Officers Pattern (See Fig: 13.)

The 'Regulations for the Dress of General, Staff, and Regimental Officers of The Army' published in 1855 describe the 'Albert' pattern helmet as follows;

"Gilt brass, the front and back peaks ornamented with a scroll wreath; a band of the same character round the bottom and up the back of the helmet; front ornament, within a shield, a diamond cut silver star upon which is a garter bearing the title of the regiment, and encircling the cypher V.R.; above the shield a crown, and below it a wreath of olive and oak extending upwards. A chin-strap of plain chain, lined with black leather, fastening on each side to a rose ornament. On the top of the helmet a socket for the plume". It then goes on to describe the helmet for the 1st and 6th regiments of Dragoons, and the plume colours of the various regiments, which I shall refer to later. N.B. I have always been under the impression that the left hand wreath was of laurel, however as the official description as given above states **olive,** and I am not much of a botanist I shall bow to their superior knowledge of matters flora and describe the left hand wreath as being of olive hereafter in this chapter.

Whilst the above is reasonably descriptive and is probably quite adequate for the purpose for which is was produced, far more detailed information has over the years become available relating to the various parts of the helmet, how they are affixed and its overall construction. The following detailed description includes the additional information that was acquired by the author whilst in the process of stripping down a helmet to its component parts for the purpose of cleaning/restoration.

Figure 13: 1st (King's) Dragoon Guards officers 1847 pattern. A fine example of this regiments 'Albert' pattern helmet. N.B. The plume is a modern replacement. Author's collection. Photo: Author.

Figure 13a: 1st (King's) Dragoon Guards officers 1847 pattern. The plume removed to show the plume holder finials. Author's collection. Photo: Author.

The Skull (See Fig: 14.)
This was normally made of copper/gilt for the seven regiments of Dragoon Guards, being formed in two separate parts, and constructed in a like manner to that of the 1842 Household Cavalry helmet. The front and rear peaks were bound with gilt metal, and were secured to the skull sections by small rivets which appeared to be attached to the back of the 3/4 inch wide leaf and scroll band that encircled the waist of the helmet. On some helmets there was a very small rivet positioned on the upper part of each side of the front peak binding, assumedly as an additional means of securing the binding to the peak itself. The foliage that decorated the peaks was attached by six small rivets to the front peak (See Fig: 16D.), and five small rivets for the back peak. This foliage decoration was however of a different pattern to that on the 1842 Household Cavalry helmet, being far less profuse, and located close to the peak binding, and did not therefore cover the whole of the front peak. Both inner peaks were covered with dark green skiver.

The rear skull seam was covered by a gilt metal tapering one inch wide oak-leaf band that extended downwards from the rear finial of the foliated plume base holder to terminate beneath the edge of the rear peak binding. It was affixed in place by the rear stud of the foliated plume base passing through a corresponding hole at the top of the rear seam band, and then on through a hole in the skull, being secured with a brass nut and washer. This band was also fitted with a short stud positioned half way down its length, being secured with a brass nut, and by a metal bend-over two pronged tab close to its base which passed through a slot in the skull, the prongs then being opened outwards and flattened.

N.B. On the early pattern helmets the skull appears to have been taller, and more dome shaped than on later examples, and it also appeared to be narrower when viewed from the front. Additionally, within the skull at the top of the dome where the plume stem entered the helmet it had the appearance of having been strengthened, and was surrounded by small ventilation holes. The thin metal triangular shaped backing plate referred to in the section describing the plume holder, was not fitted to this pattern of helmet.

The Plume Holder
Similar to the Household Cavalry pattern, it was of gilt/brass and in two separate pieces. These consisted of a foliated socket, (See Fig: 15A.), having seven, or more commonly eight short finials, and was fitted with a tapering inner funnel which prevented the plume stem from being pulled too far down into the socket. The finialed socket fitted into a shorter one having four large upright finials, (See Fig: 15A.), which was permanently attached to a foliated pattern base with eight leaf pattern terminals. The inner finialed socket (complete with tapering funnel), was attached to the foliated base by means of two small studs at its lowest part which passed through parallel holes in foliated base, where it was secured by two small brass nuts.

The complete plume mount was attached to the skull by a similar method as on the Household Cavalry helmet, however on some Dragoon Guards skulls, there was the addition of a thin metal triangular shaped backing plate (See Fig: 14.), which was positioned over the front and side studs on the base of the plume mount, onto which brass nuts and washers were attached. This backing plate was not however passed over the rear stud of the plume mount base, as

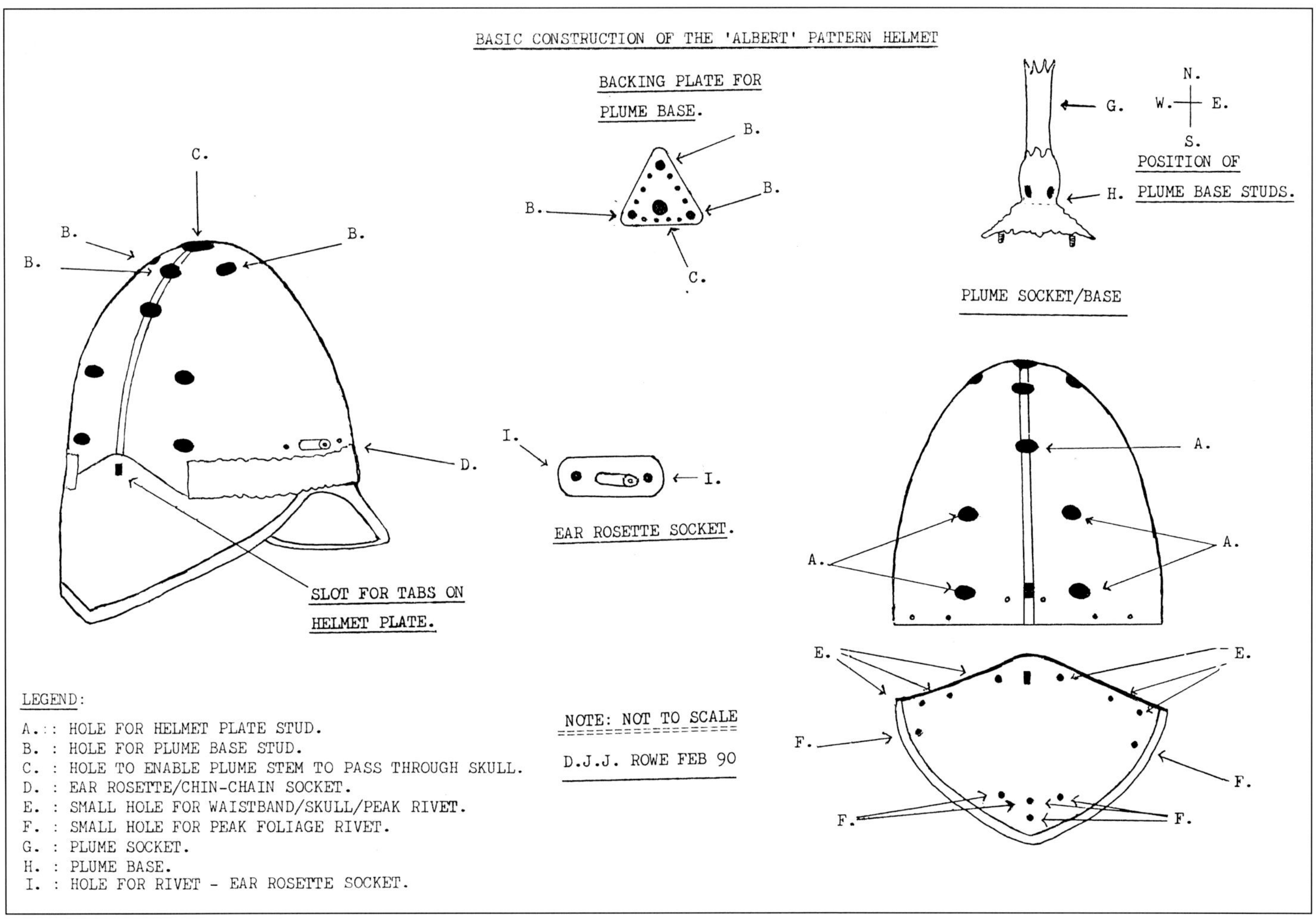

Figure 14: Basic construction of the 1847 'Albert' pattern helmet for both Dragoon Guards and the 1st and 6th Dragoons. Author.

Figure 15: 4th (Royal Irish) Dragoon Guards officers 1847 pattern. An early example of the officers 1847 pattern helmet complete with original plume. c. 1855-1871. Author's collection. Photo: Courtesy of the National Army Museum.

Figure 15a: Side view of helmet with plume removed to show the tall 'dome' shape of the skull. Author's collection. Photo: Courtesy of the National Army Museum.

ROYAL IRISH DRAGOON GUARDS

this stud was used as the means of securing the top of the rear oak-leaf seam band.

It is of interest to note that the height of the finialed plume socket, when measured from the lowest part of the foliated plume mount base, to the tip of the finials varies by as much as an inch on some helmets, and this difference in height can clearly be seen in the helmets illustrated in Fig: 18. It is possible that this difference is merely a makers variation, however it is also conceivable that it is related to the physical stature of the wearer, an officer of say 5ft 2 inches wearing a helmet fitted with the taller of the two plume sockets, thereby increasing his overall height. N.B. The stature of an officer and the height of his head-dress is known to have been taken into account for the 2nd Dragoons (Royal Scots Greys), as the Dress Regulations of 1900 give three differing heights for the officers bearskin, details of which will be given later in chapter six.

The Headband and Lining

As with the helmets of the Household Cavalry the headband was made of either what appears to have been hard leather, or alternatively of pressed felt. The headband measured approximately two inches in depth and was secured to the skull by the method used on the Household Cavalry helmet. The lining which was sewn onto the headband was of either quilted cloth, usually beige in colour edged with brown velvet, of brown or red leather and having a silk upper section of similar colour, or alternatively of soft leather, but without the silk upper section. Adjustment for size and comfort was achieved by loosening, or tightening the one, or two drawstring/s fitted to the lining.

The Helmet Plate

In gilt metal, within a wreath of olive leaves (left), and oak leaves (right), a rococo shield surmounted by a 'Victorian' crown having depressed arches. Upon the shield an eight-pointed silver diamond-cut star surmounted by the central device, this being a gilt metal oval shaped strap bearing the regimental title (see below) with the Royal Cypher 'V.R.' (Victoria Regina) within the strap. N.B. With all due deference to the compiler of the 1855 Dress Regulation, as the 'Garter' referred to in the text of this book does not bear the Motto of the Order of the Garter, I respectfully suggest that the term **strap** is more appropriate.

The aforementioned helmet plate had a crown measuring approximately 2 1/2 inches (2 5/8 inches) from outer arch to outer arch, with the wreath measuring approximately 5 1/4 inches (6 1/8 inches) when measured across the centre, (from olive leaves to oak leaves). There was also a slightly smaller pattern helmet plate, thought to have been introduced sometime later, or possibly being a makers variation, although this has not been confirmed. This pattern of plate had a crown which measured approximately 2 1/8 inches (2 1/4 inches), with the wreath measuring approximately 4 3/8 inches (5 1/4 inches) when measured as described above. N.B. Measurement of the crown and the wreath was achieved by the following methods. (1) By the use of a dividing compass, this being the first measurement given, and by (2) By using a thin piece of twine, which permitted the curvature of the helmet plate to be included in the overall width, the later measurements being those shown within the brackets. The helmet plate/badge consisted of three separate pieces, these being the crown/wreath/rococo shield, the diamond-cut star, and the central device.

On early pattern helmets the central device (strap/royal cypher) was affixed to the shield by means of four very thin metal pins positioned at north, south, east and west, which when passed through corresponding holes in the shield were flattened with the points of the pins pointing towards each other. This also secured the diamond-cut star in place. An alternative, later method of securing the device to the shield, was by passing the two small lugs attached to the centre device (positioned at east and west) through corresponding slots in both the star and the shield, then placing a small 'oblong' shaped washer over each lug. The device was finally secured by passing a thin brass pin through the minute hole at the end of each lug. N.B. With the exception of the oblong shaped washers, this was similar to the method used on the centre device assembly on the Household Cavalry helmet plate.

Opposite, Figure 15b: Close up view of the helmet plate. Authors collection. Photo: R. Biondi.

The Regimental Titles on the Strap

The following are the regimental titles as they appeared on the strap described above, when reading from left to right:

1st Dragoon Guards	Kings Dragoon Guards
2nd Dragoon Guards	Queens Dragoon Guards
3rd Dragoon Guards	Prince of Wales Dragn. Guards (as spelt on strap)
4th Dragoon Guards	Royal Irish Dragoon Guards (See Fig: 15B.)
5th Dragoon Guards	P.C.W. Dragoon Guards (See Fig: 16A.)
6th Dragoon Guards	The Carabiniers
7th Dragoon Guards	Dragoon VII Guards

The complete helmet plate was affixed to the skull by means of either of the following methods. (1) Three short studs to the reverse of the plate, they being located with one stud behind the crown, one behind the centre of the olive wreath, and one behind the centre of the oak wreath. (2) Five short studs at the reverse of the plate, they being positioned as follows. One stud behind the crown, one to the upper rear of the olive wreath, one to the lower rear of olive wreath, one to the upper rear of the oak wreath, and one to the lower rear of oak wreath, with a two pronged bend over blade (tab) positioned behind the point where the oak and olive wreaths met. For either pattern of plate the method of securing the plate to the skull was the same as for the Household Cavalry. N.B. On a 5th Dragoon Guards pattern helmet in the authors collection there is an additional short, gilt metal foliated band measuring approximately 3/4 inches in width, positioned below the front terminal of the plume mount base and extending down beneath the top of the helmet plate crown, which covers the front seam joint of the skull. This fitment is all belonging and contemporary with the rest of the helmet, it being held in place by the front stud of the plume base mount, and the short stud positioned behind the crown that surmounts the helmet plate.

The Ear Rosettes

On the early pattern helmets examined by the author, they were all fitted with the large 'Albert' pattern rosette, being similar in appearance to the Household Cavalry pattern (See Fig: 9.G), being with, or without the raised (proud) centre. Both these pattern of rosette were of gilt/brass and measured 2 1/4 inches in diameter having a threaded stud soldered to the reverse.

The Chinchain

As mentioned earlier the official description was "a **chinstrap** of plain chain lined with black leather", however it is not unusual for the backing leather to be of the same colour as the leather of the skull lining, e.g. red leather is known to have been used on both the head lining and the chinchain backing on some of the helmets of the 4th Dragoon Guards. Also to occasionally be found are chinchains faced with black leather having a black velvet backing, and on hel-

Opposite, Figure 16A: Close up of the helmet plate. Note the abbreviated regimental title on the strap. Photo: R. Biondi.

Figure 16: 5th (Princess Charlotte of Wales's) Dragoon Guards officers 1847 pattern. A post 1855 example complete with original plume. Compare the size of the plume rosette, illustrated with pattern fitted to the plume in Fig: 15. Photo: R. Biondi.

P.O.W. DRAGOON GUARDS

Figure 16c: Side view of helmet with plume removed to show the shape of the skull. Compare this skull with that of the 4th Dragoon Guards helmet illustrated in Fig: 15A. Photo: R. Biondi.

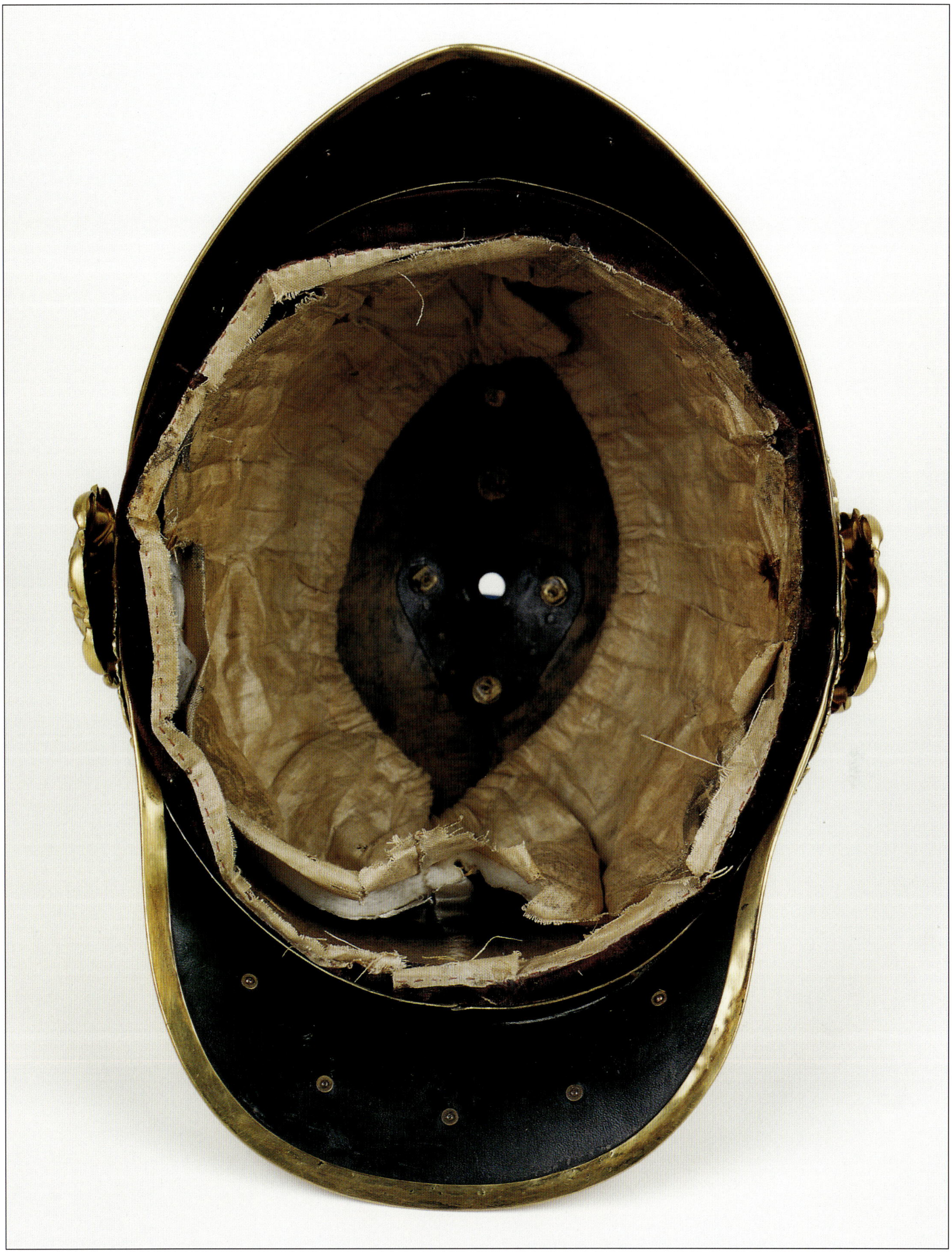

Figure 16d: Inside view of the skull showing the age worn lining. Photo: R. Biondi.

mets having a red/scarlet head lining, the velvet backing to the chinchain was often of the same colour.

The standard width of the chain/backing appears to have been approximately one inch wide, however helmets do sometimes turn up having narrower chinchains, although it may well be that these are a replacement fitting. To enable the chain to be hooked onto the ear rosette socket, various methods were used, these being (1) At each end of the chinchain there was either two/three loose additional links, (2) There was a hole in the leather strap between the last, or penultimate link, or (3) There was a thin brass tag complete with a hole at each end of the chain.

The Plume

Upon the introduction of this pattern of helmet the plume was of originally of black horsehair for all seven regiments of Dragoon Guards, and the *Regulations for the Dress of General, Staff, and Regimental Officers of The Army of 1855* describe the plume as follows, "Plume-horsehair, with a rose at top, standing five inches above the top of the helmet". However no mention is made of the horsehair 'thistle' type brush which supported the long falling hair plume, nor of the method of securing the plume to the helmet.

The basic construction of the plume was similar to the Household Cavalry pattern, except that for some unknown reason there was not a brass square 'ball' located above the threaded shaft at the base of the stem. Additionally on the Dragoon Guards helmets, the height of the 'thistle' brush was quite noticeably shorter than the brush on the 1842 pattern Household Cavalry helmet. However the method of attaching the plume to the helmet was the same.

Feather Plume

In the excellent book (20) by John and Boris Mollo on the British Cavalry in the Crimea, there is a photograph of a watercolour painting[14] by the artist W. Buckler of an officer of the 5th Dragoon Guards c. 1853 in dismounted review order holding his helmet. In this photograph/painting it can be clearly seen that the helmet is fitted with a feather plume which appears to be black in colour.

The Plume Rosette

This fitment was made of gilt/copper, or alternatively of gilt/brass, and had a threaded socket to the centre of the underside to enable it to be screwed onto the top of the plume stem. In appearance and dimensions it was identical to the ear rosette illustrated in Fig: 9.B., and was often the pattern having the raised (proud) centre.

Figure 18a: Officers 1855 pattern plumes. 4th Dragoon Guards (left), and 5th Dragoon Guards (right). Author's collection. Photo: R. Biondi.

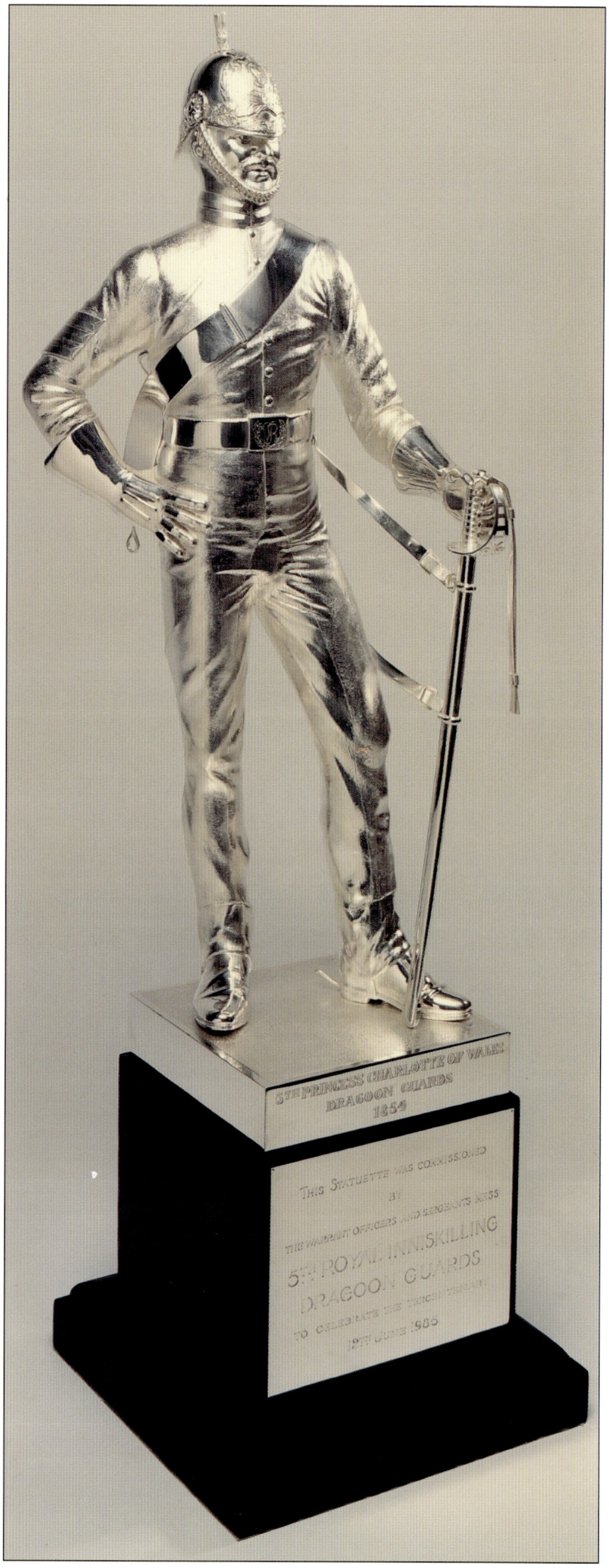

Figure 17: 5th (Princess Charlotte of Wales's) Dragoon Guards. A silver statuette of a private c. 1854 commissioned by the 5th Royal Inniskilling Dragoon Guards regiment. A splendid example of the goldsmiths and silversmiths art. Photo: Courtesy of Meilling Gartrell Goldsmiths and Silversmiths.

Figure 18: Officers 1847 pattern helmets, 5th (left) and 4th (right). Note the noticeable difference in height of the plume sockets. Author's collection. Photo: R. Biondi.

The Other Ranks Pattern

The Skull

The skull was very similar in appearance to the officers pattern, but being made of brass, which in addition to making it stronger, (replacement only once every four years) also made it heavier. The foliage to the peaks, the waist band, and rear seam band were also all in brass and were affixed by the method described earlier in this chapter. On the other ranks helmet only the front inner peak was lined with skiver.

The Plume Holder

Again similar to that on the officers helmet and affixed to the skull by the same method, one noticeable difference however being that the inner brass socket was not secured to the outer one by means of two small brass studs at its base as on the officers helmet, but was permanently affixed in place. With one exception, on the many helmets of this pattern examined by the author there was neither an inner triangular plate, nor any evidence of the inner area where the plume stem entered the skull having been strengthened as on the officers pattern helmets.

The Headband and Lining

The headband was as for the officers helmet, the lining however differed considerably as it was of brown leather, having some seven sections (leaves) which met in the centre of the skull. At the end of each of these sections was a small, metal reinforced hole, through which a drawstring was passed and then tied. Adjustment was achieved by tightening or loosening this drawstring.

The Helmet Plate

A brass rococo shield surrounded by an olive and oak-leaf pattern wreath surmounted by a crown, similar if not identical in appearance to the officers pattern plate. To the centre of the shield an eight pointed **white metal beaded star**, upon which was mounted the die-stamped, brass, oval shaped strap with centre device. The plate was made up of the same number of separate pieces, and secured to the helmet as mentioned above for the officers pattern.

The Ear Rosettes

The standard 'Albert' pattern rosette in brass, but not having the proud (raised) centre.

The Chinchain

A one inch wide brass linked chain backed with brown leather.

The Plume and Rosette

The plume was similar in appearance to that of the officers pattern, the main difference noted by the author being, that on the rank and files plume, the rosette was of brass and was considerably smaller in size. Additionally the rosette did not have a stud socket fitment to its underside, but was permanently soldered/brazed to the top of the plume stem.

The 1855 'Albert' Pattern Helmet

The Helmet Plate

Sometime during the period that this helmet was in service there occurred for at least three of the regiments, a slight variation to the centre device of the helmet plate. Whilst the Royal Cypher of 'V.R.' remained at the centre, on some helmets of the 5th, 6th and the 7th regiments, the centre device was not a die-struck fitment, but was made with the gilt metal 'V.R' being a separate piece. The cypher was attached to a backing plate within the garter, by thin pins/wire affixed to its reverse being passed through parallel holes in the backing plate and then bent over and soldered into position. The centre device was then affixed to the helmet plate by the previously described lugs/pin method. This pattern of plate was made up of four component pieces, these being the crown/wreath/rococo shield, the star, the centre device/strap, and the 'V.R.' cypher.

The Ear Rosette

Helmets of both the 1st (King's) Dragoon Guards, and the 7th (Princess Royals) Dragoon Guards have been seen by the author with either the standard 'Albert' rosette being fitted, or with one of a different pattern, this second version being illustrated in Fig: 9.I., which incidentally, was the pattern used on the later 1871 officers pattern helmets by both the aforementioned regiments.

The Plume

It was on page sixty-four of the *Regulations for the Dress of General, Staff, and Regimental Officers of The Army of 1855* that the first known official notification of a change to the plume colour for most regiments was announced, the description reading as follows:" *Plume-horsehair, with rose at top, standing five inches above the top of the helmet. The several regiments distinguished, as under, by the colour of the plume*":

1st (King's) Dragoon Guards	*Red.*
2nd (or Queen's) Dragoon Guards	*Black*
3rd (P.W.) Dragoon Guards	*Black and Red*
4th (R.Irish) Dragoon Guards	*White.*
5th (P.C.W.) Dragoon Guards	*Red and White*
6th (Carabiniers) Dragoon Guards	*Black*
7th (Princess Rls) Dragoon Guards	*Black and White*

No mention however, was made of which of the two colours was to surmount the other, for those regiments having a plume of more than one colour, nor was there any mention of which of the two colours the 'thistle' brush was to be. It is, I consider, important that such detail is not omitted, for this information would be of interest to those making a study of both helmets, and uniforms in general, and I therefore offer the missing information for the three regiments concerned:

3rd (P.W.) Dragoon Guards	Black over red with a red brush
5th (P.C.W.) Dragoon Guards	White over red with a red brush
7th (Princess Rls) Dragoon Guards	Black over white with a white brush

N.B. With regard to the new plume colours being announced in the 1855 regulations, John and Boris Mollo in their book referred to earlier in the chapter, state as follows when referring to the plume colours quoted in the regulations of 1857, *"Coloured plumes were in fact specified, but until 1857 all regiments wore black"* (20).

The Plume Rosette

Over the years helmets have appeared at auction salesrooms being fitted with a rosette that was dissimilar to the standard 'Albert' pattern rosette, this rosette being of a smaller differing pattern. Additionally many contemporary photo-

Figure 19: 2nd (Queen's Bays) Dragoon Guards c. 1847-1871 other ranks pattern helmet. Note that the star is the hobnailed pattern and not diamond-cut, as on the officers helmets. Author's collection. Photo: Courtesy of the National Army Museum.

graphs taken c. 1865 and after, of officers in full dress uniform holding or wearing their helmet, show that a smaller sized plume rosette was now being worn by some regiments, this rosette being similar in appearance that illustrated in Fig: 9.C.

The 1871 Pattern Helmet

The Officers Pattern

Towards the close of the nineteenth century it was not unusual for the ruler of a continental power to be given the Colonelency of a British regiment, and for British Royalty to hold a similar appointment in a foreign army. That said, perhaps one of the most unexpected men ever to wear the officers pattern helmet of a British Dragoon Guards regiment was the Emperor of Austria, His Imperial and Royal Apostolic Majesty Francis Joseph I. K.G. Emperor of Austria and Hungary[3], who held the appointment of Colonel-in-Chief of the 1st (King's) Dragoon Guards from the 25th March 1896 until the outbreak of the First World War. On the outbreak of the war in August 1914, the Emperor wrote to the regiment *"conveying his sorrow at the coming conflict and stated that if any member of the K.D.G's should happen to be taken prisoner by Austro-Hungarian troops he should be informed of the fact instantly by the regiment"* (21).

Another ruler of a continental country who was so honoured was H.M. Albert I, King of the Belgians, who was appointed Colonel-in-Chief of the 5th (Princess Charlotte of Wales's) Dragoon Guards on the 11th August 1915. N.B. H.M. Leopold III, King of the Belgians was appointed Colonel-in-Chief of the 5th Royal Inniskilling Dragoon Guards on the 30th March 1937 (6).

A great many Dragoon Guards officers had rewarding careers and went on to achieve fame and high military rank, amongst them being the following:

> Lt General Robert Stephenson Smyth Baden-Powell Bt[4] G.C.M.G., G.C.V.O., K.C.B., O.M., Kt., LL.D., (22) who commanded the 5th Dragoon Guards in 1897.
>
> Field Marshal Sir William Robertson Bart[5] G.C.B., G.C.M.G., G.C.V.O., D.S.O., D.C.L., LL.D., who served in **the ranks** of the 16th (The Queen's) Lancers from 1877 to 1888, when he was commissioned into the 3rd (Prince of Wales's) Dragoon Guards.
>
> Lt General Adrian Carton de Wiart[6] V.C., K.B.E., C.B., C.M.G., D.S.O. A Belgian, with an Irish grandmother, he enlisted in Paget's Horse and went to South Africa at the outbreak of the war there, was later give a commission in the Imperial Light Horse, and in 1901 was commissioned in the 4th (Royal Irish) Dragoon Guards. Lt 1904, Captain in 1910, he also held the post of Adjutant of the Royal Gloucester Hussars. Just before the First World War he was with the Camel Corps in Somaliland fighting the dervishes where he received wounds in the left eye which later had to be removed.

In his book on head-dress (3) W.Y. Carman writes as follows when referring to the 1871 pattern helmet. *"In April 1871 a new pattern helmet was approved for the heavy cavalry. The foliage on the peak was discontinued and a narrow brass edge sufficed"*. He goes on to say *"the elaborate backing plate with crown and wreath disappeared leaving the regimental device on a twelve pointed plate, cut steel for officers, rayed for men"*.

Dress Regulations 1874

The section from the above dress regulations that relates directly the full dress helmet and plume, is reproduced below as it was printed in this book. Although somewhat lacking in finite detail, it was probably sufficient for the requirements of both the helmet manufacturer and the military outfitter/tailor who supplied the head-dress to the officers in the late 1870s, and was an improvement of previously published dress regulations:

> *"Helmet for Dragoon Guards-Gilt brass, with a scroll wreath along the bottom in front, and up the back. A diamond-cut silver star in front, with the regimental device or number in the centre, within a garter bearing the title of the regiment. Plain gilt burnished chain, lined with black leather, and fastened on each side with a gilt rose ornament. A gilt plume-socket on the top of the helmet.*
>
> *Plume-Horsehair, of the colours stated below for each regiment, with rose at top, rising 6 inches above the top of the helmet and then falling as far as the bottom.*

Regiment	***Colour of Plume***
1st Dragoon Guards	*Red*
2nd Dragoon Guards	*Black*
3rd Dragoon Guards	*Black and Red*
4th Dragoon Guards	*White*
5th Dragoon Guards	*Red and White*
6th Dragoon Guards	*White*
7th Dragoon Guards	*Black and White.*

Regarding the colours of red and white as given for the 5th Dragoon Guards above, I respectfully suggest that this is inaccurate as the predominate colour (upper) of this regiments plume was white and not red as inferred by this description. If using the above as a plume colour guide, then for the 3rd Dragoon Guards 'black and red' infers that the plume was black **over** red which is correct, and for the 7th Dragoon Guards 'black and white' infers black **over** white which again is correct. I mention this point not to be pedantic, but to point out an error which was repeated through all the following dress regulations, even the 1934 version.

Owning an original painting by a famous military artist of the Edwardian era, that illustrates an officer of the 6th Dragoon Guards in review order, I noticed that the artist had made an error in detail when painting the helmet plate centre. This leads me to belief that the artist concerned consulted the then current dress regulations as a source of reference, and took what was quoted as being totally accurate, which was in fact not the case.

In respect of the colour of the plume for the 5th Dragoon Guards, as I would not wish such an error to be perpetuated by artists and model makers of the present and future, I respectfully bring this matter to the reader's attention. N.B. prior to 1873 the plume of the 6th Dragoon Guards was black in colour.

With regard to the above description for the helmet, no mention is made of the design on the 'scroll wreath along the bottom in front', this description apparently referring to the laurel-leaf waist band, and 'up the back' referring to the rear seam band. There is also no mention of the differing pattern plume sockets, of the head lining, what form the regimental device took, nor of the differing pattern ear and plume rosettes.

Dress Regulations 1883

With the publication of the 1883 regulations came several changes in the description for the helmet, which redressed some of the earlier omissions. Some of this additional information is quite significant, and therefore reproduced below is the amended description of the helmet as printed in these regulations. I have also identified the changes and the additional information by placing same in bold text.

> *"Helmet for Dragoon Guards-Gilt brass,* ***bound round the edge. At the top, a cross-piece base*** *and a gilt plume socket,* ***4 inches high from the point of insertion in base. A laurel wreath above the front peak, and an oak-leaf band up the back.*** *A diamond-cut silver star in front:* ***on the star in gilt metal, a garter, pierced with the motto, Honi soit qui mal y pense, or the designation of the Regiment. In the 4th Dragoon Guards, the garter is pierced with the motto "Quis separabit". Within the garter,*** *the regimental device or number. Plain gilt burnished chain* ***3/4 inch wide,*** *mounted on* ***black patent leather,*** *and fastened on each side with a gilt rose ornament".*
>
> ***"Plume-Horsehair, of the colour stated below for each regiment. The plume rises 2 inches from point of insertion in the socket, and falls as far as the bottom of the helmet. A gilt rose at the top, screwed on to the metal stem of the plume".***

Although far greater detail was included in this description, there was still no mention that there where at least two differing pattern plume sockets, what type of head lining was used, nor, that for two regiments the silver star that formed a major part of the helmet plate differed from those of the other regiments, neither was any mention made of the different pattern ear and plume rosettes etc. The full details of the above mentioned omissions, together with

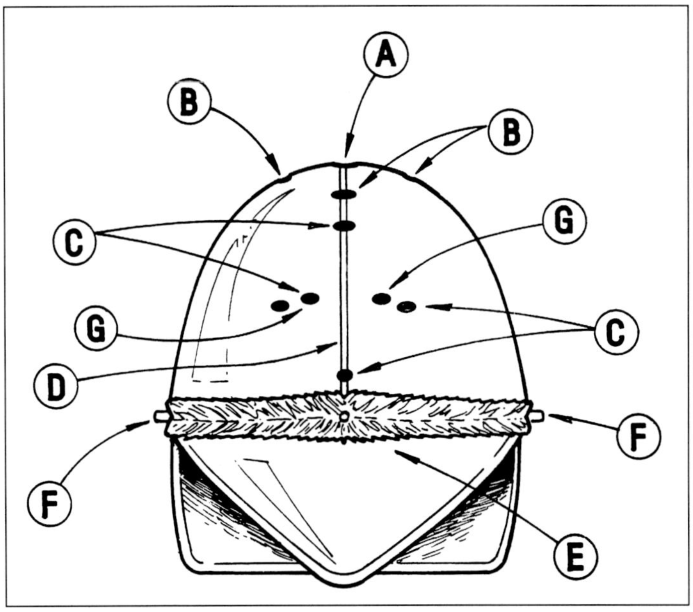

Figure 20: Basic construction of the 1871 pattern helmet for both Dragoon Guards and the 1st and 6th Dragoons. A. hole to enable the plume stem to pass through the skull; B. holes for plume base studs; C. holes for helmet plate studs; D. centre seam; E. waist band; F. ear rosette/chinchain socket; G. holes to enable the lugs that attach the strap/garter to the helmet plate to pass through the skull. Not to scale. Author.

additional information relating to this pattern of helmet acquired during my research into this subject are as follows.

The Officers Pattern Helmet (See Fig: 21.)

The Skull

Of gilt/copper and made in two sections (See Figs: 20. and 21D.), the brim of the peaks being bound in gilt metal, the inside of both front and back peaks

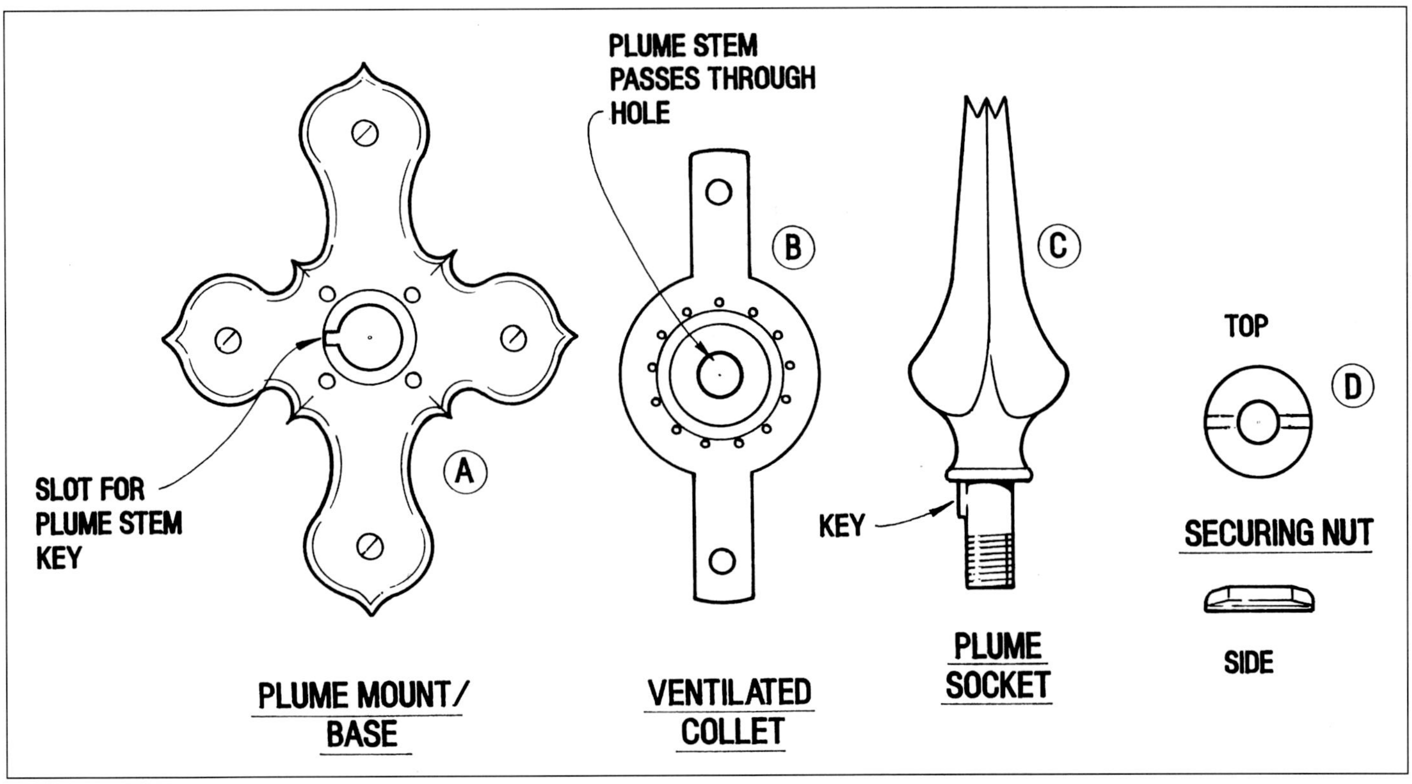

Figure 20a: The plume base, plume socket, and collet as fitted to the 1871 officers pattern helmet. Author.

being lined with green skiver, with the skull being constructed in the same manner as the Household Cavalry helmets. Above the front peak a gilt metal laurel-leaf band being approximately 5/8 inches wide at the sides and 1 1/2 inches wide at the centre, being attached to the skull by means of three, double pronged bend-over tabs, one at either end, and one at the centre of the reverse of the wreath. The rear seam joint was covered by a gilt metal oak-leaf pattern band measuring 1 inch in width which extended downwards from beneath the rear terminal of the crosspiece base of the plume holder to terminate beneath the edge of the rear peak binding. It was secured by the top of the band by being soldered to the skull, and additionally held in place by the rear stud of the crosspiece base, as on the Household Cavalry helmets. It was further secured by means of a small stud with a brass nut to the centre, and another small stud fitted with a circular brass 'nut' towards the bottom of the band.

The Plume Holder

"A cross-piece base and a gilt plume socket, 4 inches high from point of insertion in base". Hardly a well defined description of this fitment, there being no mention of the taller plume socket as fitted to the helmet of the 2nd Dragoon Guards and the 1st, and 6th Dragoons, nor of the spike that has been known on rare occasions to have been fitted in place of the plume socket.

The plume holder consisted of (1), a gilt/brass cross-piece base having four terminals positioned at north, south, east and west, beneath each of which was a short stud (See Fig: 20A.), there being a hole at the top of the base with a keyway cut into it (See Fig: 20A.) (2), A gilt/brass fluted socket, having a key located above the thread at its base. (3), A steel collet, and (4), a brass circular 'nut'. N.B. It is not unusual to find that the underside of the plume mount base, and that the bottom of the socket is indented with the number of the regiment, e.g.'3' to indicate 3rd Dragoon Guards.

The plume holder was assembled by passing the studs beneath the cross-piece base, through corresponding holes in the dome of the skull, with the steel collet (See Fig: 20A.), being placed over the studs at north, and south position, all four studs then being secured with brass nuts and washers. The threaded stem of the plume socket was then passed down through the hole/keyway/collet, ensuring that the key on the stem was correctly located in the keyway of the plume base, to prevent the socket accidentally being turned sideways. The brass circular 'nut' was then placed onto the threaded part of the stem and tightened, thereby securing the complete plume holder to the skull section.

As mentioned earlier the 2nd Dragoon Guards had a different pattern plume socket which consisted of a fluted socket similar to the one described above, below which was a medium sized oval shaped ball (smaller in size than the bulbous shaped ball on the Household Cavalry plume holder). Below this ball was a short tube, at the base of which was a small disc having a milled edge (all one piece), which joined the plume mount base as described above. (See Fig: 25.B.) This pattern of plume holder was approximately 4 1/4 inches in height, being some 3/4 inches taller than the socket not having the ball fitment. N.B. At a world famous London Auction House in 1988 an officers helmet of the 7th Dragoon Guards was offered for sale having a plume holder similar to the above, but with the ball beneath the socket being smaller and rounder than the ball on the 2nd Dragoon Guards plume holder. However as this pattern of plume holder was normally only to be found on the yeomanry helmets, it may be that this holder was a replacement (See Fig: 25.D.).

In addition to the three aforementioned pattern of plume holders, there was also an alternative top mount, this being in the shape of a spike. The spike was fitted in place of the fluted socket and was not capable of accepting a plume stem (See Fig: 25.F). It was mounted above a smaller, rounder ball than the one beneath the socket on the 2nd Dragoon Guards plume holder, but was however fitted with the same pattern plume mount base. The author however, has only seen an example of this pattern of holder on one dragoon guards helmet, this being in a photograph showing a helmet of the 6th (Carabiniers) Dragoon Guards. N.B. This spike pattern top mount with base, was also fitted to the officers foreign service helmet of the 13th Hussars during the mid 1870s. The spike was also fitted to a similar pattern helmet worn by the rank and file of the 4th Dragoon Guards whilst in India c. 1895/96, and to the foreign service helmet of the musicians in the band of the 5th Dragoon Guards whilst also on service in India c.1903/04.

Figure 20b: 1st (King's) Dragoon Guards. 'Officers for the Cape' 12th January 1901. Note: Captain E.A. Williams whose helmet is illustrated in Fig: 21. is seated second from left in the middle row. Photo: Courtesy R.G. Harris.

The Headband and Lining

Both the headband and the ear rosette socket were of similar design and construction as on the Household Cavalry helmet. The lining was generally of beige padded cloth/silk, although brown padded cloth, scarlet padded silk, soft tan calf with a silk upper section were also used. On some very late pattern helmets, chamois leather was used in place of cloth/silk. Adjustment for comfort and fit was as previously described

A possible aid to identifying the name of the officer who once owned a particular helmet, may sometimes be found on the tailor's paper label which on some helmets may be located at the front inner of the skull on the actual headband, being normally hidden from view by the silk lining. Examples seen by the author have had a date, the tailor's reference number, followed by the officers surname and in some case his head size, or a combination of any of these four. Given this information it may be possible by searching through the various volumes of either the *Monthly Army List*, or *Harts Army List* to more positively identify the officer concerned, and to trace his various military appointments. Four known examples of a name being on the tailors label that have been successfully identified and researched are as follows:

The Life Guards: Label: "25/6/25 Lord Allenby 7 3/8 full", being identified as the helmet of Field Marshall Sir Edmund Allenby, Colonel of the 1st Life Guards (26).

1st (King's) Dragoon Guards: Label: "3?4 Williams" which the author is

confident is the helmet that was once the property of Captain E.A.Williams[7], K.D.G.'s.
6th Dragoon Guards: In 1995 a helmet at a London salesroom (27) had a tailors label that read: "'347 Annesley 18/6/12", which was identified by the auctioneers as having once belonged to James Howard Adolphus Annesley C.M.G., D.S.O.[8]
Lothian and Border Horse: Label: "47 Linlithgow 7 1/4 Full", being the helmet formerly belonging to the 2nd Marquis of Linlithgow K.G., K.T., P.C., G.C.S.I., G.C.I.E., O.B.E., D.L., T.D.[9]

I cannot emphasis to strongly that **extreme caution must be exercised** if looking for the tailor's label within the lining. These linings will invariably be in a very fragile condition and should be handled with great care, as the lining **may tear or split if handled indelicately.**

The Helmet Plate

As with most matters relating to the finite detail of military uniforms and accoutrements, there are nearly always exceptions to the rule, none more so than in respect of the centre device on the officers helmet plates. Below is given a full description of the helmet plate of all seven regiments of Dragoon Guards, the details of which have been taken from helmets in the authors collection. When compared with the official descriptions given in the *Dress Regulations 1900* reproduced later in this chapter, it will be seen that there are some considerable differences between what was meant to be, and the centre devices that were actually fitted to the officers helmets.

1st to 3rd Dragoon Guards

A silvered diamond-cut twelve pointed star measuring approximately 5 1/8 inches from tip to tip (north to south), and 4 3/4 inches (west to east), often referred to as a Garter Star, on the reverse of which was four short threaded studs being positioned north, south, east and west. N.B. The bottom (north) stud was smaller than the other three, possibly because when the helmet plate was fitted to the skull of the helmet this stud passed through a hole close to the headband. Upon the star a gilt metal elliptical shaped garter pierced with the motto "Honi Soit Qui Mal Y Pense" backed with translucent blue enamel. Within the centre of the garter the regimental device or number as detailed below. The helmet plate was assembled by placing the enameled backing plate within the garter, and then by passing the lugs located at either side of the garter through corresponding slots in the star where it was secured by a very thin brass pin being pushed through a minute hole at the end of each of the garter lugs. The complete helmet plate which was attached to the skull by the same method as on the Household Cavalry helmets, was made up of four separate pieces these being the silvered star, the pierced garter, the enameled backing plate, and the centre device. e.g. the Royal Cypher. N.B. The backing plate (enamel ground) onto which the red and blue enamel was laid was usually of sterling silver. N.B. Unlike on the Household Cavalry garter, the edges of this garter did not have a rope pattern border.

1st (King's) Dragoon Guards (See Fig: 21.)
In silver The Crest of England (a Lion over a Victorian Crown) on a red translucent enamel ground, or alternatively, in silver the Royal Cypher (Intertwined V.R.) also on a red enamel ground. I would suggest that the 'Crest of England' centre device was adopted first as this appears on a helmet illustrated in a copy photograph I have, the head-dress having belonged to an officer who was gazetted to the regiment on the 8th March 1871.

Unique to this regiment was the tripartite silver scroll pierced with the title "Kings Dragoon Guards" in gilt which was positioned beneath the lower part of the star. To the reverse of the scroll were three very small studs, being located one at either end, with one to the centre of the scroll. As with the helmet plate the studs passed through parallel holes in the skull where it was secured with small brass nuts. It would seem logical to assume that as the pierced garter was backed with enamel, that the title scroll also would have a similar backing. However on the scroll fitted to the helmet in the author's collection, and on other title scrolls examined on helmets in both private collections and militaria shops there was absolutely no evidence on an enamel backing having ever been fitted. N.B. In order that this scroll could be secured in position on the skull it was necessary for the very tip of the bottom point of the garter star to be **flat and not diamond-cut.**

2nd (Queen's Bays) Dragoon Guards (See Fig: 22.)
The star, and the garter as on the 1st Dragoon Guards plate, but having within the garter in silver, the Royal Cypher (V.R.) on a red enamel ground.

3rd (Prince of Wales's) Dragoon Guards (See Fig: 24.)
The star, and the garter as on the 1st Dragoon Guards plate, but having within the garter in silver, The Prince of Wales's plume (feathers) including the motto "Ich Dien" on a red enamel ground. N.B. There is a known variation of this pattern helmet plate, being almost identical in appearance, except that it was very nearly half sized, measuring only some 2 1/2 inches x 2 1/4 inches, which was fitted to the foreign service (tropical) pattern helmets worn by the officers of this regiment.

4th (Royal Irish) Dragoon Guards (See Fig: 28.)
The Most Illustrious Order of St. Patrick[11], being a silvered diamond-cut **eight** pointed star. upon which was a gilt elliptical shaped circlet pierced with the motto 'Quis Separabit' and MDCCLXXXIII' on a pale blue solid enamel ground. Within the circle on a silvered ground, the Cross of St. Patrick in red translucent enamel. Upon the cross a silver shamrock-leaf, having the three leaves in green translucent enamel, with upon each leaf a silver crown, overlaid with red and blue translucent enamel. The plate/badge, which was made up of four separate pieces, consisting of the star, the pierced circlet and the cross, the silvered and enameled backing plate (ground), and the silver and enameled shamrock, was assembled, and fitted to the skull as previously described. N.B. Possibly due to the considerable amount of intricate silver and enamel work that comprised this helmet plate, it is not unusual to find that the enamel is in a damaged condition and/or that the stalk of the shamrock-leaf is either bent or missing completely.

With regard to the garter having the pierced motto as mentioned above, as the 5th, 6th, and 7th Dragoon Guards had the title of the regiment in place of a motto, I would suggest that for these regiments the term strap is more appropriate, and it will therefore be substituted in my description of the helmet plate for these three regiments.

5th (Princess Charlotte of Wales's) Dragoon Guards (See Fig: 29.)
This was numerically the first regiment not to have a motto, or an enamel backing to the centre of the device. The plate consisted of a silvered twelve pointed diamond-cut star upon which was a gilt metal elliptical shaped strap inscribed "P.C.W. Dragoon Guards". Within the strap on a frosted gilt metal ground was the numeral "5" in silver, which was secured to the ground (backing) by passing two thin pins attached to the back of the numeral through corresponding holes

in the ground, the pins then being bent to face each other and soldered in place. The strap/ground had a short tag positioned on each side, east and west, and was secured to the star as described earlier. On the star of the helmet plate in the authors collection, there were to the reverse three studs only, the bottom (north) stud being replaced by a double pronged bend-over blade, which I would suggest was a makers variation. The plate/badge consisted of three separate pieces, these being the star, the strap/ground, and the silvered numeral.

6th Dragoon Guards (Carabiniers) (See Fig: 31.)
A silvered **rayed** twelve pointed star, upon which was mounted a gilt elliptical shaped strap bearing the title "The Carabiniers", the words of the title being silvered. Within the strap a silvered 'Royal Crest', also known as The Crest of England, (as previously described) on a frosted gilt ground. There were two slightly differing types of 'Crest', the early pattern having a wide crown with voided arches, the later version being slightly less wide with **solid arches**. Both these patterns of crown that were used on the Royal Crest, were most distinctive being more similar in appearance to the 'Imperial' (Tudor), than the 'Victorian' crown generally in use at this time. On an early pattern helmet plate in the authors collection, the 'Royal Crest' device has on its reverse two short lugs with minute holes at the end of each lug. These lugs are positioned one slightly above the other, the crest being secured to the strap/backing by a thin brass 'pin'. The strap itself is affixed to the star by means of two lugs as on the 5th Dragoon Guards strap, with the addition of a further lug with a minute hole, at the bottom of the strap. This additional lug is secured to the star by a very short metal rod positioned north to south being passed through the small hole at the end of the lug. To the reverse of the star are three studs at north, east, and west, with a bend-over two pronged tab at the south position, the complete helmet plate being attached to the helmet in a similar method as described for the Life Guards officers helmet in chapter four. The plate/badge was made up of three separate pieces, consisting of the rayed star, the strap/ground, and the Royal Crest device. N.B. There is an excellent representation in stone, on an officers helmet surmounting the regiments war memorial on Chelsea Embankment, London[15]

7th (Princess Royal's) Dragoon Guards (See Fig: 35.)
A silvered twelve pointed diamond-cut star, upon which was mounted a gilt elliptical strap inscribed "The Princess Royal's Dragoon Guards", the wording of the title being in silver. Within the strap the Royal Cypher (intertwined V.R.) on a gilt ground, being attached to the ground by similar means as on the 5th Dragoon Guards helmet plate. The star had four studs to the reverse, the studs being positioned as for the 1st Dragoon Guards plate, and was secured to the helmet as previously described. The plate/badge was made up of three separate pieces, these being, the star, the strap/ground, and the Royal Cypher.

Figure 21: 1st (King's) Dragoon Guards officers 1871 pattern helmet with correct officers pattern plume as worn by Captain E.A. Williams c. 1900. Note: See Fig: 22. for an example of the 'V.R.' Royal Cypher that was used as an alternative centre device for the 1st D/Guards. Author's collection. Photo: R. Biondi.

HONI SOIT QUI MAL Y PENSE
KINGS DRAGOON GUARDS

Opposite, Figure 21a: Close up view of the helmet plate. Note the tripartite scroll bearing the regimental title.

Figure 21b: Offset view of the helmet. Note the fullness of the officers pattern plume.

Figure 21c: Side view of helmet. The correct pattern of ear rosette as fitted to this helmet, is just visible beneath the edge of the plume.

Figure 21d: Helmet plate and scroll removed from skull of helmet. N.B. It is just possible to see the manufactured holes to the front of the skull, made to accommodate the helmet plate studs. Author's collection. Photo: Author.

Opposite, Figure 22a: Close up view of the helmet plate. Note that one tip of the star is absent (upper right). This is something to look for if purchasing a similar helmet.

Figure 22: 2nd Dragoon Guards (Queen's Bays) officers 1871 pattern helmet complete with officers pattern plume c. 1900. Author's collection. Photo: R. Biondi

HONI SOIT QUI MAL Y PENSE

Figure 22b: Offset view of helmet. Note the ball beneath the socket on the plume holder.

Figure 22c: Side view showing the correct pattern ear rosette fitted to the helmet.

Figure 23: 2nd Dragoon Guards (Queen's Bays) officer c. 1890 in full dress uniform. Photo: Courtesy of R.G. Harris.

Figure 24: 3rd (Prince of Wales's) Dragoon Guards officers 1871 pattern c. 1900. Note. The plume fitted to this helmet is an associated other ranks pattern and is therefore incorrect. Author's collection. Photo: R. Biondi.

Figure 24a: Offset view of the helmet. Compare this associated, other ranks pattern plume with the 'fuller' officers pattern plume illustrated in Fig: 21B.

Figure 24b: Side view of helmet with plume removed to show the correct pattern of ear rosettes and width of chinchain (one inch wide version). Photo: R. Biondi.

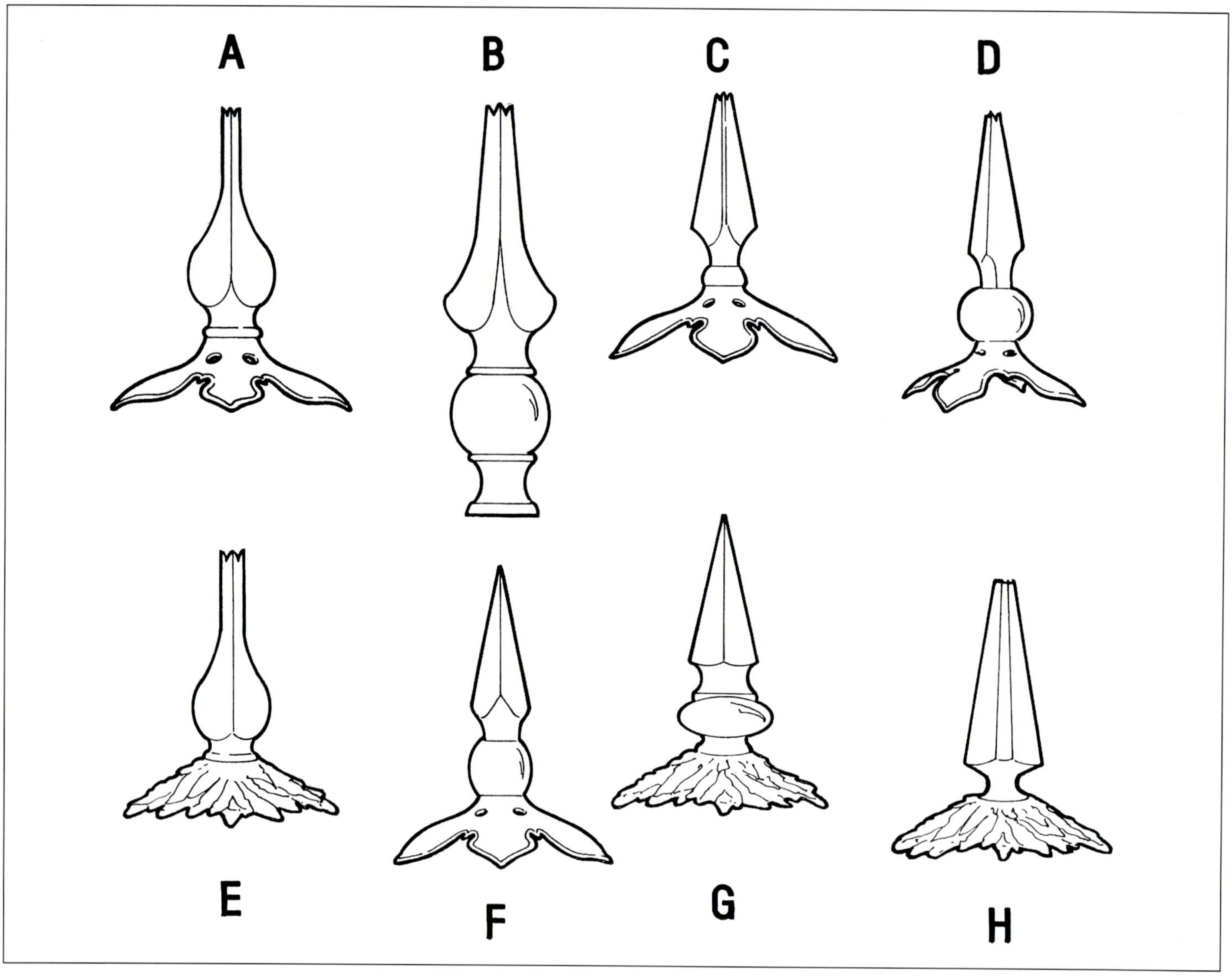

Figure 25: Types of the 1871 pattern officers plume socket, for the helmet of Dragoon Guards and the 1st and 6th Dragoons. Author.

Figure 26: Examples of officers and other ranks pattern chinchains. Life Guards (other ranks) c. 1842. 7th Dragoon Guards (officers) c. 1900. Life Guards (officers) c. 1996. and Blues and Royals (officers) c. 1996. Author's collection.

Figure 27: Major General E.C. Bethune K.C.B. C.V.O. Colonel of the 4th (Royal Irish) Dragoon Guards c. 1908. Lt 1875: Gordon Highlanders, Captain 1887: 6th Dragoon Guards, Major 1895: 16th Lancers, Colonel 1900, Major General 1908, Lieutenant General 1913. Photo: Courtesy of R.G.Harris.

Opposite, Figure 28a: Close up view of the helmet plate showing the fine detail of the centre device, including the crown on each petal of the shamrock.

Figure 28: 4th (Royal Irish) Dragoon Guards officers 1871 pattern. A late example in almost mint condition c. 1922. Note. The plume fitted to the helmet is a modern replacement. Author's collection. Photo: R. Biondi.

QUIS SEPARABIT

Figure 28b: Side view of helmet which shows the correct medium sized ear rosettes fitted.

Figure 29: 5th (Princess Charlotte of Wales's) Dragoon Guards officers 1871 pattern. A late example c. 1922, the condition of which would indicate that this helmet was hardly ever worn. Note. The plume is a modern replacement. Author's collection. Photo: R. Biondi.

P.C.W. DRAGOON GUARDS
5

Opposite, Figure 29a: Close up view of the helmet plate. Note: This is the only regiment that had a numeral as part of the centre device on the officers pattern helmet.

Figure 29b: Offset view of the helmet. Note the unmarked condition of the gilt metal skull.

Figure 29c: Side view showing the correct pattern of ear rosettes fitted to the helmet.

Figure 30: Colonel R.S.S. Baden-Powell in the full dress uniform of the 5th (Princess Charlotte of Wales's) Dragoon Guards c. 1899. Of interest is the profuse 'field rank' Austrian knot cuff decoration reaching as far as the elbow. Photo: Courtesy of R.G. Harris.

Opposite, Figure 31a: Close up view of the helmet plate in which can be seen the centre device which has a crown with non-voided arches.

Figure 31: 6th Dragoon Guards (Carabiniers) officers 1871 pattern helmet complete with original plume. Author's collection. Photo: R. Biondi.

THE CARABINIERS

Figure 31b: Offset view of helmet. Compare the slimness of this officers pattern plume, with the fuller version officers plume illustrated in Fig: 35B.

Figure 31c: Side view of helmet in which can be seen the correct pattern ear rosette. Note. This version of rosette is also fitted to the 1st, and the 7th Dragoon Guards officers pattern helmet.

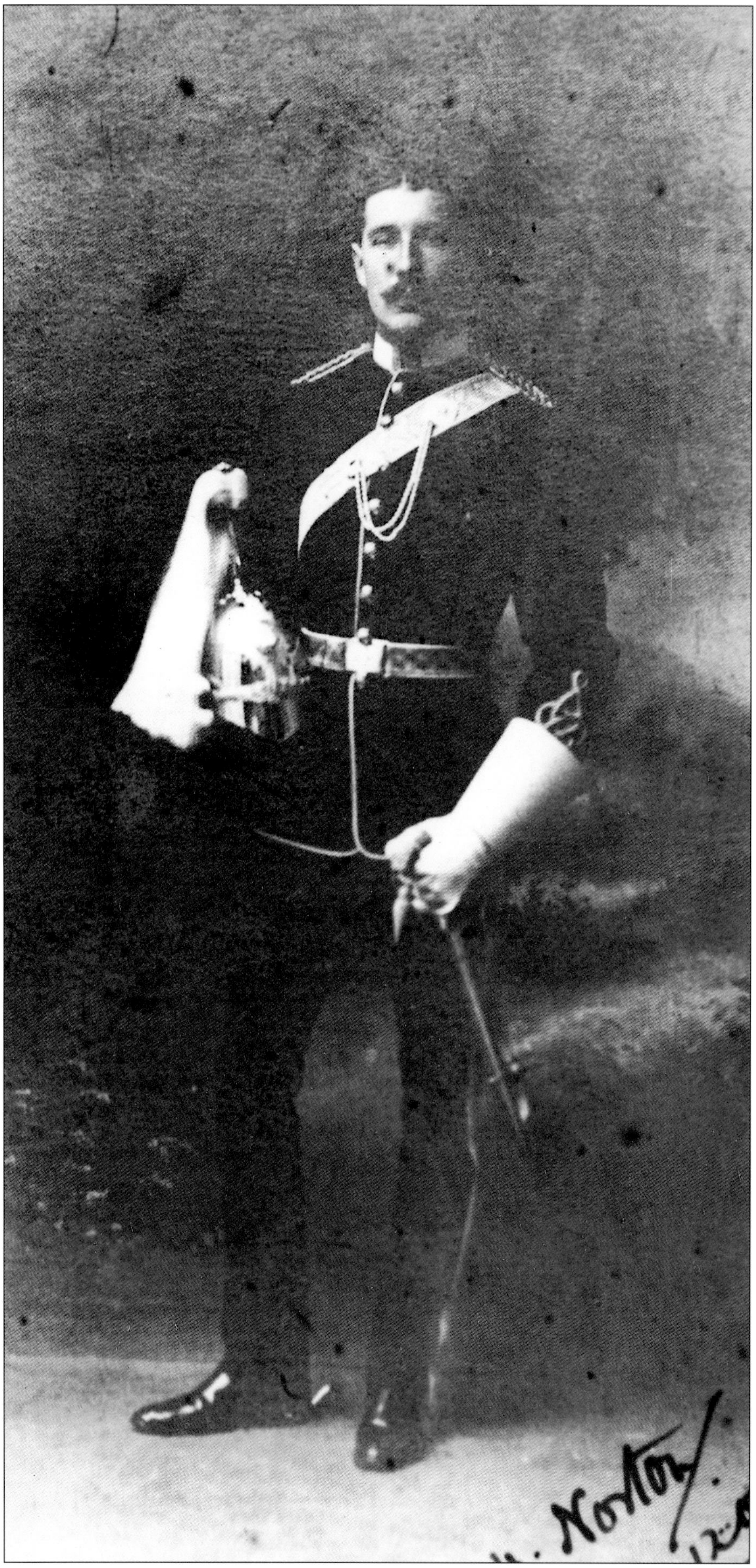

Figure 32: 2nd Lieutenant J.H. North of the 6th Dragoon Guards (Carabiniers) in dismounted review order c. 1903. Note the crossbelt with prickers and chains, normally only worn by officers of Hussar, or Lancer regiments. Photo: Courtesy of R.G. Harris.

Figure 33: 6th Dragoon Guards (Carabiniers), officers 1871 pattern helmet showing the silk head lining, the underside of the cross-piece base of the plume holder, and the reverse side of the helmet plate. Author's collection. Photo: Author.

Figure 34: A subaltern officer of the 6th Dragoon Guards (Carabiniers) c. 1885 in review order. Of particular interest is the length of the plume fitted to the helmet. Photo: Courtesy of R.J.Marrion.

Figure 35: 7th (Princess Royal's) Dragoon Guards officers 1871 pattern helmet, pre 1902, complete with officers pattern plume. Compare the size of the plume rosette with the pattern illustrated in Figs: 21. and 22B. Author's collection. Photo: R. Biondi.

THE PRINCESS ROYAL'S DRAGOON GUARDS

Opposite, Figure 35a: Close of view of the helmet plate showing the intertwined 'V.R.' Royal Cypher..

Figure 35b: Offset view of the helmet showing the correct pattern of ear rosettes fitted.

Figure 35c: Side view of helmet, in which can be seen the one inch wide chinchain.

The Ear Rosettes

As any collector of head-dress will be aware, these fittings being simple to remove, are also easily exchanged or replaced. As the ear rosettes for the officers helmet tended to vary in pattern depending on the regiment concerned, I give for each regiment a reference letter, which denotes the pattern of rosette that one might reasonably expect to be found fitted to an officers helmet that is in untouched condition. This reference letter refers to a pattern of rosette that is illustrated in Fig: 9. N.B. On many pattern of ear and plume rosette fitted to helmets of both Dragoon Guards and Dragoon officers, the highlights of the rosette were of burnished gilt with the remainder being in matte gilt:

1st Dragoon Guards:	Medium sized	Type: I
2nd Dragoon Guards:	Small sized	Type: J
3rd Dragoon Guards:	Small sized	Type: J
4th Dragoon Guards:	Medium sized	Type: H
5th Dragoon Guards:	Small sized	Type: J
6th Dragoon Guards:	Medium sized	Type: I
7th Dragoon Guards:	Medium sized	Type: I

The above information was acquired over a period of many years by examining helmets in both private collections, and regimental museums, and by close examination of contemporary photographs of officers holding or wearing their helmet. N.B. It is of interest that the illustration of an officers helmet of the 3rd Dragoon Guards as shown in Plate 4. of the *Dress Regulations 1900,* which one might reasonably expect to be accurate, does it fact show the helmet as having the **other ranks** pattern ear rosette.

The Chinchain

As described in the *Dress Regulations 1883*, the chinchain was 3/4 inches wide on black leather, however it is known that it is also possible to find the chinchain being backed with red leather, particularly if the head lining was of this colour. It is also possible that a helmet may be fitted with an other ranks brown leather backed chinchain, the original chain either being in too poor a condition as to be of any use, or having at some time been lost. Whilst other ranks chinchains do occasionally turn up in auction sales, or at militaria dealers premises, replacement officers pattern chinchains are very difficult to obtain from any source. (See Fig: 26.), for a selection of differing pattern chinchains.

The Plume

The plume was bound to a square steel stem which was threaded at the base to accept the 'wing' nut. It was also threaded at the upper part of the stem where the binding of the hair commenced, onto which was screwed a gilt metal half cup, and again at the top of the stem onto which was screwed the plume rosette. N.B. It is not unknown for the stem to be stamped with a number to indicate the regiment concerned, e.g. 7 DG.

The colour of horsehair plume for all seven regiments has already been given under the section relating to the *Dress Regulation of 1874,* however these regulation make no mention of the shredded whalebone or yak hair plume favoured by the officers of some regiments. There is very little information available regarding these alternative materials or why they were adopted in favour of the usual horsehair plume. To my knowledge over the past thirty years very few helmets having either of these types of plumes have been sold in auction salesrooms, there was however a helmet of the 1st Dragoon Guards with a red shredded whalebone plume sold in 1970, a helmet of the 6th Dragoon Guards with a white shredded whalebone plume sold in 1974, and a helmet of the 5th Dragoon Guards having a white over red yak hair plume was sold in 1991.

Figure 36: Officers 1871 pattern plumes of 1st, 6th, and 7th regiments of Dragoon Guards. Note the slimness of the 6th Dragoon Guards plume compared to the other two. Author's collection. Photo: R. Biondi.

A point worthy of consideration is the difference between the officers and the other ranks plume, as on all the officers plumes I have seen the plume tended to be fuller, and the hair softer and sleeker than on the other ranks pattern. Additionally on a **regular** officers plume both the gilt plume rosette and the gilt half cup located under the plume (as mentioned earlier) both unscrew and can be removed whereas similar fitments on the other ranks plumes were of brass and were permanently affixed to the stem. N.B. The rosette and half cup are not always removable on a **yeomanry** officers plume.

At the risk of repeating myself I emphasize that due to makers variations it is possible to find a helmet which has fittings etc., with measurements that do not conform to those quoted in this book. I also suggest that it might be prudent not to treat every description given in the various dress regulations produced over the years as being 'gospel'.

In respect of the above, the *Dress Regulations of 1883, and 1900* both state that the plume *"rises 2 inches from point of insertion in socket and falls as far as the bottom of the helmet"*. However, having measured for myself the

Figure 37: Types of plume. Left an officers pattern of the 1st Dragoon Guards, and right an other ranks pattern of the 3rd Dragoon Guards. Note the fullness of the officers pattern plume. Author's collection. Photo: R. Biondi.

height that the plume actually rises from the point of insertion to the bottom of the plume rosette, on plumes of the 1st, 2nd, 6th and 7th Dragoon Guards I found that the height was in fact **2 5/8** inches. With regard to the length of the plume, I have examined a great many helmets complete with plume, of various regiments, where its length fell well short of that described above. Additionally the study of contemporary photographs of officers wearing their helmets, has shown that the plume length tended to vary quite considerably (See Fig: 34.).

The plume was secured to the helmet by means of either the 'hooped' fly nut as described in chapter four (1842 pattern helmet), or one of very similar design, but having two short rods in place of the hoop.

The Plume Rosette

As with the ear rosettes, many regiments seemed to favour a differing pattern of plume rosette. Therefore to aid identification, each pattern of known plume rosette has been given a reference letter of either A, B, C, D, E, or I, using a similar method as for the ear rosettes:

1st Dragoon Guards;	Small sized.	Type: E
2nd Dragoon Guards:	Small sized.	Type: E
3rd Dragoon Guards:	Small sized.	Type: E
4th Dragoon Guards:	Medium sized.	Type: C. or D
5th Dragoon Guards:	Small sized.	Type: E
6th Dragoon Guards:	Medium sized.	Type: C. or D
7th Dragoon Guards:	Large sized. Similar to ear rosette.	Type: I

Dress Regulation 1900

With the publication of these dress regulations came a slightly amended description of the helmet and plume from the particulars that were given in the 1883 edition. Below are extracts from the new regulations with the important changes being in bold text. N.B. The new sealed pattern date for both the helmet and plume was given as 23rd August 1898.

For the skull of the helmet, gilt or **gilding metal** is substituted for gilt-brass. The chinchain is to be **1 inch wide**, mounted on black patent leather, **lined with velvet. Furniture gilt or gilding metal.** For the plume, **steel stem with screw and 'fly' nut.** For the helmet plate the text reads "*A diamond-cut silver star in front; on the star in gilt or* ***gilding metal****, the garter pierced with the motto 'Honi soit qui mal y pense', or an* ***elliptical ring*** *with the designation of the regiment.* ***Within the garter or ring the regimental device or number. (For detailed description see Appendix I.) In the 6th Dragoon Guards the star has plain rays***". N.B. There is now no description given of the motto of the 4th Dragoon Guards.

The Appendix I. referred to above, gives details of the badges and devices authorised to be worn on buttons, collars of tunics and frocks, on full dress head-dress, on the waist plate, on the pouch, and on the field cap. However as this book is not concerned with buttons, waist plates, and tunics etc., I have only reproduced the head-dress details (as printed).

1st (King's) Dragoon Guards

On the Garter star, in silver, the Garter with motto in gilt or gilding metal, pierced on a ground of blue enamel. Within the Garter on a ground of red enamel, the Royal Cypher in silver.

2nd (Queen's Bays) Dragoon Guards (See Fig: 22A.)

On the Garter star, the Garter, with motto pierced on a blue enamel ground; within the Garter the Royal Cypher in silver on a ground of red enamel.

3rd (Prince of Wales's) Dragoon Guards

On the Garter star, in silver, the Garter with motto in gilt or gilding metal, pierced on a ground of blue enamel; within the Garter, in silver, the Prince of Wales's plume, on a scarlet enamel ground.

4th (Royal Irish) Dragoon Guards (See Fig: 28A.)

On the Garter star, in gilt or gilding metal, a circle inscribed Quis separabit, MDCCLXXXIII, on a blue enameled ground. Within the circle, on a **white ground**, the Cross of St. Patrick. On the cross a shamrock-leaf in green enamel, with a red enameled Crown on each petal.

5th (Princess Charlotte of Wales's) Dragoon Guards (See Fig: 29A.)

On the Garter star, in gilt or gilding metal, an elliptical ring inscribed "P.C.W. Dragoon Guards". Within the ring "5" in silver.

6th Dragoon Guards (Carabiniers)

In silver, the Garter with motto in gilt, or gilding metal, pierced on a ground of **blue enamel**. Within the Garter, on a ground of **red enamel, the figure "6" in silver**. The star has plain rays.

7th (Princess Royal's) Dragoon Guards

On the Garter in silver, an elliptical ring, with "the Princess Royal's Dragoon Guards" in burnished gilt or gilding metal on a **silver blue enamel** ground. Within, on a ground of **red enamel the figure "7" in silver.**

There are in my opinion a few important anomalies in the above descriptions, and I therefore list my observations below:

1st Dragoon Guards:

No mention is made of the silver tri-part scroll bearing the title of the regiment.

4th Dragoon Guards:

I have never seen, nor heard of the existence of a centre device of this regiment having 'a white ground' as described, and assume that this part of the 'specification' was not carried out by the makers of the helmet plate.

5th Dragoon Guards:

No mention is made of the type of ground the numeral "5" was surmounted upon.

6th Dragoon Guards:

Again I have never seen, nor do I know of any collector or militaria dealer who has seen a helmet plate for this regiment as described above, and I feel confident that the plate as described above was never adopted.

7th Dragoon Guards:

As above for 6th Dragoon Guards.

H.M. Reserve Regiment of Dragoon Guards

Very little appears to been recorded about the head-dress of the reserve regiments raised during the South African War of 1899 to 1902. That cap badges for the reserve regiments of Dragoon Guards, Dragoon, and Lancers were produced is not in doubt, however regarding the helmet plate for the full dress head-dress there seems to be differing opinions. Hugh King, a well respected collector of head-dress badges and co-author of a book on military badges, (28) that must be the definitive work on this subject, describes the officers full dress helmet plate for Her Majesty's Reserve Regiment of Dragoon Guards thus. "On the Garter Star the Garter with the motto pierced on a blue enamel ground. Within the Garter the letters **RR** in silver on a red enamel ground".

The subject of whether full dress helmet plates were ever worn by the reserve regiments, was raised in a letter to the *Crown Imperial Society* (29) in 1983, when the writer of the letter referred to an article on head-dress which had appeared in the society's journal of September 1982, the article including a reference to the helmet plates of the Reserve Regiments. The writer queried the information given in the article regarding the other ranks of these regiments wearing reserve regiment helmet plates bearing the Royal Cypher (VR and EVIIR), which in my opinion has a bearing on whether or not the officers of these regiments actually wore full dress uniforms.

This same writer also referred to Army Order No 78 of April 1900 which details clothing to be provided to these regiments, and he states that *"a study of the individual items show that 'full dress' was not included in the issue and that the only headgear referred to is the field cap or glengarry".* He goes on to refer to Item No.2 of Army Order 79 which gives details of the officers full dress uniforms, and states *"provision of full dress is not necessary, but officers* ***may*** *provide themselves with the full dress of their respective regiments"*, and goes on to describe the badge to be worn on the full dress head-dress. The writer continues by stating that *"since these army order make it clear that other ranks badges were to be similar to officers there is no reason to suppose that their helmet plates would have been of a different pattern, if they had, had full dress issued. However one can hardly imagine that at that time other ranks would have been allowed to parade in full dress if the officers were not similarly dressed".* The above I respectfully suggest is sound reasoning based on common sense.

In the same edition of the Journal of *The Crown Imperial Society* the author of the aforementioned article on head-dress replied to the letter mentioned above and suggested that *"It is of course conceivable that these plates were not, in fact, ever worn upon the 1871 helmet by other ranks, or perhaps only in small quantities"*, and goes on to say that *"The existence of an example with the usual fittings (with screw-fittings), however, would seem to indicate that the idea was at least contemplated"*, all of which, I feel would also apply to the officers pattern helmet.

Having corresponded with Hugh King regarding this matter he was unable to provide any additional information, he did however express the opinion that *"there is a strong feeling that some (helmet plates) were not proceeded with".* I share this view and am of the opinion, that as with the description for the helmet plate of the 6th, and the 7th Dragoon Guards as given in the Dress Regulations of 1900, that although proposed these particular pattern plates were never adopted/worn.

Figure 38: 3rd (Prince of Wales's) Dragoon Guards other ranks 1871 pattern helmet having the flat top to the numeral '3'. Photo: Courtesy of G.Frost.

The Warrant Officers (Senior N.C.O.'s) Helmet

As mentioned in chapter two, the Warrant Officers (Regimental Sergeant Major, Bandmaster etc.) of certain regiments of Dragoon Guards wore an officers pattern helmet, whilst those holding a similar position in one of the other regiments wore the other ranks pattern. It does not seem unreasonable that for those Warrant Officers who wore the other ranks pattern helmet that the skull and fittings would be of gilt, rather than brass, although I have as yet been unable to confirm this.

The Other Ranks Helmet (See Fig: 38.)

As with the 1847 'Albert' pattern helmet, the new helmet for the rank and file was very similar in general appearance to that of the officers. There were of course many small differences, not the least of which being the quality of the helmet and its fittings, details of which are given below. N.B. One of the better known manufactures of the other ranks helmet was Firmin and Sons, London, who are now based in Birmingham, England.

The Skull

Whilst the overall shape of the skull on most other ranks pattern helmets closely resembled that of the officers, there was also another, very minutely differing shaped skull. This pattern of skull which in my opinion is less pleasing to the eye, had, at a casual glance the appearance of being not unlike a 'dome' shaped bell'. The front peak also differed slightly on this pattern of skull as it was shallower, with a less pronounced 'V' to its centre, however the basic design and construction of both the front waist band, and the rear seam band were unchanged. This shape of helmet is also known to have been used at some period in time for the officers helmets of the 1st, 2nd, 3rd and 6th regiments, and although not confirmed it is possible that this skull was either an early pattern, or a makers variation.

The actual skull was made of brass, being constructed in the same manner as for the officers helmet. However the pattern of waist leaves above the front peak differed, being slightly less defined than on the officers helmet, with the front peak only being lined with skiver. The rear seam band was attached to the skull by bend over pins within the skull, and by two small rivets to the inner rear peak. As mentioned earlier in chapter two, it is possible to find issue marks stamped onto the inner rear rim (peak binding) of some helmets given details of the regiment to which the helmet was issued and a service number.

The Plume Holder

For the other ranks helmet there was only one pattern of plume holder, this being the version not having the ball beneath the socket, an illustration of which may be seen in Fig: 25(A). The underside of the plume holder base was fitted with four studs as on the officers helmet, however on passing these studs through corresponding holes in the skull, a thin metal support plate, being similar in shape to the plume base terminals (See Fig: 20.A.), was placed over the studs before the nuts were secured in place. Onto the threaded base of the plume socket, which protruded down through the top of the skull was placed a round brass lock 'nut' having two short 'wedges' which when held between finger and thumb enabled the lock nut to be screwed onto the plume socket thereby securing it in place. N.B. On the other ranks pattern plume holder it was not always possible to separate the socket from the base.

The Headband and Lining

The headband was of similar materials, and construction as for the officers helmet. The lining however differed in that it was of brown leather, being not unlike the lining of the other ranks helmet of the Household Cavalry, having eight sections (leaves) each with a small, metal supported hole through which the drawstring was passed. It did not however have the additional, Household Cavalry buckle and strap fitment.

The Helmet Plate

A white metal twelve pointed rayed star, upon which was mounted a brass garter. In his book on Cavalry Head-Dress (3) Bill Carman advises that 'The new pattern helmet plate was sealed on the 20th March 1884, and originally the garter was gilt for non commissioned officers, but around 1897 the garter was to become brass for all other ranks'. It is thought that prior to the introduction of the 1884 pattern plate that 'old' plate from the 'Albert' helmet was worn on the new helmet, although this has yet to be confirmed.

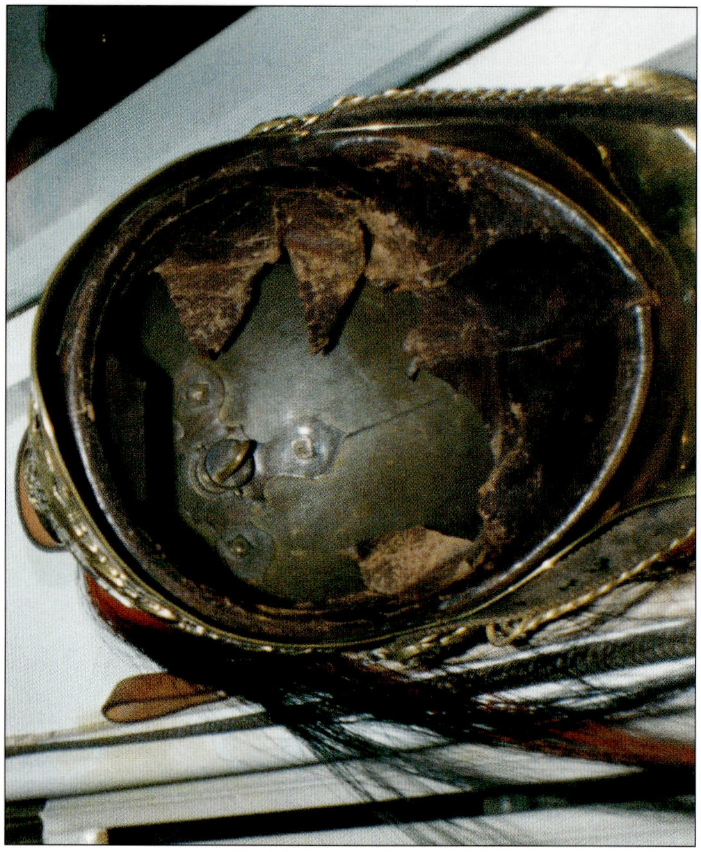

Figure 38a: Inside view of the helmet in which can be seen the head lining, the plume holder supporting plate, and the plumes 'fly' nut. Photo: Courtesy of G.Frost.

As on the helmet plate for officers of the 1st to 3rd Dragoon Guards, the other ranks pattern garter bore the motto "Honi.Soit.Mal.Y.Pense, but unlike the officers pattern it was **not pierced**. Within the garter, on a ground of either black leather, or black japanned metal, was a brass numeral denoting the seniority of the regiment. It is possible to find a helmet plate with the leather backing completely missing, the leather probably having perished through wear and tear, or old age, and it is not unknown for someone to have painted the backing with black paint in an attempt to make the fact that the leather is missing less noticeable.

There are several variations for the numeral, one pattern having a flat surface, with another having curved edges to the face of the number. For the 3rd Dragoon Guards there is a numeral '3' having a flat top, and another version with a rounded top, (See Fig: 38.). There are also helmet plates having a replacement numeral of a dubious nature, and therefore if in doubt, and if permitted, I would suggest that the plate is removed from the helmet and the fixings on the back of the plate examined to ensure that they are in untouched condition and that the method of affixing the numeral in place is contemporary with that of the garter and rayed star.

The helmet plate consisted of four separate pieces, these being the rayed star, the garter, the numeral, and the leather or japanned metal backing to the numeral. The garter had two bend over tabs located north and south, as did the numeral. The position of these tabs in descending order was (1): for the garter. (2 & 3): for the numeral, and (4): for the garter. Each tabs passed through a corresponding slot in the rayed star and was then bent over and inwards. The complete helmet plate was attached to the skull by means of the four studs as on the officers helmet.

The Ear Rosettes

The author has only ever seen one pattern of ear rosette fitted to an other ranks helmet and that is the pattern illustrated in Fig: 9.(K)., which was of brass with the usual threaded stud to the reverse.

The Chinchain

The brass chinchain measured approximately 17 1/4 inches in length by 3/4 inches wide and was mounted on black or alternatively dark brown leather. N.B. The chinchain on an other ranks pattern helmet is frequently found to have been restored by the use of new leather or worse, has been replaced by a modern replacement chain. For the collector, I would suggest that a helmet fitted with either of the above is preferable to having no chain at all fitted and it will serve its purpose whilst the owner seeks a genuine replacement item from such sources as fellow collectors, auction sales, or militaria shops.

The Plume and Plume Rosette

The colour of the plume for the rank and file was not unnaturally the same as for the officers, the exceptions being the band and trumpeters, whose plume colours will be discussed later in this chapter.

It was in the quality of the plume that the difference was apparent, the other ranks plume being less full, and with a less defined shape. The rosette, (See Fig: 54.) was identical for all regiments as was the half-cup, both of which were of brass instead of gilt, with neither of these fitments being removable as they were either brazed or silver soldered to the plume stem. The plume rose some 2 inches from the point of insertion in the plume socket, this being 5/8th of an inch less in height than that of known examples of the officers plume.

Reserve Regiment

There are in existence other ranks helmet plates attributed to being of the Reserve Regiment of Dragoon Guards. These plates were comprised of the standard pattern twelve-pointed rayed star in brass/gilding metal, mounted upon which, in a similar metal was the garter with the motto as on the regular regiments helmet plate. Within the garter in brass/gilding metal was the voided Royal Cypher of 'V.R.' on a black leather ground.

To the reverse of the star in place of the normal four threaded studs were **metal loops**, through which were passed split pins to secure the plate to a helmet. It has been suggested that these helmet plates were in fact worn on the blue cloth helmet, and also by the Military Mounted Police. However if these helmet plates really are of the reserve regiment of Dragoon Guards I can see no reason why it should be thought that a cavalry regiment would wear the blue cloth helmet favoured by the infantry, it making far more sense to acknowledge the possibility that they were worn by the M.M.P.

Foreign Service Helmet

At a Sussex Auction House salesroom in 1987 there appeared an other ranks helmet plate described as *'An interesting HM Reserve Regiment's Trooper's brass HP'*. This plate consisted of a standard pattern brass rayed plate with garter and motto, having a separate numeral '3' to the centre mounted upon three thin bars. There was however no provision for either the leather or japanned backing as mentioned above. In view of the aforementioned controversy regarding the reserve regiment helmet plates, I sought the views of Hugh King regarding this most unusual plate, and it was his understanding that *'they were worn abroad on the white sun helmet' (foreign service helmet)*. As previously mentioned it has already been established that the officers of the 3rd Dragoon Guards had an undersized version of the full dress helmet plate that was worn on the F.S. helmet and it therefore seems reasonable that the troopers of this regiment would also have a helmet plate for their version of the this helmet.

Cavalry Musician's Plumes

It was generally the practice for trumpeters in cavalry regiments to have different colour plumes to those of the rest of the regiment in order that they might easily be recognised. Additionally the musicians in the band also wore different colour plumes, and to confuse this matter even further it is known that in some regiments the kettle drummer wore a differing colour plume to the remainder of the band. The following are the plume colours as worn by band members of the various regiment c. 1900 as given in W.Y. Carman's book (3):

Regiment	Plume colour
1st Dragoon Guards	White
2nd Dragoon Guards	White
3rd Dragoon Guards	White
4th Dragoon Guards	Black and White
5th Dragoon Guards	Red
6th Dragoon Guards	Red
7th Dragoon Guards	Black

Musicians of some cavalry bands are also known to have worn the foreign service helmet when in review order whilst serving abroad with their regiment, and there are photographs showing this helmet fitted with either the ball and spike fitment as illustrated in Fig: 25.F., or with this helmet complete with the full dress plume, possibly by using the plume holder from the metal full dress helmet.

1902 and Onwards

Some time after the accession to the throne by King Edward VII, the Royal Cypher on the officers helmet plate centre for the 1st (King's), the 2nd (Queen's Bays)[10] and the 7th (Princess Royals) Dragoon Guards changed from 'V.R.' to 'E.R.VII', however on the centre device of the 6th (Carabiniers) Dragoon Guards the crown to the Crest of England remained unchanged. N.B. With regard to the centre device on the helmet plate for the 1st Dragoon Guards, whilst there are many existing examples having the Crest of England with the 'Victorian' crown surmounted by a lion, I have been unable to find any evidence either photographic or otherwise to indicate that a post 1902 version having a 'Kings' crown was ever made.

The helmet plate for the other ranks of the seven regular regiments was unaffected by the change of crown and cypher, however there are in existence many examples of the plate thought to be that of the Reserve Regiment of Dragoon Guards bearing the Royal Cypher of King Edward VII.

Dress Regulations 1911/Change of Royal Cypher

The 1911 Dress Regulations give no change of wording for the helmet plate devices, however some time after the Coronation of King George V on 22nd June 1911, the Royal Cypher to the centre of the helmet plate changed to G.R.V. for the 1st (King's), the 2nd (Queen's Bays) and the 7th (Princess Royals) Dragoon Guards.

Delhi Durbar 1911

A most interesting tale was told to me some years ago by my friend Frank Mitchell a retired schoolmaster, relating to the Delhi Durbar which took place on the 12th December 1911. Apparently the late King George V was an extremely punctual person, whilst his wife was known for always being late. The King had all the clocks in the royal houses set half-an-hour fast to compensate for his wife's lateness, but this ploy did not work and she continued to annoy him by her lateness.

Came the day of the Delhi Durbar and the King was already a full hour late for this official engagement due to his wife's 'dallying', with the poor soldiers being stood at attention on parade, in the blazing mid-day Indian sun wearing their full dress uniforms complete with helmets. As is known, when worn properly the cavalry helmet touches the wearers nose and every cavalryman on parade that day had his nose burnt by the hot peak of his helmet. Apparently in later years those same cavalrymen would proudly point to the enduring scar on their nose which proved that they were present at this most historic occasion.

The Amalgamations of 1922

For the accountants, bankers, and stockbrokers April 1922 heralded a new 'financial' year and the possibility of exciting things to come, not so for the heavy cavalry for in that month, of that year, the results of 'The Geddes Axe' came crashing down, and with it the loss of the proud regimental titles of five of the Dragoon Guards regiments and of one regiment of Dragoons.

Following the above amalgamation the titles for the remaining five regiments of Dragoon Guards were as follows: 1st King's Dragoon Guards, The Queen's Bays (2nd Dragoon Guards), 3rd Carabiniers (Prince of Wales's Dragoon Guards), 4th/7th Dragoon Guards, and 5th Inniskilling Dragoon Guards.

1929: Sealed Pattern Helmet Plate

The helmet plate for the 3rd Carabiniers (Prince of Wales's Dragoon Guards) was sealed in 1929, however photographic evidence shows no visible change from the pattern that was originally sealed way back in 1900 (30).

1930 Crimped Plumes

A copy photograph in my collection of a mounted troop of the 3rd Carabiniers Prince of Wales's Dragoon Guards) c. 1930 (31) shows that the plumes of the troopers are all crimped. This practice was popular in some of the Lancer regiments and was achieved by binding the dampened plume within a pair of wooden crimping sticks, the inner surfaces of which were undulating, having a saw-tooth surface. When the plume was dry, it was removed from the crimping sticks, and had a most noticeable 'wavy' appearance. N.B. There was also a pair of narrow, straight boards that were used to keep the plume straight when not actually on the helmet, assumedly these sticks being used when there was no requirement for the plume to be crimped.

Dress Regulations For The Army 1934

The text describing the helmet in the above publication is identical to that given in the *Dress Regulation 1900,* with the exception that for the 5th Inniskilling Dragoon Guards the helmet is described thus: *'Of the same pattern as for Dragoon Guards, but* ***of white metal****, with gilt or gilding metal ornaments'.*

The description for the plume is also identical to that given in *Dress Regulation 1900*, however the plume colours are now given as:

Regiment	Colour of Plume
1st King's Dragoon Guards	*Red.*
2nd Queen's Bays	*Black.*
3rd Carabiniers	*Black and Red.*
4th/7th Dragoon Guards	*White.*
5th Inniskilling Dragoon Guards	*Red and White*

However it is in the descriptions of the helmet plate devices for some of the regiments that we see some quite dramatic changes, the details of which are reproduced below, with the additions/amendments in bold text.

1st King's Dragoon Guards

Centre device as per the *Dress Regulation 1900 and 1911.*

The Queen's Bays (2nd Dragoon Guards)

Centre device as per the *Dress Regulations 1900 and 1911.*

3rd Carabiniers (Prince of Wales's Dragoon Guards)

On the Garter star, in silver, the Garter with the motto in gilt or gilding metal pierced on a ground of blue enamel; within the Garter in silver, ***on crossed carbines,*** *the Prince of Wales's Plume* ***and coronet*** *on a scarlet enamel ground.*

4th/7th Dragoon Guards

On the silver Garter star an oval in gilt pierced with "Quis Separabit"[11] *and* ***MCMXXII*** *on a ground of* ***royal*** *blue enamel. In the centre on a white enamel ground the* ***Cross of St. George in gold and red enamel; superimposed on the Cross the Princess Royal's coronet in gilt and red enamel.***

5th Inniskilling Dragoon Guards

In gilt or gilding metal *the Garter Star with an elliptical ring, inscribed* ***"Inniskilling Dragoon Guards."*** *Within the ring "5" in silver.*

There are several anomalies in the above descriptions for the 4th/7th Dragoon Guards centre device and my observations are as follows. Once again white enamel is described as the colour of the ground to the Cross, which itself is described as being as the **Cross of St. George**. This I find most puzzling as this was an 'Irish' regiment and the 'old' 4th Dragoon Guards centre device displayed the **Cross of St. Patrick.**

In respect of the above I have no knowledge of any collector, museum, or militaria specialist that has ever seen or heard of the existence of the above described centre device for the 4th/7th Dragoon Guards, nor the centre device as described for the 3rd and 5th regiments, and it is my opinion, although not confirmed, that these three devices were in fact never worn or even manufactured.

With regard to the white metal skull for the helmet of the 5th Royal Inniskilling Dragoon Guards as quoted in the *Dress Regulations 1934,* it appears that there is some question with regards to whether gilt or white metals skulls where actually used. Colonel Sir Mike Ansell C.B.E., D.S.O.[12] who served in this regiment as a young subaltern and later became Colonel of the regiment, recalls in his book 'Leopard' (33) that brass helmets were worn with the full dress uniform at a Searchlight Tattoo in 1929. Of particular interest in this book is an copy photograph which shows the then Lieutenant Mike Ansell, leading the mounted members of the 'Musical Ride' troop along a deserted road. Although all the members of this group are in khaki service dress, they are wear-

Figure 39: Senior N.C.O.'s of the 5th Royal Inniskilling Dragoon Guards in review order c. 1958 at York. Author's collection. Courtesy of John Collins.

ing their full dress helmets minus plume, the exception being Lt Ansell who is wearing a service dress peaked cap.

In Colonel Ansell's books 'Soldier On' (34) there is an excellent photograph of him in his full dress uniform as Colonel of the regiment c. 1957-1962, holding his helmet. This prompted me to try to establish whether the skull was actually of gilt or white metal, and to find out if the title as described in the *Dress Regulations 1934* was identical to the title on the strap on his helmet plate. In August 1990 having traced his residence I telephoned his home and spoke to a Mrs. Hermione Wynn, who identified herself as the Colonel's secretary. Having explained the reason for my interest in the helmet I enquired if it might be possible to clarify the colour of the skull and the strap inscription, to which the kind lady replied that she was *'looking at the helmet which was placed on the mantlepiece, and that she would go and look for me'*. Her reply to my questions was that the skull was gold in colour and that the title read 'P.C.W. Dragoon Guards'. This together with Col. Ansell's reference to brass helmets as mentioned above, would appear to indicate that the use of a white metal skull was short lived, if ever adopted for use by this regiment

Continuing with this regiments helmet, a photograph in my collection depicting a mounted officer c. 1925 (35) wearing review order clearly shows that his helmet has both the plume holder, and the ear rosettes from the former 6th (Inniskilling) Dragoons helmet. In another photograph of the officers of this regiment c. 1929 (36) in dismounted review order, it can clearly be seen that all the helmets of the seated, senior officers, have the ball beneath the socket, pattern of plume holder, whilst the helmets of the standing, subaltern officers, all have the alternative plume holder without the ball beneath the socket. Additionally the plumes of the subalterns, also all appear to have been crimped in the manner previously described.

Finally with regard to the helmets of this regiment, an officers **gilt** metal helmet seen at a London Militaria dealers showroom in 1994, was fitted with the ball beneath the socket pattern plume holder as used on the former 6th Dragoons helmet. I was permitted to closely examine the inside of this helmet and all the fittings etc. appeared to be contemporary and in untouched condition, and my conclusion was that this was a rare post 1922 example of a 5th Inniskilling Dragoon Guards helmet.

Mechanization 1936

In October 1936 the process of converting the Queen's Bays (2nd Dragoon Guards) into a light tank regiment commenced, and by March 1937 the regiment's horses were reduced to forty officers chargers, and fifty-three troop horses.

Change of the Royal Cypher in 1937

King George VI succeeded to the throne on 10th December 1936, with the Coronation taking place on 12th May 1937. Some time after this date came yet one more change of Royal Cypher for both the 1st (King's), and the 2nd (Queen's Bays) Dragoon Guards, this time to that of 'G.R.VI.' However the change of cypher no longer effected the 7th (Princess Royals) as they now formed part of the 4th/7th Dragoon Guards, and the amalgamated regiment bore the helmet plate of the 'old' 4th (Royal Irish) Dragoon Guards.

Mechanization 1937

The last mounted parade of the 1st King's Dragoon Guards took place at Secunderabad, India on the 23rd October 1937. The 3rd Carabiniers (Prince of Wales's Dragoon Guards) were also in India, being stationed at Sialkot, when they were notified that they were to become a light tank regiment. In January 1938 they said 'farewell to their horses', the conversion from horse to tank being completed in March 1939.

Mechanization 1938

The last mounted parade of the 4th/7th Royal Dragoon Guards took place at Dreghorn Loan, Edinburgh, Scotland on the 15th August 1938. This was also the year that the 5th Royal Inniskilling Dragoon Guards 'Trooped the Standard and Guidon' of the regiment for the last time. This mounted parade took place at the Cavalry Barracks, Colchester Garrison, Colchester, Essex, with the officer, and escort to the Standard and Guidon parading in mounted review order complete with helmets and plumes, the remainder of the regiment wearing khaki service dress. There were still however occasions when an appearance in mounted review order was permitted, as shown in a photograph taken at York in 1958 clearly illustrates. (See Fig: 39.) N.B. Colchester Cavalry Barracks still exists today looking very much as it must have done way back in 1938, although it is no longer used by the cavalry, and sadly it is rumoured that the barracks are to be demolished in the not too distant future.

Amalgamation of the 1st and 2nd Regiments 1959

On the 1st January 1959 the 1st King's Dragoon Guards and the Queen's Bays (2nd Dragoon Guards) the only two regiments of Dragoon Guards unaffected by the 1922 mergers were finally amalgamated to become known as 1st The Queen's Dragoon Guards.

Amalgamation of the 3rd/6th Regiment 1971

For the former 3rd, and the 6th regiments a further merger took place on the 6th July 1971 at Queen's Park, Edinburgh, Scotland, when the 3rd Carabiniers (Prince of Wales's Dragoon Guards) and the Royal Scots Greys (2nd Dragoons), Scotland's only regular cavalry regiment amalgamated to form the Royal Scots Dragoon Guards.

1973: Princess Anne's & Captain Phillips Wedding

A rare occasion to see an officer wearing dismounted review order arose in the 15th November 1973 when Her Royal Highness Princess Anne married Captain Mark Phillips[13],who was a serving officer in 1st The Queens Dragoon Guards (the former 1st King's Dragoon Guards, and The Queens Bays, 2nd Dragoon Guards). Captain Phillips wore the dismounted review order uniform, and carried an officers pattern helmet throughout the ceremony.Although having studied a great many photographs that appeared in newspapers and magazines at that time, it was regrettably not possible to positively identify the centre device on Captain Phillips helmet, however what could be clearly be seen was that the helmet had the ball beneath the socket, pattern of plume holder, which was the pattern used on the helmet of the former Queens Bays (2nd Dragoon Guards). Captain Phillip's best man also wore review order dress, and carried his full dress helmet, which could be seen as having the plume socket without the ball. It is reasonable therefore to assume that the helmet of Captain Phillip's best man was from the former 1st King's Dragoon Guards.

Amalgamation/Merger of 1992

Amongst the many amalgamations announced under the "Options for Change" in 1992 was the merger of the 4th/7th Royal Dragoon Guards and the 5th Royal Inniskilling Dragoon Guards which took place on the 1st August 1992, the newly formed regiment being named The Royal Dragoon Guards.

Figure 40: Musicians of the 4th/7th Royal Dragoon Guards at the Cavalry Sunday Memorial Parade held at Hyde Park May 1976. Note the black over white plumes. Author's collection. Photo: Author.

Musicians Helmets and Plumes

1st Queen's Dragoon Guards

The musicians of both the 1st and 2nd regiments of Dragoon Guards continued to wear white plumes up until, and after amalgamation in 1959, when the helmet plate of the former 1st King's Dragoon Guards was taken into use by the newly formed 1st The Queen's Dragoon Guards. Sometime after the new regiment was formed, and certainly by 1985, the Bandmaster (Warrant Officer Class One) began wearing a helmet having the ball beneath the socket, pattern of plume holder, whilst the remainder of the band wore the helmet with the alternative plume holder. The Bandmaster also took to wearing a scarlet hair plume.

3rd and 6th Dragoon Guards

For the 3rd (Prince of Wales's) Dragoon Guards the plumes of the band changed to yellow c. 1902, and remained that colour until the change to black over red. A contemporary photograph taken c. 1927 of the Bandmaster in dismounted review order shows that he wore an officers pattern helmet with black over red plume.

With the amalgamation of the 3rd Carabiniers and the Royal Scots Greys in 1971, the musicians of the newly formed Royal Scots Dragoon Guards took into wear the black bearskin with crimson feather plume worn by the former Royal Scots Greys. The kettle-drummer/bass drummer however is permitted to wear the famous white bearskin with scarlet feather plume.

Figure 41: Musicians of the 4th/7th Royal Dragoon Guards at the Royal Tournament, July 1991. Note the plumes are no longer black and white as shown in Fig: 40. Author's collection. Photo: Author.

4th and 7th Dragoon Guards

The plume of the band of the 4th (Royal Irish) Dragoon Guards changed to black c. 1902, and at this time the musicians plume for the 7th (Princess Royal's) Dragoon Guards was said to have changed to white. A newspaper photograph c. 1937 of the mounted band of the 4th/7th Dragoon Guards band taken during a musical ride at Edinburgh Castle shows the musicians wearing white plumes. However at some period in time, the plume for the musicians of the amalgamated regiment changed to black over white, as may be seen in a photograph taken by the author at the Cavalry Sunday Memorial Parade in May 1976 (See Fig: 40.). The musicians helmets bore the other ranks pattern plate of the 'old' 4th regiment, with the helmet of the Bandmaster at this time being the officers pattern, of the former 4th (Royal Irish) Dragoon Guards, complete with a white plume. N.B. The Bandmasters plume at this period was very similar, if not identical to the plume of The Life Guards.

Sometime between 1976 and 1986 the plumes of the musicians changed from black over white to white, as shown in a photograph of the Trumpet Major taken in 1986. This photographic illustration which appeared in the regimental magazine (38) clearly shows that his helmet has the ball beneath the socket, pattern of plume holder, and is fitted with a plume similar to that of The Life Guards. However a photograph taken by the author of musicians performing at the Royal Tournament of 1991 shows that their helmets have the alternative pattern plume socket (See Fig: 41.).

5th Inniskilling Dragoon Guards

The musicians of the amalgamated regiment continued to wear red plumes in their helmets, as did the Commanding Officers trumpeter. However sometime towards the end of the 1960s the band suffered a serious loss when the helmets of the band were stolen from their motor coach whilst they were stationed in Germany, and at that time they were unable to replace them (39). This loss might explain why, when the band appeared at the Cavalry Sunday Memorial Service in May 1976 they were dressed in No 1. Dress (blues), complete with green topped peaked caps.

However by the time that the band made an appearance at the 1991 Royal Tournament they had by then acquired replacement helmets having Dragoon Guards pattern brass skulls, strangely however the helmets were fitted with the ball beneath the socket, pattern plume holder. The red plumes worn by the musicians looked very much to be of the Blues and Royals pattern, and it is therefore possible that the ball and socket of the plume holder (but not the plume holder base) where of Household Cavalry pattern, although this has yet to be confirmed.

NOTES

[1] Of interest is the choice of words on a recruiting notice of the 18th century for the 3rd (The Prince of Wales's) Dragoon Guards. The wording on this notice would not I feel be acceptable in today's enlightened society, however it is reproduced here exactly as it was apparently written: *"Any Young Man having Unfortunate Connections with the Opposite Sex should join this Great Regiment where he will lead a life of Jollity and Ease"*.

[1B] This series of cigarette cards includes illustrations of officers helmets of the 2nd Dragoon Guards 1818 to 1834 (the card gives dates as 1822 to 1831). 4th Dragoon Guards 1834 to 1843. 6th Dragoon Guards 1843 to 1847. 5th Dragoon Guards 1855 to 1871. Life Guards 1815, and 1st Life Guards 1871 (card gives date as 1860).

[2] Brigadier James York Scarlett was born the second son of James, 1st Lord Abinger in 1799. He was a former Commanding Officer of the 5th (Princess Charlotte of Wales's) Dragoon Guards and was given command of the Heavy Brigade despite being allegedly 'blind as a bat', and having had no personal experience of war. He was beloved by all and a well respected soldier.

[3] There is an excellent black and white photograph of an original painting depicting the Emperor in dismounted review order, with his helmet placed upon a 'stand' alongside him, in the SFAHR Journal of Spring 1986 (6).

[4] Lieutenant Colonel Robert Stephenson Smyth Baden-Powell born 22nd February 1857 was the hero of the Siege of Mafeking, which was relieved on the 17th May 1900 (the 216th day of the siege). He went on to become a Lieutenant General, and later founded the Boy Scout Movement.(94)

[5] Field Marshall Robertson was Colonel of the 2nd Dragoons (Royal Scots Greys) from 1916 until 1925, Colonel of the 3rd/6th Carabiniers from 1925 to 1929, and Colonel of the Royal Horse Guards from 1929 until his death in 1933 (23). A real example of the saying, *'A Field Marshal's baton in every private's knapsack'*.

[6] Carton de Wiart's returned to the 4th Dragoon Guards, and in 1915 whilst serving with this regiment he received a most serious wound which lost him his left arm. His Victoria Cross was awarded for most conspicuous bravery, coolness and determination whilst commanding the 8th Gloucesters in the capture of La Boiselle in 1916. His military career was however far from over for he served again during the Second World War, was taken prisoner by the Italians, escaped, was recaptured, and released a year later. He reached the rank of Lt General, and was appointed Colonel of the 4th/7th Royal Dragoon Guards, a position he held until his death. A few years ago when visiting the premises of the Army Museums Ogilby Trust, based at that time in Aldershot, Hampshire, the author saw Lt General de Wiart's full dress helmet on display, which regrettably was minus both the plume socket and its plume. N.B. The 4th Dragoon Guards are accredited with being the regiment who fired the first shots of World War One.

[7] E.A. Williams was commissioned into the 1st Dragoon Guards with the rank of Captain on the 4th July 1900 having transferred from the 18th Hussars. He saw service with Bethune's Mounted Infantry during the Boer War, and was killed in action at Orebyfontein, Orange River Colony on the 9th November 1901 (25). See Fig: 21., for an illustration of the helmet worn by Captain Williams.

[8] J.H.A. Annesley was commissioned into the 18th Hussars in 1893, and transferred to the 3rd Dragoon Guards in 1905. He later commanded the 6th Dragoon Guards (Carabiniers) from 1913-1914.

[9] The Marquis of Linlithgow (Victor Alexander John Hope) in the County of Linlithgow or West Lothian, was commissioned into the Lothians and Border Horse on the 1st June 1908 (24), and saw service during the First World War as a Captain with this regiment. Mentioned in despatches, he commanded a Battalion of the Royal Scots 1916-1920 (22A) and later rose to command the 1st Lothians and Border Armoured Car Company 1920-1926. Hon. Colonel Lothians and Border Yeomanry: 6th October 1926. He was appointed Viceroy and Governor-General of India 1936 to 1943 (24). N.B. See Fig: 56 for an illustration of his helmet.

[10] With regard to the centre device of the 2nd Dragoon Guards, several years ago I saw a helmet with the enamel backing to the ER VII cypher being almost orange in colour. I at first thought that the backing had been re-enamelled and that the red colour had 'come out wrong'. However having since seen at least three other helmets with this peculiar colour enamel backing, I reserve my judgment on this matter.

[11] "Quis Separabit" (Who shall separate us?). N.B. The Order of St. Patrick was instituted in 1783, the first Grand Master being Lord Temple, afterwards Marquis of Buckingham. It consisted of the Sovereign, a Grand Master, and twenty-two Knights. (99).

[12] Colonel Ansell's father was Lieutenant Colonel George Kirkpatrick Ansell, who commanded the 5th (Princess Charlotte of Wales's) Dragoon Guards from 1911 until he was killed in action leading two squadrons of the regiment in a most successful charge against the enemy at N'ery on 1st September 1914.

[13] Captain Phillips connection with the cavalry can be traced back to his mother's father who was Brigadier John Tiarks. He joined the 1st King's Dragoon Guards in 1915, commanded the regiment during the period 1936 to 1939, and was Colonel of the Regiment from 1953 to 1958. He was also Colonel of the then newly formed 1st Queens Dragoon Guards from 1958 to 1960 (37).

[14] This watercolour by W. Buckeler is in the possession of the National Army Museum, Chelsea, London.

[15] This memorial is sited at the junction of Chelsea Embankment and Chelsea Bridge Road, and is within walking from the National Army Museum. It was erected in remembrance of the officers and men of the regiment who sacrificed their lives during the Boer War. It has bronze relief plaques, and the aforementioned helmet in stone which is a tribute to the skill of the stonemason, and is well worthy of a visit.

The Chinchain

The chinchain for both regiments was as described for Dragoon Guards 1847.

The Plume

Prior to the introduction of the new plume colours, as detailed in the regulations of 1855 both regiments worn black plumes, being similar in appearance and construction to the plumes of the Dragoon Guards regiments. However sometime after 1855 the 6th Dragoons plume colour changed to white, the 1st Dragoons however retained their black plumes.

The Plume Rosette

The early pattern plumes of the Royals were first adorned with the large 'Albert' pattern rosette as illustrated in Fig: 9.B., however some later pattern helmets are known to have been fitted with the version of rosette illustrated in Fig: 9.C. This smaller rosette was also the pattern that was generally fitted to helmets of the 6th Dragoons, that have been examined by the author, or seen in photographs.

The 2nd Dragoons

During this period the description of the bearskin for the 2nd (Royal North British) Dragoons, as given in the previously mentioned regulations, read as follows *'The Second or Royal North British Dragoons, have permission to wear a bear-skin cap with a white hackle feather, nine inches long, thistle (gilt) on the front of cap according to sealed pattern'.* N.B. During the Crimean campaign the bearskin was worn by the regiment, but minus the hackle feather.

The Other Ranks Pattern Helmet

It proved to be far more difficult to obtain accurate information regarding the finite detail of the other ranks pattern helmet of the 1st and 6th Dragoons, than it did for the Dragoon Guards regiments, possibly because there were only two, rather than seven regiments. There appeared to be less photographs available as a source of reference, of either the helmet itself, or of Dragoons wearing this pattern of head-dress, additionally on the rare occasions that an other ranks helmet was offered for sale by auction, the description given in the salesroom catalogue was either vague, or lacking in detail. However despite the these restrictions some information was gathered and this is given below.

The 1847 Pattern Helmet

Skull and Plume Mount etc.

The skull, plume holder, peak decoration, waist, and rear seam band, together with the ear rosettes were all in brass and were as described for the other ranks pattern helmet of the Dragoon Guards, with the headband, lining, chinchain, the number of component parts, and the method of construction also being similar.

The Helmet Plate

For the 1st Royal Dragoons the helmet plate consisted of the standard 'Albert' pattern wreath with shield, surmounted by a crown, and measuring 5 1/4 inches (6 1/8 inches), and 2 1/2 inches (2 5/8 inches) respectively, upon which was mounted an eight pointed white metal hobnailed star. To the centre of the star was a die-struck brass centre device, being a strap bearing the title 'The Royal Dragoons' with the intertwined Royal Cypher 'V.R.' to the centre.

Figure 42: 6th (Inniskilling) Dragoons officers 1847 pattern. A very scarce post 1855 example having the 'castle' at the centre of the strap of the centre device, in place of the more usual 'V.R.' Royal Cypher. Courtesy of Frank Mitchell Photo: Author.

For the 6th Dragoons, a similar pattern wreath with shield, crown, and star was used, with the centre device consisting of the cypher surrounded by a strap bearing the title 'Inniskilling Dragoons'. For both regiments the helmet plate consisted of three separate pieces, these being the wreath/rococo shield/crown, the hobnailed star, and the centre device. N.B. There is no known evidence to indicate that the other ranks helmet was fitted with the smaller pattern helmet plate, that was fitted to the officers pattern helmet, and although not confirmed it is reasonable to presume that the star on the helmet plate for the 6th Dragoons was in white metal, as for the Royals Dragoons.

The Post 1855 Pattern Helmet

The metal used to form the skull was gradually changed from brass to white metal, however, the details relating to the waist and rear seam band, ear rosettes and chinchain remained unchanged.

The Plume Mount

On an helmet of the 6th Dragoons examined by the author at a Sussex auction salesroom in 1984, the plume mount was affixed to the skull by means of brass bend-over blades in place of the more common, stud and nut method of affixing the plume base to the skull. This fitment looked to be both genuine and contemporary with the rest of the helmet, and the author has subsequently seen other helmets of this regiment having this method of attaching the plume mount to the skull.

The Helmet Plate

Regarding the 6th Dragoons helmet mentioned above, the helmet plate was also affixed to the skull by four brass bend-over blades, this fitment also having the appearance of being genuine and contemporary with the rest of the helmet. N.B There is also a version of this helmet plate having two screw studs to the reverse, with a pair of flat blades behind the crown.

The Plume Rosette

On most other ranks helmets examined by the author the plume rosette was considerably smaller than the officers version, and did not unscrew from the plume stem, however plumes fitted with the standard pattern 'Albert' brass plume rosette as illustrated in Fig: 9.B. are also known to exist.

Variations

1st (Royal) Dragoons

In 1987 a helmet of this regiment was sold at a reputable militaria shop in London having two distinctive features that differed from the standard pattern other ranks helmet. The centre device consisted of a die-struck **silvered/white metal** titled strap with intertwined 'V.R.', the quality of which was such that I was of the opinion that it might be a genuine item, and not a 'made up' one. Additionally this centre device appeared to be contemporary with the oak and olive leaf wreath, the rococo shield, and the star. Secondly the lining to this helmet was of silk, and not of leather as one would have expected on an other ranks helmet. However as the lining was in what appeared to be unused condition, this may have been a replacement, which might possibly have some bearing on the authenticity of the silvered centre device. There is however also, the possibility, that this helmet was once worn by a senior N.C.O., such as the Regimental Sergeant Major.

6th (Inniskilling) Dragoons

A helmet plate sold at a Buckinghamshire auction salesroom was described as *'Officers helmet plate. A very fine 1847-71 example, large gilt wreath half laurel, half oak; within the wreath an ornate gilt shield surmounted by a Crown. On the shield, an eight pointed* ***gilt hobnailed star*** *mounted with a gilt strap inscribed "Inniskilling Dragoons". VR to centre'.* My observations on this item where, that as the centre device was die-struck and the Royal Cypher was not a therefore a separate piece, it is unlikely that this was an officers pattern plate. It might however have been an early version senior N.C.O's plate, although this has yet to be confirmed.

The 1871 Pattern Helmet

The Officers Pattern

The three regiments of Dragoons were not to be outdone by their senior colleagues the Dragoon Guards, when it came to having members of a royal household as their Colonel-in-Chief. The 1st (Royal) Dragoons had Kaiser H.I.M. William II German Emperor, King of Prussia[5] as it Colonel-in-Chief from the 5th May 1894 (6) until the outbreak of the First World War, this position remaining unfilled until King George V became Colonel-in-Chief in 1922. An additional royal connection with the regiment involved H.S.H. Prince Francis of Teck who was commissioned Lieutenant in 1891, and Captain in 1894.

For the 2nd Dragoons, H.I.M. Nicholas II Emperor of Russia held the appointment of Colonel-in-Chief of this regiment from 8th December 1894 (61) until his death. Further royal connections with the regiment occurred when H.R.H. Prince Arthur of Connaught was commissioned Captain in 1907, Major in 1913, and in 1921 became Colonel-in-Chief of the regiment. His son The Earl of MacDuff followed in his fathers footsteps, being commissioned 2nd Lieutenant in 1935, and Lieutenant in 1939 (6). More recent royal connections are Her Majesty Queen Elizabeth II as Colonel-in-Chief of the Royal Scots Dragoon Guards (Carabiniers and Greys), and H.R.H. the Duke of Kent who commanded this newly formed regiment in the late 1970s.

Not to be outdone by the 1st, and 2nd regiments the Inniskillings had as their Colonel-in-Chief from 22nd June 1897 Arthur William Patrick Albert, Duke of Connaught and Strathearn[6] (Third son of Queen Victoria) (6). The National Army Museum, Chelsea have some excellent photographs of the Duke's full dress helmet, the front view of which really shows off the helmet plate to perfection (51). Field Marshall Edmund Allenby who has already been mentioned in Chapter 4, commenced his military career in this regiment, being gazetted 2nd Lieutenant C.1882, he was appointed Adjutant of the regiment in 1889, and Brigade Major of the 3rd Cavalry Brigade at the Curragh in 1898 (7). However perhaps the most famous officer ever to serve in the 'Skins' was Captain L.E.G. Oates[7] who perished on Captain Scott's ill fated expedition to the South Pole in 1912.

Dress Regulations 1874

The paragraph describing the helmet of the Dragoon Guards has already been quoted in full in chapter 5, and it is therefore not considered necessary to repeat it again here. I do however reproduce the paragraph, albeit brief though it is, relating to the helmet of the 1st and 6th Dragoons, which was deliberately omitted from my earlier reference to the Dress Regulations of 1874, and additionally I reproduce the description given for the bearskin cap of the 2nd Dragoons as quoted in these regulations, both these paragraphs being reproduced as printed.

Figure 43: 1st (Royal) Dragoons officers 1847 pattern. A post 1855 example in almost perfect condition. Note: The plume is a good quality modern replacement. Author's collection. Photo: R. Biondi.

Figure 43a: Offset view of helmet. Note the gilt 'hobnailed' star.

Figure 43b: Side view of helmet with the plume removed to show the shape of the skull. Note the ear rosettes, which are the correct pattern having the 'proud' (raised) centre.

Figure 43c: The rear view of the helmet in which can be seen the rear seam band, and the profuse decoration to the edge of the rear peak.

Figure 44: Dragoon officers helmet post 1855 pattern with the plume mount and helmet plate removed. Of interest is the small strengthening plate positioned behind the crown of the helmet plate. Author's collection. Photo: Author.

Figure 45: Inside view of an officers 1855 pattern helmet in which can be seen both the silk lining, and plume base fitment. Author's Collection. Photo: R. Biondi.

Helmet for 1st and 6th Dragoons

'Of the same pattern as for Dragoon Guards, but of white metal with gilt ornaments'.

As with the description for the helmet of the Dragoon Guards the above official description gives very little detail of the helmet plate, the distinctive shape plume holder, or the pattern of ear rosettes etc. fitted to the helmet of the 1st, and 6th Dragoons, and therefore this omitted information is given below.

Cap for 2nd Dragoons (Scots Greys)

'Black bearskin, 10 inches high; with a gilt thistle in front; and a gilt grenade on the left side, as a plume socket, bearing the badge of St. Andrew, with the Royal Arms above, and the word "Waterloo" below. Plain gilt burnished chain, lined with black leather'. 'Plume-White hackle feather, 9 inches long'.

The Helmet Skull for the 1st and 6th Dragoons

Whilst the skull was of white metal instead of gilt, the number of component parts, and method of construction was the same as for the Dragoon Guards pattern helmet, with all fittings being in gilt metal. It is not unusual however to find an officers helmet of either of the two regiments having a **silver plated, copper** skull, this being both lighter and of better quality than the white metal version.

The Plume Holder

Again the number of component parts and method of affixing the plume holder to the skull was the same as for the Dragoon Guards, with the helmets of both the 1st and the 6th Dragoons having the identical pattern plume holder that was fitted to the 2nd **Dragoon Guards** helmet. This fitment, in gilt metal was the pattern having, in ascending order, a milled edge at its base, a short stem, and a medium sized ball, all being beneath the fluted socket (See Fig: 25.B.). This version of plume holder measured 4 1/4 inches in height and was 3/4 inches taller that the version fitted to the helmets of the 1st, and 3rd to 7th regiments of Dragoon Guards.

1st Dragoons - Plume Holder Variations

At an auction sale in 1972 a helmet of the 'Royals' was sold which was not fitted with the type of plume holder mentioned above, in its place there being a gilt spike above a small round ball, the spike not being capable of accepting a plume stem (See Fig: 25.F.). A further variation was seen in an auction salesroom in 1983 when another 'Royals' helmet was sold, this time the gilt metal plume holder was similar to the 'spike' version but was capable of accepting the plume stem, (See Fig: 25.D.) and in fact a plume was fitted to this helmet. N.B. The later pattern plume holder is the type generally to be found on yeomanry helmets.

The Headband and Lining

The headband and method of attachment to the skull was as for the Dragoon Guards helmet, with the lining usually being of beige padded/quilted cloth or soft quilted silk, although soft red leather with a silk upper section was occasionally used. Adjustment for fit was achieved by loosening or tightening the one/two fitted drawstrings.

The Helmet Plate

For both regiments the helmet plate consisted of a twelve pointed gilt **hobnailed** (beaded) star upon which was the regimental centre device, these being:

1st (Royal) Dragoons (See Fig: 46C.)

A silvered metal elliptical strap bearing the title 'The Royal Dragoons', and within the strap on a silvered metal ground The Crest of England in gilt metal. The complete helmet plate was comprised of four separate pieces, these being the hobnailed star, the strap, the silvered ground, and the Crest of England.

6th (Inniskilling) Dragoons (See Fig: 48A.)

A gilt metal elliptical strap bearing the title 'Inniskilling Dragoons', and within the strap on a silvered metal ground the Royal Cypher 'V.R.' (intertwined) in gilt metal. This helmet plate was also comprised of four separate pieces, these being the hobnailed star, the strap, the silvered ground, and the Royal Cypher. N.B. For both the above helmet plates the method of assembly, and affixing to the skull of the helmet was as for the Dragoon Guards helmet.

A helmet of the Inniskilling's that was sold at the London Arms Fair in 1986 was fitted with a most dubious helmet plate, the centre device consisting of a gilt garter **pierced** with the motto *'Honi Soit Qui Mal Y Pense* on a **blue enamel ground,** and within the garter a silver **Castle on a red enamel ground**. Whilst the plume holder, ear rosettes, and other fittings all looked to be of the correct pattern, the plume however was a replacement other ranks version. Having examined this helmet very closely, it is my unconfirmed opinion that this was not a genuine helmet plate centre device, but was a 'made up' item.

The Ear Rosettes

The 1st Dragoons

The Royals seemed to have been 'spoilt for choice' when it comes to the pattern of ear rosette fitted to the officers helmet. A pre 1902 version in the author's collection is fitted with the pattern illustrated in Fig: 9.J, whilst a post 1902 version has the pattern illustrated in Fig: 9.H. Both these patterns are correct for this regiment, as confirmed in an illustration of the officers of the regiment c. 1896 that appeared in a volume of *'The Navy and Army Illustrated'* of that year, in which the pattern of ear rosettes can be seen on the helmets being held by the officers.

6th Dragoons

For the 'Skins' the pattern illustrated in Fig: 9.H. was fitted. This version appears to have been favoured by the regiment, as some of the late, 'Albert' pattern helmets were also fitted with this pattern of rosette.

The Chinchain

As for the Dragoon Guards helmet, although in the 1st Dragoons red **morocco** leather is also known to have been used to back the chinchain.

The Plume

Black for the 1st Dragoons, and white for the 6th. A Victorian period plume of the Royals in the author's collection has extremely fine hair, and is has been suggested that this example was made from the mane rather than the tail of a horse, the former apparently being finer hair.

The Plume Rosette

For both the Royals and Inniskillings the plume rosette was normally than pattern illustrated in Fig: 9.C. in gilt metal.

Figure 46: 1st (Royal) Dragoons officers 1871 pattern, pre 1902. Note the ball beneath the socket pattern of plume holder and the slimness of the officers pattern plume. Author's collection. Photo: R. Biondi.

Figure 46a: Offset view of the helmet. Note the inner rear peak of this helmet has not been lined with skiver.

Opposite, Figure 46c: Close up view of the helmet plate, which clearly illustrates the correct pattern hobnailed (beaded) star.

Figure 46b: Side view of the helmet in which can be seen the smaller (Type: 9.J.) of the two known pattern of ear rosettes that are correct for this helmet.

THE ROYAL DRAGOONS

Figure 47: 'A Seasoned Campaigner' Sir F. Marshall. K.C.M.G.[8] Colonel of the 1st Dragoons 29th March 1890. Courtesy of R.G. Harris.

Figure 48: 6th (Inniskilling) Dragoons officers pattern. An early version of this helmet with original officers pattern plume c. 1880. Author's collection. Photo: R. Biondi.

INNISKILLING DRAGOONS

Opposite, Figure 48a: Close up of the helmet plate in which can be seen the hobnailed star and the intertwined 'V.R.' Royal Cypher to the centre device. Note. It is though that the cypher changed to the Castle over V.I. pattern sometime after 1880.

Figure 48b: Offset view of the helmet in which can be seen the medium sized plume rosette (Type 9.C.).

Figure 48c: Side view of the helmet showing the correct pattern of ear rosette for this regiments, officers pattern helmet.

Dress Regulation 1900

This was the first time that details of the helmet plate for the 1st and 6th regiments was published in the Dress Regulations, and the following particulars are reproduced as originally published, together with the slightly amended description for the helmet, and chinchain, with the relevant changes being in bold text. Also given are details of the bearskin for the 2nd Dragoons (R.S.G) which by this time was far more informative.

1st (Royal)Dragoons (See Fig: 46A.)
'In gilt or gilding metal the Garter star. On the star the Crest of England on a burnished silver ground within an elliptical ring in silver inscribed "The Royal Dragoons"'.

6th Dragoons (See Fig: 49.)
On a gilt or gilding metal beaded Garter star, an elliptical ring inscribed "Inniskilling Dragoons" in burnished letters on a frosted ground. Within the ring, in silver the Castle over "V.R." on a frosted gilt or gilding metal ground'.

'Helmet for 1st and 6th Dragoons of the same pattern as for Dragoon Guards, but of white metal, with gilt ***or gilding metal*** *ornaments.' 'Plain burnished chain,* ***1 inch wide, mounted on black patent leather, lined with velvet*** *and fastened on each side with a rose ornament'.*

2nd Dragoons
'Cap for 2nd Dragoons-Black bearskin, a grenade fitted with a spring on the left side as a plume socket. Plain burnished chain, lined with patent leather, backed with velvet'. 'For officers not exceeding 5 ft 6 in. in height, 9.1/2 in high.

5ft. 6in.	"	*5' 9"*	"	*10"*	"
5'9 "	"	*6'0"*	"	*10.1/2"*	"
6'0 " and upwards				*11"*	"

Plume – White hackle feather, 10 inches high to the top of the plume.
For device on grenade see Appendix I.'
The relevant section of Appendix I reads as follows:

Figure 49: 6th (Inniskilling) Dragoons officers pattern. A late version helmet. Compare this helmet plate centre device with the one illustrated in Fig: 48A. Author's collection. Photo: Author.

Figure 49a: 6th (Inniskilling) Dragoons, officers late pattern helmet with the ear rosettes, chinchain, and helmet plate removed from skull of the helmet. Author's collection. Photo: Author.

Figure 49b: Captain Valerio Alwy Magawly Cerati de Calry. D.S.O.[9] 6th (Inniskilling) Dragoons c. 1910/1912. Note the Castle & VI to centre of helmet plate. Courtesy of R.G. Harris.

A grenade in gilt or gilding metal. On the grenade the Royal Arms. In the centre below, St. Andrew and Cross, between sprays of rose, thistle and shamrock; on a scroll beneath the word "Waterloo".[19A]

1902 and Onwards

With the death of Queen Victoria in 1901 and the Coronation of King Edward VII came a slight alteration to the centre device on the helmet plate of the Royal Dragoons, this being changed from 'Lion over Victorian crown' to 'Lion over King's (Tudor or Imperial) crown'. The centre device for the 'skins' however was unaffected.

Reserve Regiment of Dragoons
The helmet plate for the above regiment is described in Hugh King's book on head dress-badges (28) as being *'On the Garter Star the Garter with the motto pierced on a blue enamel ground. Within the Garter the letters RR in silver on a red ground'*. Although details of the motto are not given in Hugh's book I am given to believe that the motto was *'Honi Soit Qui Mal Y Pense.'*

The Warrant Officers (Senior N.C.O.'s) Helmet
Despite extensive research and studying a great many photographs I have been until to establish if the Warrant Officers of Dragoon regiments wore officers, or other ranks pattern helmets, and therefore make no observations on the helmets worn by the gentlemen holding this rank.

The Other Ranks Helmet

The Skull and Fittings

A skull of white metal, with the peak binding, waist band, rear seam band, plume holder, chinchain and ear rosettes all being in brass, and of the same pattern as for the other ranks of the Dragoon Guards, as also was the headband and lining. N.B. Whilst the plume holder for both regiments was normally identical to that fitted to the Dragoon Guards helmet, an other ranks pattern helmet on display at the Household Cavalry Museum, Windsor, is fitted with a plume holder having a small ball beneath the socket as illustrated in Fig: 50A. This fitment is very 'out of place' on this helmet, however the plume holder does seem to be contemporary with the rest of the helmet, and I can offer no explanation as to why this pattern of holder was fitted.

The Helmet Plate
A brass twelve pointed rayed star, upon which was mounted a white metal garter (not pierced) with the motto *'Honi.Soit.Qui.Mal.Y.Pense'*. Within the garter on either a black leather, or a lack japanned metal ground, the regimental number being either the numeral one, or six in brass, dependent upon the regiment concerned, (See Fig: 50.) for an illustration of the 1st Dragoons helmet. The helmet plate consisted of four separate pieces, these being the rayed star, the garter, the leather or japanned metal ground, and the numeral, and was assembled and affixed to the skull of the helmet as described for the Dragoon Guards. N.B. A version of the garter exists which does not have a dot between each word of the motto, this version being fitted to a helmet of the 6th Dragoons.

Figure 50: 1st (Royal) Dragoons other ranks pattern. Note the correct other ranks pattern ear rosettes fitted to this helmet. Photo: Author.

2nd Dragoons - Bearskin
A black bearskin similar to that of the officers, but being lower in height and of a lesser quality, and having a white metal 'Horse of Hanover' to its rear. Leather head lining, with a brass, leather backed chinchain.

The Plume and Rosette
The plume for the 1st Dragoons was black, with the 6th Dragoons having a white plume, both plumes having a small brass rosette which was identical to that on the plume of the other ranks of the Dragoon Guards regiments. (See Fig: 54.). The 2nd Dragoons wore a white hackle (feather plume) to the left side of the bearskin, that fitted into a brass flaming grenade, similar in pattern to that of the officers.

Cavalry Musician's Plumes

The plumes for trumpeters and the musicians in the band of the 1st Dragoons were white, although the plume for the Kettle-drummer of c. 1895 was reported as being black over white (52). For the 6th Dragoons, red and white plumes were worn by the bandsmen as early as c. 1870, and for the 2nd Dragoons a scarlet feather plume was worn by the musicians of their band.

Reserve Regiment of Dragoons

The above helmet plate is described in Hugh King's excellent book on head-dress badges (28) as follows. *'On a twelve pointed star the Garter. Within a voided centre the Royal Crest in gilding metal with a black leather backing to the Royal Crest'.* N.B. My previously expressed observations regarding the helmet plate of the Reserve Regiment of Dragoon Guards applies equally to the above described Dragoon helmet plate.

Mechanization of the 1st (Royal) Dragoons 1940/41

The Royal Dragoons were serving in Palestine when news of their proposed mechanization to an armoured car regiment was received, their last horse inspection taking place just before Christmas of 1940.

For the Royal Scots Greys (2nd Dragoons) it was to be May 1941 before news arrived that they were to become an armoured regiment, they being the last cavalry regiment in the British Army to be mechanized (65).

Figure 50a: 1st (Royal) Dragoons other ranks pattern. Compare the pattern of plume holder fitted to this helmet with the standard pattern holder fitted to the helmet in Fig: 50. Photo: G. Frost. Courtesy of the Household Cavalry Museum.

NOTES

[1] Sergeant Charles Ewart, an expert swordsman captured the Eagle of the 45th Regiment early on in the engagement, cutting down the French standard bearer and two other French soldiers. Sergeant Ewart died in 1846.

[2] Major Henry Dalrymple White was appointed to command of the Inniskillings when his commanding officer was killed in an accident. This occurred when the 'Europa', the ship transporting Lieutenant Colonel Willoughby Moore and some other members of the 6th Dragoons to the Crimea, caught fire and was totally destroyed, with the loss of Lt Colonel Moore, and eighteen others, plus all the horses, the baggage, and equipment (42). Lieutenant Colonel White as he then became, was first commissioned as Cornet (2nd Lieutenant) in 1838 in the 6th Dragoons. He was then promoted Lieutenant 1839 (43): 6Dns. Captain 1844: 6Dns. Major 1848: 6Dns. Lieutenant Colonel June 1854: 6Dns., and Brevet Colonel November 1854. He eventually rose to the rank of full General in 1879, and was Colonel of the 2nd Dragoon Guards in 1873, until appointed Colonel of the 6th Dragoons in 1874 (44). He was honoured with the awards K.C.B. and C.B. N.B. Up until 1871 officers purchased their commissions, however by the post Crimea period an officer had to spend some time in each rank before purchasing his next commission. Prior to 1860 the "advertised" price of a Cornet's commission was £850, and a Major's was commission £4,575 (23).

[3] Lieutenant Colonel Henry Darby Griffiths C.B. was born on the 5th July 1810 (47) and commissioned Ensign (2nd Lieutenant) 1828: The 4th or King's Regiment. Lieutenant 1832: 35th Sussex Regiment of Foot. Captain 1839: 2nd Dragoons. Major 1846: 2Dns. Lieutenant Colonel August 1854: 2Dns. Colonel (In the Army) November 1854 (49). He rose to the rank of full General in 1880 (48), and was Colonel of the 2nd Dragoons: 31st March 1866, and Colonel of the 5th Lancers: 1st January 1872 (46).

[4] Lieutenant Colonel John Yorke C.B. was born on the 11th June 1814, and was commissioned Cornet 1832: 1st Dragoons. He was promoted to Lieutenant 1834: 1Dns. Captain 1841: 1Dns. Major 1849:1Dns. Lieutenant Colonel 1853: 1Dns. He rose further to become a full General in 1877 (49), and was Commandant of the Royal Military Asylum from 1st April 1864 to 30th September 1866, and Colonel of the 19th Hussars: 6th May 1872 (49).

[5] There is a really excellent painting of Kaiser Wilhelm II in the officers mess at Comberemere Barracks, Windsor, which depicts the Kaiser as Colonel-in-Chief of the regiment, in dismounted review order holding his helmet, this painting being reproduced in colour in the 'Regiment' Magazine (50).

[6] H.R.H. Arthur William Patrick Albert, Duke of Connaught and Strathearn (1850-1942) either served in, or was Colonel-in-Chief of a great many regiments, including several regiments of foreign powers. The following are some of the cavalry regiments he was connected with in one way or another. Captain 1874: 7th Hussars. Major 1875: 7th Hussars. Hon. Colonel 1883: 13th Bengal Lancers. Hon. Colonel 1886: Royal East Kent Mounted Rifles. Hon. Colonel 1891: 1st Bombay Lancers. Colonel-in-Chief 1897: 6th Inniskilling Dragoons. Colonel-in-Chief 1904: 31st Duke of Connaught's Own Lancers. Hon. Colonel 1908: South Irish Horse (6).

[7] Lawrence Edward Grace Oates was born 17th March 1880, the son of William Edward and Caroline Anne Oates, and was educated at Willington School, Remenham Prep School, and Eton. He was first gazetted to the 2nd Volunteers Battalion of the Suffolk Regiment c. 1896, later being gazetted to the 3rd Militia Battalion of the Prince of Wales's (West Yorkshire Regiment) c. 1897. He was commissioned 2nd Lieutenant in the 6th Dragoons in 1900, Promoted to Lieutenant in 1902 and to Captain in 1910. He distinguished himself in the Boer War in which he was severely wounded. In 1910 he joined Captain Scott's Antarctic expedition as the keeper of the expedition's ponies. His body was never found, and the relief expedition built a cairn inscribed *"Hereabouts died a very gallant gentleman, Captain L.E.G. Oates, of the Inniskilling Dragoons. In March 1912, returning from the Pole, he walked willingly to his death in a blizzard to try and save his comrades, beset by hardships. This note was left by the Relief Expedition of 1912" (98).* N.B. See chapter eleven regarding the sale of his helmet.

[8] Lieutenant General F. Marshall K.C.M.G. Born 26th July 1829. Cornet 1849:1st Dragoon Guards. Lieutenant 1851: 1DG. Captain 1859: 2nd Life Guards. Major 1863. Lt Colonel 1868. Major General 1877. Lt General 1884. Colonel of the 1st (Royal) Dragoons 29th March 1890.

[9] Captain Valerio Alwy Magawly Cerati de Calry. D.S.O. Born 25th August 1883. 2nd Lieutenant 1902: 3rd Northumberland Fusiliers. Lieutenant 1905: 3rd Northumberland Fusiliers. Lieutenant 1907: 6th Dragoons. Captain 1910: 6th Dns. Adjutant 1912: 6th Dns. Temporary Major April 1916: 7th Rifle Brigade. Acting Lieutenant Colonel September 1916: Rifle Brigade. Killed in Action 10th August 1917. See Fig: 49B. for an illustration of this officer in full dress.

[94] The following is an abridged extract relating to the bearskin of the 2nd Dragoon (Royal Scots Greys) that originally appeared in 'The Regiment Journal' No 16 Vol 1. on the 18th July 1896, which it is hoped will be of interest to readers. 'The bearskin is ten inches high, a white horse at the rear, and a gilt grenade on the left side as a plume socket, bearing the badge of St. Andrew with the Royal Arms above and the word "Waterloo" below. Plain gilt burnished chain lined with black leather. Plume, white hackle feather nine inches long. The Officers wear no ornaments, save the grenade at the side. The head-gear is black bear-skin on a leather foundation, weight about two pounds. The price of the Officers is fifteen guineas, whilst those of the men fluctuate according to the supply available. Messrs Hawkes and Company, of Piccadilly, construct quite a number of caps, both for officers and men of the Scots Greys'.

7

Regiments: The Yeomanry

Introduction to the Yeomanry

The yeomanry can trace its history back to 1761 albeit that it was not properly organised until 1794. The command was on a county basis with the regiments at that time consisting of the county gentlemen (officers) and farm workers (other ranks), all of which provided their own horses.

Many regiments sprang up when a threat to the nation arose such as the Napoleonic war, only to be disbanded once the threat had ceased, and by 1870 there came reductions with those regiments having fewer than four troops being disbanded (53).

In 1885 the War Office drew up a 'Yeomanry Table of Precedence' for the first time, the results of which were in many cases unpopular, as many regiments would not have been pleased with their 'ranking' in this list. Further changes took place with the Defence Act of 1888 which amended the terms of service for the yeomanry so that all ranks were liable for service anywhere in Great Britain, with a further change occurring in 1893 when all yeomanry regiments were ordered to reorganise on a squadron basis (53).

By 1897 their were 38 regiments on the official establishment, with a further 2 regiments being classed as Volunteer Light Horse. The uniforms of the yeomanry followed those of the regular regiments of cavalry, albeit in many cases being far more elaborate with, 11 regiments dressed as Dragoons, 25 as Hussars, 1 as Lancers, and 1 as Mounted Rifles,(1) with the 2 regiments of Volunteer Light Horse being dressed similar to Dragoons.

With the outbreak of the Boer War in 1899, the need arose for more additional mounted troops, and as a result several new yeomanry regiments were raised, not the least amongst them being the Westminster Dragoons, and City of London Yeomanry (Rough Riders).

Under the Militia and Auxiliary Forces Act of 1901, together with Army Order 109, the name of the Yeomanry Cavalry was changed to the Imperial Yeomanry. For many regiments this resulted in a change to their title such as, the Montgomeryshire Yeomanry Cavalry becoming the Montgomeryshire Imperial Yeomanry, and the Shropshire Yeomanry changing to the Shropshire Imperial Yeomanry, which in both cases resulted in a change to the title as borne on the strap of the centre device, of the helmet plate.

In 1908 the yeomanry became a part of the newly formed Territorial Force and those regiments who had changed their title to include the word 'Imperial' should in theory have changed again, and indeed a great many regiments did so. However, a very limited number of regiments retained the word 'Imperial' on their helmet plates, the Norfolk Yeomanry having been known to have kept their tri-part scroll bearing the title 'King's Own Norfolk **Impl** Yeomy on the helmets through to, and during the reign of King George V, and the Westminster Dragoons appear never to have removed the letters I.Y. from their helmet plate.

Although not always the case, the post of Adjutant to a yeomanry regiment was frequently held by an officer seconded from a regular cavalry regiment, as were the permanent staff posts such as the Regimental Sergeant Major, and the Squadron Sergeant Majors, some known examples of the period c. 1897 to 1911 being given below:

Yeomanry Regiment		**Adjutant**
Yorkshire Dragoons	c. 1897.	Capt. L.J. Richardson. 14th Hussars (54).
East Kent Mount Rifles	c. 1902.	Major E.M. Lafone. 4th (Queen's Own) Hussars (55).
Norfolk Yeomanry	c. 1905.	Captain J.F. Champion 14th King's Hussars (56).
North Somerset Yeomanry	1907.	Captain O.W. Brinton. 21st (Empress of India's) Lancers (57).
Duke of Lancaster's Own	1909.	Captain A.W.B. Spencer. Yeomanry 13th Hussars (58).
Staffordshire Yeomanry	1911.	Captain H.B. Towse. Royal Scots Greys (59).
		Permanent Staff
3rd County of London Yeomanry (Sharpshooters)	1903.	R.S.M. Lesney. 13th Hussars (60).
3rd County of London		S.S.M. Eatwell. 3rd Dragoon Guards (60)
3rd County of London		S.S.M. Morris. 15th Hussars (60).
3rd County of London		S.S.M. Taylor. 17th Lancers (60).

What is most interesting is that contemporary photographs tend to show the permanent staff i.e. the R.S.M. and S.S.M.'s wearing the uniform of the yeomanry regiment to which they are seconded, whilst the regular officer serving with the same yeomanry regiment wears the full dress uniform of his parent regiment. The most likely explanation for this is that, whilst the full dress yeomanry uniforms of the R.S.M. and S.S.M's would have been an official issue to them, the officer (Adjutant), would have been expected to meet the cost, of the additional expense incurred by providing the full dress yeomanry uniform out of his own pocket.

Having in previous chapters given a brief description of the full dress uniform of the Household Cavalry and the Dragoon Guards it is reasonable to expect that similar information would be given on the uniforms of the yeomanry regiments. However as this chapter covers some twenty-five regiments it is not practical to do justice to all the differing pattern shoulder belts, pouches, waist belts etc. that were used, and therefore information has been restricted to the colour of the tunic and the pantaloons (breeches), as worn by the other ranks of the particular regiment concerned, together with the date these details refer to, where known. N.B. The date given after the uniform details refers to a period that this uniform was worn, and not the date it was first adopted by the regiment.

Also within this chapter I have included a 'thumbnail' history relating to the formation of each regiment accompanied by its official acceptance date, together with some of the changes of regimental title that occurred up until the outbreak of the First World War, together with the address of the regimental headquarters as at 1914 (90). N.B. The official acceptance date is the date of the earliest troop that formed the regiment (89).

Yeomanry Bands

Following in the footsteps of their brother-in-arms, the regular cavalry, many yeomanry regiments had a band, whilst the more ambitious, and perhaps affluent regiments, emulated the 'regulars' by having a mounted band complete with drum horse. Information relating to these bands is very scarce, and I have therefore only given a plume colour for a particular regiments band where the information has been taken from an authoritative source such as R.G. Harris's booklet on drum banners (62).

Dress Regulations were not published for officers of the Yeomanry, and the head-dress of the these regiments did not necessarily follow a regulation pattern. Their head-dress often ranged from obsolete pattern helmets, long since discarded by the regular cavalry, through to the current pattern of helmet being worn by the these regiments. Two notable examples of the former are the Glasgow Yeomanry and the North Somerset Yeomanry, each of which continued to wear the 'Albert' pattern as their full dress head-dress, albeit with minor variations up until, and quite possibly long after the First World War, although this has not been confirmed. It is the authors personal opinion that when selecting a new pattern of head-dress for his regiment the Commanding Officer might well have chosen to visit a helmet supplier and upon viewing his stock of fittings, past and present, selected a skull and then added the plume holder, ear rosettes and other fittings that appealed to him. This might explain the mix of obsolete and new parts that make up some of the helmets worn by the yeomanry regiments.

A considerable amount of the detailed information given on the yeomanry helmets in this chapter was obtained when closely examining actual examples of the items concerned, many of which were owned by private collectors. The exceptions being the Fife Mounted Rifles, Imperial Yeomanry, The Lancashire Mounted Rifle Volunteers, and The Sussex Light Horse where limited information was obtained from examining photographs, and in the case of the Imperial Yeomanry by verbal details being supplied by an owner of one of this exceedingly rare helmets, of which there are only two examples known to exist.

As with the helmets of the regular cavalry the yeomanry helmet has been 'broken down' into its component parts, these being the skull, plume holder, headband and lining, helmet plate, ear rosettes, chinchain, plume, and plume rosette. However as the method of attaching the plume mount, headband and lining, the helmet plate, ear sockets, and other fittings to the skull was very similar to that of the Dragoon Guards helmet, it is not considered necessary to repeat these details within this chapter.

Regarding the other ranks pattern helmet, as this was frequently very similar in appearance to that of the officers, and often fitted with identical member parts albeit of a lesser quality, I have reduced the number of 'component part headings' by including the ear rosette and the chinchain under the same heading as the skull and the plume holder.

The Individual Component Parts of the Helmet

The Skull

The description of the skull is given under the regimental heading for each of the individual regiments. However although on most of the yeomanry helmets the waist and rear seam band conformed to that on the helmets of the Dragoon Guards and Dragoons, several of these volunteer regiments had unique pattern waist bands, and these will be described in full, when giving an account of the helmet concerned. For those regiments having the regular cavalry pattern waist and rear seam band, the following describes the two acknowledged patterns of these fitments, which hereafter will be referred to as Type: K., and Type: L.

Type: K. The 'Albert' pattern waistband which measured 3/4 inches in width, being of a leaf and scroll pattern and completely encircling the waist, with the rear seam band being a tapering one inch wide band of oak-leaf pattern, both these fitments being either in gilt or silvered metal for the officers, and brass or white metal for the other ranks.

Type: L. The 1871 pattern laurel-leaf waistband measuring approximately 5/8th inches in width at the sides, and 1 1/2 inches in width at the centre, being position above the front peak and extending from ear socket to ear socket. The rear seam band was of oak-leaf design and measured one inch in width. and again both these bands are to be found in either gilt/brass or silvered/white metal dependent upon the regiment concerned.

Plume Holders

It is when researching the various patterns of plume holder that the peculiarities of the Yeomanry helmet become most evident, for unlike the officers helmets of the Dragoon Guards and the Dragoons, on whose helmets only two versions and one version respectively were generally to be found, the yeomanry helmet may be fitted with any one of eight varying type of plume holder dependent on the regiment. As always there is the 'exception to the rule' which in this case was the Hampshire Yeomanry/Carabiniers, on whose helmets at least three differing pattern of socket were fitted.

Below is listed a brief description of the eight known patterns of plume holder, together with two known pattern of spikes, each of which as been given a code letter for easy reference, which will be referred to in the following text, as and when appropriate:

> Type: A. Having the standard cross-piece base with four terminals (hereafter referred to as the plume base), surmounted by a fluted tapering socket, as illustrated in Fig: 25.A. N.B. This is the pattern of holder fitted to the officers helmets of the 1st, 3rd, 4th, 5th, 6th, and 7th Dragoon Guards.
>
> Type: B. Plume base as described above, surmounted by a medium-sized sphere, above which was a fluted tapering socket, as illustrated in Fig: 25.B. N.B. This is the pattern of holder fitted to the officers helmet of the 2nd Dragoon Guards, and the 1st, and 6th Dragoons.

Type: C. This pattern consisted of the standard plume base, surmounted by a tapering fluted socket that was narrower at its base than either Type A or Type B and is illustrated in Fig: 25.C. N.B. To my knowledge this pattern was only ever made in silvered/white metal.

Type: D. The standard plume base surmounted by a small sized sphere, above which was a narrow tapering fluted socket similar in appearance to the socket on Type C. This is illustrated in Fig: 25.D.

Type: E. This pattern differed totally from the four previously described plume holders in that the base was of a leaf pattern, above which was a fluted socket of Type A, as illustrated in Fig: 25.E. This version, was what appears to be a 'marriage' of an 'Albert' pattern base with an 1871 pattern socket.

Type: F. Again the standard plume base, but this time surmounted by a small-sized sphere above which was a narrow tapering fluted spike, similar in general appearance to Type D, but **not being capable of accepting the stem of a plume**. Illustrated in Fig: 25.F.

Type: G. A leaf pattern 'Albert' style base similar in appearance to Type E. However, it differed in that the base was surmounted by a small-sized inverted half-cup, above which was a medium-sized oval shaped sphere, which itself was surmounted by a narrow tapering fluted spike which was **not capable of accepting a plume stem**. Illustrated as in Fig: 25.G.

Type: H. A leaf pattern 'Albert' style base having a six -sided tapering socket, that was capable of accepting a plume stem, as illustrated in Fig: 25.H.

Type: I. The 'Albert' pattern plume holder as described previously in chapter 5, and illustrated in Fig: 15.

Type: J. Similar to the above pattern, but having a leaf patterned four sided round socket **without finials** above a floriated base, as illustrated in Fig: 58. N.B. Unlike plume holder Type: I., the four-sided round socket, **did not sit within a shorter four finialed socket**.

The Headband and Lining

The headband, was similar to that on the Household Cavalry, Dragoon Guards and Dragoons helmets. It was made of pressed felt, or alternatively of hard leather, and was attached to the skull of the helmet by the two ear rosette sockets which were themselves secured to the skull by small rivets. As this particular fitment appears to have been very similar, if not identical on most 'Albert' pattern and 1871 pattern helmets, no further reference will be made to the headband so as to avoid unnecessary repetition.

The officers pattern lining was generally of quilted beige cloth, or beige silk, with either one or two drawstrings with which to adjust the lining for comfort and fit. Reference will however be made to the type of head lining fitted to each regiments helmet, as frequently on the officers pattern, various slightly differing types of head lining were fitted. N.B. The type of head lining listed for each regiment is the pattern known to have been fitted to this particular helmet, it is however always possible that other types of linings were fitted.

On all of the other ranks pattern yeomanry helmets examined by the author the headband and lining were of the pattern fitted to the Dragoon Guards and Dragoons helmets, and therefore no further reference will be made to this fitment within this chapter.

The Helmet Plate

Full details of each regiments helmet plate, for both the officers and the other ranks patterns, are given under the individual regimental heading. To again avoid repetition, I list below the various types of crown that may usually be found on a yeomanry helmet plate, each pattern of crown having been given a code letter ranging from M to R, which will be used in the text of this chapter when referring to a pattern of crown, as appropriate.

The centre device (where applicable) was secured to the helmet plate in a similar manner as on the officers plate of the 5th, and 6th Dragoon Guards, details of which were given previously in chapter five. However on the helmets of the yeomanry, the methods used to attach the complete plate to the skull of the helmet were many and varied, and tended to differ from regiment to regiment. The following few examples give an indication of the differing number of studs/bend-over **twin** blades (tabs) that were fitted to these plates to secure the plate to the helmet, although it is possible that many other variations were used. For the Hertfordshire Yeomanry officers plate pre 1902 there was **one stud**, plus two bend-over twin blades, the Shropshire Yeomanry officers plate also pre 1902 had **three studs** but no blades, the other ranks plate of the Westminster Dragoons c. 1903 was fitted with three studs plus one twin blade, the Montgomeryshire Yeomanry officers plate c. 1908 had just **four studs**, whilst the Yorkshire Dragoons officers plate pre 1902 pattern had **five studs**, plus one twin blade.

Types of Helmet Plate Crown

Type: M. A large St. Edward's crown of similar design to that on the 'Albert' pattern Dragoon Guards helmet measuring 2 1/2 inches in width by 1 7/8 inches to 2 5/16 inches in height as illustrated in Fig: 55. The Hertfordshire Yeomanry helmet.

Type: N. A medium sized crown with rounded raised arches measuring 2 1/8 inches in width by 2 inches in height, as illustrated in Fig: 51. The Berkshire Yeomanry helmet plate.

Type: P. A medium sized crown stylised similar to the "Imperial" pattern crown and measuring 1 7/8 inches in width by 2 inches in height as illustrated in Fig: 58. The Staffordshire Yeomanry helmet. N.B. Type: P appears to be a variation of Type: N.

Type: Q. A small squat crown having a slight dip to the arches measuring 1 3/4 inches in width by 1.1/2 inches in height as illustrated in Fig: 61A. The Yorkshire Dragoons helmet.

Type: R. A small 'King's pattern crown made in various sizes, as found on the helmet plate of the Essex Yeomanry, and the Westminster Dragoons (See Figs: 52. and 60.)

The Ear Rosettes and Chinchain

Details of the particular pattern of ear rosette fitted to each regiments helmet, together with the chinchain details are given under the individual regimental heading. N.B. where an officers ear or plume rosette was silver plated, the highlights such as the centre and outer petals of the rosette were normally of burnished silver with the remainder being in matte silver. This burnishing effect was also applied to the officers gilt metal rosettes.

The Plume and Plume Rosette

Once again it is under the individual regimental heading that the colour/s of plume, and the pattern of rosette fitted will be found.

The Yeomanry Regiments

For ease of reference the regiments are not listed by County or by order of precedence, but by their regimental title, therefore the 2nd County of **London** Yeomanry is not listed under the County of London, but by its more widely known name The Westminster Dragoons.

Also included within this list are the titles of four corps/regiments of mounted rifles whose existence, with the exception of the Fife Light Horse was generally for a short period only. Although not strictly yeomanry in the true sense of the word, these regiments dressed in a similar fashion to Dragoons, and wore either a leather helmet, an 'Albert' pattern helmet, the 1871 pattern helmet or a variation of same, and it is hoped that the limited information given on the head-dress of these regiments will be of interest to helmet collectors.

The endnotes relating to the text on the head-dress of the Household Cavalry, Dragoon Guards, and Dragoons are to be found at the end of their relevant chapter. Endnotes for all of the yeomanry regiments covered within this chapter have also been placed at the end of the chapter (see pages 180-181).

Alphabetical List of Regiments Covered

Berkshire Yeomanry Cavalry
Derbyshire Yeomanry
Duke of Lancaster's Own Yeomanry
Essex Yeomanry
Fife Light Horse
Glasgow Yeomanry
Hampshire Yeomanry
Hertfordshire Yeomanry
Herfordshire Light Horse
Lancashire Mounted Rifles
Lothians & Berwickshire Yeomanry
Lothians & Border Horse
Montgomeryshire Yeomanry Cavalry
Norfolk Imperial Yeomanry
Northamptonshire Yeomanry
North Somerset Yeomanry
Shropshire Yeomanry Cavalry
South Salopian Yeomanry
Staffordshire Yeomanry
Suffolk Yeomanry
Sussex Light Horse Volunteers
Sussex Yeomanry
Westminster Dragoons
1st West Yorkshire Yeomanry
2nd West Yorkshire Yeomanry
Yorkshire Dragoons

Royal Berkshire Yeomanry Cavalry

The first Troop in the county was raised in Abingdon in 1794[1] they being officially accepted on the 20th April 1794 (89), with the 1st Berkshire Cavalry being formed of four Troops in 1804, only to disappear in 1828. In 1831 the Hungerford Troop was re-raised, and they became the Berkshire (Hungerford) Yeomanry Cavalry (63). Other titles by which the R.B.Y.C.'s predecessors have been known include Berkshire Cavalry, First Regiment of Yeomanry Cavalry in the County of Berkshire, Eastern Berks Cavalry, and Hungerford Corps of Yeomanry Cavalry.

It is of particular interest that serving with this regiment in the late 1880's was one R. Caton Woodville (1856 -1927), the famous and well respected artist who exhibited at the Royal Academy, being best known for his paintings of military battle scenes, amongst which are *"Saving the Guns-Maiwand", "The Battle of Tel-el-Kebir" and "The Charge of the Light Brigade".*

The Royal Berkshire Yeomanry Cavalry provided the 36th Company of the 10th Battalion Imperial Yeomanry during the war in South African of 1899 (67). N.B. All future references to the Boer/South African war refer to the conflict of 1899-1902.

Officers 'Albert' Pattern Helmet

The Skull and Plume Holder

Thought to have been adopted c. 1852, the skull on this pattern of helmet was of black japanned metal with the front and rear peak edges being bound with silvered metal, both peaks being decorated with foliated strips in like metal, with the inner peaks lined with skiver. The standard pattern waistband and rear seam band were of Type: K., in silvered metal, the plume holder being of like metal and of **Type: J.**

The Head Lining

I have been unable to ascertain what type of head lining was fitted to this helmet, however it is reasonable to presume that the lining would have been similar to the pattern fitted to a Dragoon Guards officers helmet of this period.

The Helmet Plate

A silvered rococo shield surmounted by a silvered 'Victorian' crown of Type: N. Upon the shield a twelve pointed silvered star to the centre of which was a gilt metal oval strap bearing the title "Hungerford Troop R.B.Y.C.", and within the strap 'The Seal of Hungerford' being a star above a crescent also in gilt metal. It is not known how many separate pieces made up the officers pattern helmet plate/badge.

The Ear Rosettes and Chinchain

The ear rosettes were of silvered metal of the pattern illustrated in Fig: 9.I., with the chinchain having silver coloured links mounted on black leather, being backed with black velvet. The end link of the chinchain was affixed to the right hand ear rosette by means of a small 'ring' which was secured to the lower petals of the rosette, and not by placing the end link of the chain over the ear rosette socket as was the normal practice. The left hand rosette had a silvered hook which hung down from, and was secured behind its lower petals, onto which to secure the 'loose' end of the chinchain.

The Plume and Plume Rosette

A white horsehair plume of the 'Albert' pattern complete with 'brush', capped with a medium sized silvered metal rosette.

Other Ranks 'Albert' Pattern Helmet

The Skull, Plume Holder, Ear Rosettes, and Chinchain

A black japanned skull with all fittings, including the plume holder, which was of **Type: J.**, being in white metal. The ear rosettes were also of white metal, and of the same pattern as described for the officers, with the chinchain having white metal links and being backed with leather.

The Helmet Plate (See Fig: 51.)

The helmet plate was similar to the officers pattern, the star being of hobnailed (beaded) white metal with the centre device consisting of the strap and 'Seal of Hungerford' this being a one piece die-struck item in brass. The helmet plate consisted of three separate pieces, these being the rococo shield/crown, the hobnailed star, and the brass centre device.

The Plume and Rosette

An 'Albert' pattern plume of white horsehair, capped by a white metal rosette.

Officers Helmet c. 1887 (101)

The Skull and Plume Holder

The skull was of the 1871 pattern, and was either silver plated, or of best quality white metal, with the peak edges bound in gilt metal, with both inner peaks being lined with skiver. The waist and rear seam bands were of Type: L., both being in gilt metal. The 'Albert' pattern plume holder of Type: J. was retained, however it was **now in gilt metal**. The head lining was of quilted cloth.

The Helmet Plate

A gilt metal twelve pointed hobnailed star, often described as 'beaded', to the centre of which was a silvered strap bearing the title "Royal Berkshire Yeomanry Cavalry". Within the strap on a silvered ground, the star and crescent both in gilt metal. The plate/badge consisted of three separate pieces, these being the hobnailed star, the strap and ground, and the star and crescent device.

The Ear Rosettes and Chinchain

Gilt metal ear rosettes as illustrated in Fig: 9.I., with a gilt metal chinchain 15/16ths of an inch wide on black leather backed with black velvet, or alternatively black, or scarlet leather.

The Plume and Rosette

The regiment retained the white 'Albert' pattern horsehair plume which was now fitted with **gilt metal rosette** thought to have been of the pattern illustrated in Fig: 9.E., although the version shown as 9.C., may also have been worn.

Figure 51: Royal Berkshire Yeomanry Cavalry other ranks helmet plate c. 1852-1875. Author's collection. Photo: Courtesy of the National Army Museum.

Other Ranks Helmet c. 1887

The Skull, Plume Holder, Ear Rosettes, and Chinchain

As for the officers pattern with a white metal skull, with all fittings in brass, including a **narrow laurel-leaf patterned band that extended from below the base of the plume mount, down beneath the top of the rayed star to cover the centre skull joint.** Both the plume holder and the ear rosettes were also of the same pattern as for the officers helmet, although again in brass. A brass leather backed chinchain. N.B. The regular cavalry pattern ear rosettes, as illustrated in Fig: 9.K., are also known to have been fitted to this helmet.

The Helmet Plate

A brass eight pointed **rayed** star upon which was a white metal strap bearing the regimental title, and within the strap, the crescent and star in brass on a white metal ground. The plate/badge consisted of the same number of pieces as on the officers helmet.

The Plume and Rosette
A white horsehair plume as for the officers, but having the standard other ranks rosette in brass as illustrated in Fig: 54., although it is not unknown for a rosette similar to Type: 9.B. to have been fitted. The musicians of the band wore white over red helmet plumes. N.B. It has also been known for a **shredded whalebone plume** to be fitted to this helmet.

O.R.'s Full Dress Uniform c. 1896

A scarlet tunic with blue facings, blue pantaloons with a single broad scarlet stripe. Regimental Headquarters 1914: Reading.

The Derbyshire Yeomanry

In 1794 several Troops of cavalry were raised within the county, the first Troop formed being officially accepted on the 16th September 1794, it being decided that they should be called the Derbyshire Volunteer Cavalry, with the Radbourne Troop being raised in 1803 making a total of six Troops. Over the next few years several more Troops were raised, and amongst them in 1817 was a Troop with the impressive title of "The Alfreton Independent Troop of Gentlemen and Yeomanry Cavalry".

Over the following forty-six years various additional Troops were formed, which were either later amalgamated or disbanded, and by 1863 only the Repton and Gresley Troop, the Radbourne Troop, and the Chaddesden Hussars remained. In 1864 all three of these independent Troops amalgamated to form what was to become the Derbyshire Regiment of Yeomanry Cavalry[2] (64).

During the South African war the Derbyshire Yeomanry provided the 8th Company of the 4th Battalion Imperial Yeomanry (67).

Officers Pattern Helmet c. 1864-1910

The Skull and Plume Mount
A silver plated, or alternatively best quality white metal skull of the 'Albert' pattern, with the waist and rear seam bands being in gilt metal and of standard pattern Type: K. Additionally there was a narrow gilt metal leaf and scroll band extending from below the base of the plume mount down beneath the top of the crown to conceal the front seam joint of the skull. The peak edges were bound with gilt metal, with both peaks being decorated with gilt metal foliated strips, with the inner peaks being lined with skiver. The gilt metal plume holder was of Type: I., complete with finials.

The Head Lining
The lining was of quilted cloth with one, or two drawstrings and apparently **grey** in colour, although beige cloth was most probably also used.

The Helmet Plate
There was not a recognised helmet plate as such, in its place there being a very large one-piece gilt metal intertwined 'V.R.' Royal Cypher surmounted by a 'Victorian' crown of Type: M.

The Ear Rosettes and Chinchain
Large gilt metal ear rosettes of pattern illustrated in Fig: 9.G.,[3] with the chinchain having gilt metal links and being backed with red leather.

The Plume and Rosette
A red[4] horsehair 'brush' surmounted by a falling white over red horsehair plume of the 'Albert' pattern, capped by a large gilt rosette as illustrated in Fig: 9.B, or alternatively of Type: C. N.B. Shredded whalebone is also known to have used for the officers pattern plume.

Other Ranks Helmet c. 1864

The author has been unable to trace any photographic evidence showing the rank and file wearing the 'Albert' pattern helmet, however an actual example belonging to a fellow collector was examined briefly, with the following details being noted.

The Skull, Plume Holder, Ear Rosettes, and Chinchain
A white metal 'Albert' pattern skull with all fittings, including the seven finialed 'Albert' pattern plume holder being in brass, with the front inner peak being lined with green skiver. Large brass ear rosettes, with a brass leather backed chinchain.

The Helmet Plate
Similar to the officers version but in brass instead of gilt metal.

The Plume and Rosette
Regrettably no details are available on the plume fitted to this helmet, as this fitment was missing from the helmet examined.

Other Ranks Helmet Post 1871

The Skull, Plume Holder, Ear Rosettes, and Chinchain
A white metal 1871 pattern skull, the peak edges bound with brass. Brass standard pattern waist and rear seam bands of Type: L, complete with a brass 1871 pattern plume holder of the type illustrated in Fig: 25.A. The ear rosettes were of brass, thought to have been of the type illustrated in Fig: 9.K., although this is yet to be confirmed. Chinchain of brass links backed with leather.

The Helmet Plate
A one piece brass intertwined 'V.R.' Royal Cypher[5] surmounted by a brass crown of Type: M. N.B. On some helmets the centre seam is visible beneath the cypher.

The Plume and Rosette
A white over red 1871 pattern horsehair plume capped with the standard other ranks pattern rosette of the type illustrated in Fig: 54. in brass.

Officers Helmet Post 1911

Sometime after 1911, the Royal Cypher changed to that of King George V, being an intertwined GR&V[6], with the narrow gilt metal band that had covered the front waist joint on the helmets having the 'Victorian' crown, appearing to have been discontinued. Whilst logically the cypher on the other ranks helmets should have changed also, I have never seen nor heard of the existence of an such an example. N.B. It is most peculiar that two different pattern helmets were worn within this regiment at the same period. The officers retaining the 1847 pattern complete with 'Albert' pattern plume, whilst the rank and file wore the later 1871 pattern helmet. Surely, this is something that could only have occurred in a volunteer regiment such as the yeomanry.

O.R.'s Full Dress Uniform c. 1890

A dark blue tunic with scarlet facings, blue pantaloons with a double scarlet stripe. Regimental Headquarters 1914: No. 91 Siddall's Road, Derby.

The Duke of Lancaster's Own Yeomanry

This regiment can trace its history back to The Bolton Light Horse which was officially accepted in April 1798, the Corps undergoing several changes of title before finally being disbanded in 1816. Some twelve years later in 1828 three independent Troops of volunteer cavalry known as the Bolton, Furness, and Wigan Troops amalgamated to form "The Lancashire Corps of Yeomanry Cavalry", the distinctive title "The Duke of Lancashire's Corp of Yeomanry Cavalry" being conferred on this regiment in 1834 (58).

In 1844 the Rochdale Troop was formed, with the Worsley Troop being raised two years later. 1872 saw the disbandment of the Furness Troop, however there shortly followed the raising of three more Troops, these being the Oldham Troop in 1873, the Broughton Troop in 1877, and the Blackburn Troop in 1880.

By 1899 the regiment consisted of three squadrons, each of comprised of two Troops, these being: A Squadron: Oldham and Rochdale Troops. B Squadron: Broughton and Worsley Troops. C Squadron: Bolton and Blackburn Troops (58).

The regiment provided the 23rd (Lancaster) Company as part of the 8th Battalion Imperial Yeomanry (58).

Sometime during 1901 the regiment was styled the "Duke of Lancaster's Own Imperial Yeomanry", the 'Imperial' later being dropped from the title following the formation of the Territorial Force.

The 1857 Pattern Helmet

An interesting reference relating to the 1857 pattern helmet appeared in the booklet (58) on this regiment by the late L. Barlow and R.J. Smith, which read as follows *'A helmet of the 1847 Heavy Dragoon or 'Albert' pattern was recorded by the late L.E. Buckell, and this was almost certainly first issued to the O.R.'s about 1857. It was of black japanned **leather**[7] with brass ornaments and mounts, and had a plume of white horsehair. The officers pattern was probably of black japanned metal from the introduction, and by about 1865 all ranks had helmets of metal'.*

Officers Helmet c. 1865-1895

The Skull and Plume Holder

A skull of black japanned metal being similar in general appearance to the standard 'Albert' pattern skull, the peak edges bound with gilt metal[8], with the inner peaks being lined with skiver. The waist and rear seam bands were in gilt metal and of Type: K., with the plume holder also in gilt metal of Type: I (complete with finials). The head lining being of the standard pattern.

The Helmet Plate

The helmet plate comprised the 'Albert' pattern oak and olive wreath surrounding a rococo shield, surmounted by a large Victorian crown of Type: M., all in gilt metal. Upon the shield, and also in gilt metal, "The Arms of the County Palatine of Lancaster", this being **three lions passant guardant.** The plate/badge was made up of two separate pieces, these being the wreath/shield/crown, and the three lions passant guardant.

The Ear Rosettes and Chinchain

Gilt metal ear rosettes of the pattern illustrated in Fig: 9.H., with a gilt metal chinchain being 15/16ths of an inch in width, or alternatively one inch in width, backed with either black, or crimson leather.

The Plume and Rosette

An 'Albert' pattern white horsehair brush surmounted by a falling white horsehair plume capped by a medium sized rosette of the pattern illustrated in Fig: 9.C. in gilt metal.

Other Ranks Helmet c. 1865-1895

The Skull, Plume Holder, Ear Rosettes, and Chinchain

A black japanned skull of similar shape to the officers pattern, with the plume holder and all fittings also as for the officers helmet, but being in brass. N.B. The front peak only was lined with skiver on the other ranks pattern helmet. I have been unable to obtain information relating to the pattern of ear rosettes, the chinchain, or the plume, and plume rosette fitted to the other ranks helmet, however it is reasonable to presume that they were similar to the officers pattern with the metal parts being of brass instead of gilt metal. N.B. There is a reference at the National Army Museum to this pattern of helmet being returned for alteration in 1877 (101).

The Helmet Plate

As for the officers helmet plate, except that it was a die -struck, one piece plate in brass.

Officers Pattern Post 1896

The Skull and Plume Holder

The 1871 pattern skull was silver plated, or alternatively of best quality white metal, the peak edges being bound in gilt metal, with the inner peaks lined with skiver. Whilst the gilt metal rear seam band was of the standard pattern Type: L., the front waist band was non-standard, consisting of a **gilt metal band of laurel leaves on the left side, with a band of oak leaves on the right hand side** (when viewed from the front). N.B. This pattern was very similar in appearance to the waist band on the Household Cavalry officers helmets. The plume holder changed to the pattern illustrated in Fig: 25.A., and was in gilt metal.

The Head Lining

The lining was **dark beige silk,** or alternatively of **brown quilted cloth**, although it is likely that light beige cloth was also used.

The Helmet Plate

The only change to the helmet plate appears to be that the plate was now a **die-struck**, one piece, gilt metal version of the pattern used on the 'Albert' pattern helmet (as described above). N.B. It would seem appropriate that upon the accession to the throne of King Edward VII, that the Victorian crown would have been changed to a 'King's pattern, however the author has never seen a helmet fitted with such a plate, nor has he any knowledge of the existence or whereabouts of one.

The Ear Rosettes and Chinchain

The ear rosettes were medium sized of the type illustrated in Fig: 9.H. in gilt metal, with the chinchain measuring 15/16th of an inch in width, having gilt metal links, and being backed with red leather.

The Plume and Rosette

The 1871 pattern horsehair plume in white, was now taken into wear with the new pattern helmet, being capped by a medium sized gilt metal rosette[9] of either Type: C., or Type: I. as illustrated in Fig: 9.

Other Ranks Helmet Post 1896

The Skull, Plume Holder, Ear Rosettes, and Chinchain

A white metal skull of the 1871 pattern with the peaks being bound with brass, the front inner peak lined with skiver. The standard pattern waist and rear seam bands were also in brass, with the brass plume holder being of the type illustrated in Fig: 25.A. The ear rosettes were of brass, and of the pattern illustrated in Fig: 9.K.,[10] with the brass link chinchain being backed with leather.

The Helmet Plate

The die-struck, one piece brass helmet plate for the other ranks resembled the officers pattern plate, but was **smaller overall** having a different pattern of crown to that on the officers helmet plate, being similar in appearance to Type: Q. N.B. The plate was affixed to the helmet by means of three screw studs and two pairs of flat blades.

The Plume and Rosette

The 1871 pattern horsehair plume in white, with a brass standard pattern other ranks rosette was fitted to the helmet, with the musicians of the band wearing scarlet plumes.

O.R's Full Dress Uniform c. 1898

A scarlet tunic with blue facings, the pantaloons being blue with a single yellow stripe. Regimental Headquarters 1914: Lancaster House, Whalley Road, Whalley Range, Manchester.

The Essex Yeomanry

The year 1797 saw the first Troops of yeomanry to be raised in the county of Essex, the official acceptance date being given as 8th April 1797 (89). These Troops generally remained independent, however in 1813 six Troops were regimented, they to be known as the First Essex Yeomanry Cavalry (63).

The year 1830 saw a regiment being raised, with the title the West Essex Yeomanry,[11] only to be disbanded c. 1876/77. However the county was not without yeomanry, as there was an Essex Troop within the Loyal Suffolk Hussars, and it was with this regiment that the yeoman of Essex saw service in the South African war. N.B. The counties of Essex and Suffolk border one another.

In 1901 an Essex Yeomanry regiment was re-established having the title Essex Imperial Yeomanry, being officially accepted on the 28th October 1901 (89), with squadrons being formed at Braintree, Colchester, Southend, and Waltham Abbey. Some seven years later in 1908 with the formation of the Territorial Force the word 'Imperial' was deleted from the regiments title. N.B. The noted author of many authoritative and informative books on military dress W.Y. Carman F.S.A. F.R. HIST.S. once served in the Essex Yeomanry.

Helmet - West Essex Yeomanry Cavalry

In 1854 the artillery troop of the West Essex Yeomanry Cavalry adopted a black leather helmet with "Essex Artillery" on the plate. The 'sword' troops do not seem to have been far behind as there exist examples of a black leather helmet having a large crowned helmet plate (63). This plate was comprised of a floral wreath, to the centre of which was a crowned strap bearing the title "Essex Cavalry " with the Arms of Essex within the strap. Below the strap, and upon the wreath a tripartite scroll thought to have borne the motto 'Decus et Tutamen'. The helmet was completed by having a ball and socket pattern plume holder, a light coloured plume, chinchain and ear bosses/rosettes.

Trial Pattern Helmet

Way back in 1983 I read an article that appeared in a then current edition of the Crown Imperial Societies journal relating to the head-dress of the Essex Yeomanry. This article reported that *'The Essex Imperial Yeomanry helmet described in Crown Imperial, June 1982, now in the Hollytrees Museum at Colchester was a trial pattern submitted to a dress committee in 1906 but not adopted owing to the impending reorganisation of the yeomanry'.* It was to be some fourteen years later before I was to first visit the town of Colchester, and whilst there I naturally visited the Hollytrees Museum, only to find that the helmet concerned was not on display. A subsequent telephone call to Mr. T. Hodgson the Curator of the museum resulted in arrangements being made for me to see this most rare helmet on the next occasion that I visited the Colchester area.

Eventually I was able to again visit the Hollytrees Museum, where the 'trial pattern' helmet was made available for me to examine. The helmet turned out to be an **other ranks pattern**, and the following is a brief description of this helmet, compiled from the notes taken at the time of my visit. I was not to know at that time, that some seven months later, I would have sold my house in Aldershot, Hampshire, and have moved to a small village some ten miles outside of Colchester.

The Skull, Plume Holder, Ear Rosettes, and Chinchain

A brass 1871 pattern skull, with brass waist and rear seam bands of Type: L, the front peak only, being lined with skiver. The plume holder was of the pattern fitted to the other ranks helmets of the Dragoon Guards, as illustrated in Fig: 25.A., with the black leather head lining being similar to the pattern fitted to the other ranks helmet of the aforementioned regular cavalry regiments. The brass ear rosettes were of the pattern illustrated in Fig: 9.K., with the brass link chinchain being backed with **brown** leather.

The Helmet Plate

A white metal twelve pointed rayed star upon which was mounted a brass oval strap inscribed *'Audacter Et Sincere'*[12], and within the strap a white metal[13] shield bearing the Arms of The County of Essex being 3 seaxes (scimitars) on a brass ground. Below the helmet plate, a white metal triple-scroll bearing the title *"Essex Imperial Yeoy"* (as spelt on scroll). The plate/badge consisted of three separate pieces excluding the scroll, these being the rayed plate, the strap and ground, and the shield.

The Plume and Rosette

The plume fitted to this helmet was of the 1871 pattern, the scarlet horsehair having badly faded, with the plume rosette being absent, however I am confident that it would have been of the standard other ranks pattern.

Helmet Plate Variations c. 1911

The following, reproduced as written, is an extract from a letter sent by the regiment to Jenner and Company[14] of 56 Conduit Street, London, W.1. dated 20th February 1911 regarding the provision of full dress helmets:

> *'Dragoon Guards helmet for 12 to 30, brass troopers as dragoon guards with GS star, brass or GM circle v brass or GM scroll.' Also for exactly as above with silver-cut star, instead of G same. Also cost of die for circles as are above pattern only different motto, with Essex shield in circle. Told Piccu the officers could get a die, cost for 50/-. Also cost of scroll as pattern, but omitting "Imperial", just "Essex Yeomanry" price of scrolls above. Cost of 1 doz. silver fluted stars as D/Gds for officer helmets* (66).

The above copy letter would appear to indicate that the regiment had at one period contemplated adopting a helmet similar to the trial pattern with the *"Essex Imperial Yeoy"* title on the scroll, although this is unconfirmed. With regard to the above reference to a **silver-cut star**, I have no knowledge of such a star ever being fitted to the Essex Yeomanry officers pattern helmet, all helmets seen by the author having the **rayed** pattern star. The mention of 'circles' would appear to refer to the oval band, and the different motto referred to in this letter would I suggest relate to the pre 1908 motto that was on the band on the 'trial pattern helmet' this being *"Audacter et sincere"*. N.B. The motto changed to *"Decus et tutamen"*[15] sometime after the presentation of a new guidon in 1909.

Officers Helmet Post 1911

The Skull and Plume Holder

A gilt metal 1871 pattern skull, the peak edges being bound with gilt metal, with both inner peaks being lined with skiver. The skull was fitted with the standard pattern waist and rear seam bands of Type: L., also in gilt metal, with the plume holder being in like metal, and of the pattern illustrated in Fig: 25.A.

The Head Lining

The lining was of beige quilted cloth, grey cloth or alternatively of **scarlet quilted cotton.**

The Helmet Plate

A twelve pointed silvered rayed star, upon which was a gilt metal oval band bearing the title *"Decus Et Tutamen"* above a spray of leaves. Within the oval band in white metal a shield surmounted by a small 'King's' crown of Type: R., with the shield bearing the Arms of the County of Essex as described above, on a gilt ground. The plate/badge was comprised of three separate pieces, these being the rayed star, the oval band and ground, and the white metal shield. Positioned just beneath the star was a **single gilt metal scroll** bearing the title *"Essex Yeomanry"*

The Ear Rosettes and Chinchain

The officers helmet was fitted with standard other ranks pattern ear rosettes of the pattern illustrated in Fig: 9.K., but being in **gilt metal**, with the chinchain having gilt metal links and being backed with black leather, or alternatively mounted upon leather and backed with crimson velvet.

The Plume and Rosette

A scarlet 1871 pattern plume of horsehair having a small gilt metal rosette of the pattern illustrated in Fig: 9.E.

Other Ranks Helmet Post 1911 (See Fig: 52.)

The Skull, Plume Holder, Ear Rosettes, and Chinchain

The skull, fittings, plume holder, ear rosettes, and chinchain etc. were all as described for the 'trial pattern', the only apparent change being to the helmet plate, which was as follows.

The Helmet Plate

A white metal twelve pointed star, upon which was mounted a **die-stamped brass** oval strap bearing the title *"Decus Et Tutamen"* above a spray of leaves. Within the band a brass crowned shield bearing the Arms of the County of Essex as described previously. The plate/badge consisted of two separate pieces, these being the rayed star, and the band/crown/shield. Beneath the helmet plate a **white metal** single scroll with the regimental title as for the officers pattern.

The Plume and Rosette

A scarlet horsehair, or alternatively **shredded whalebone** plume with the standard pattern other ranks rosette in brass.

O.R.'s Full Dress Uniform c. 1908

A Green tunic with scarlet facings, green pantaloons with a double scarlet stripe. Regimental Headquarters 1914: 17 St. Isaac's Walk, Colchester, Essex.

Figure 52: Essex Yeomanry other ranks pattern post 1911. Of interest is the crown above the shield which was absent on the 'trial' pattern centre device. Author's collection. Photo: Courtesy of the National Army Museum.

Fife Mounted Rifles/Fife Light Horse

The year 1797 saw the raising of the Kirkaldy Troop, which in 1803 amalgamated with the Fife Yeomanry, only to be disbanded in 1828, and then re-raised in 1838. N.B. The regiments official acceptance date is given as the 17th June 1797 (89).

In 1860 a regiment was raised, being known as the Fife Volunteer Mounted Rifles, later to be titled the Fife Light Horse. In 1900 the regiment contributed many volunteers for the war in South Africa and formed the nucleus of the 20th Company of the 6th Battalion Imperial Yeomanry. In May of 1901 the regiment merged with the Forfar Light Horse to become the Fife and Forfar Imperial Yeomanry (68), the word 'Imperial' being dropped from the title sometime after 1908.

Officers Helmet: Fife Mounted Rifles c. 1864

The Skull and Plume Holder

A Black patent leather skull, with the front and rear peak being of similar material. On some, but not all officers pattern helmets, the front peak, and possibly the rear peak were bound with silvered/white metal, however it is not uncommon to find an officers helmet without this binding. The plume holder appears to have been of a unique pattern consisting of a silvered/white metal four-pointed star surmounted by a short, gilt metal four sided socket above a four pointed metal base. The head lining was of silk, or alternatively of quilted cotton with a silk edge.

The Helmet Plate

A four pointed silvered/white metal star, being similar in appearance to the star at the base of the plume holder, with upon the lowest point of the star the Roman numerals IX. Upon the star a gilt metal St. Andrew's Cross having five ribs to each bar of the cross, and surmounted upon the cross in white metal the 'Thane of Fife' being a mounted knight in full armour, holding his sword upright. Below the St. Andrew's Cross, tripartite scrolls (thought to have been in white metal) bearing the motto *"Pro Aris* (left scroll), and *Et Focis*[16] (right scroll), with the letters *'FMR'* superimposed upon the centre scroll. Plate/badge: six separate pieces, these being the star, the cross, the Thane of Fife, the numerals IX, the tripartite scrolls, and the letters FMR.

The Ear Rosettes and Chinchain

These were of unique pattern, being a boss upon which was the ribbed Cross of St. Andrew, with a star superimposed upon the cross. The left hand rosette had a small 'ring' secured to its lower petals onto which was attached the end link of the silvered metal chinchain, with the right hand rosette having a hook which hung down, and was secured behind its lower petals, onto which to secure the 'loose' end of the chain. N.B. The silvered metal chinchain, which had widely spaced links, was mounted upon leather and backed with brown velvet.

The Plume

A white 'Albert' pattern horsehair plume capped by a small rosette complete with a white horsehair 'brush', within a unique pattern gilt metal holder in the shape of a thistle above a small ball.

The author has been unable to obtain any information on the other ranks pattern helmet, although it is reasonable to presume that it was similar to the above, but of a lesser quality.

Officers Helmet: Fife Light Horse c. 1896-1901 (See Fig: 53.)

The Skull and Plume Holder

A silver plated, or alternatively best quality white metal skull, the peak edges being bound in like metal with the inner peaks lined with skiver. The silvered/white metal rear seam band and waist band were of Type: L, however the front waist band differed in that it **did not extend from ear to ear as was usual**, instead it was joined on each side with tripartite scrolls of similar metal, that were positioned to the front waist of the skull. This tripartite scroll bore the motto *"Pro Airs"* (left scroll), with *"Et Focis"* (right scroll), with the centre scroll having the letters *'FLH'* applied in gilt metal. The plume holder was in white metal, and was of the pattern illustrated in Fig: 25.A.

The Head Lining

There were at least two differing pattern head linings known to have been fitted to the skull, these being of beige quilted cloth, or alternatively of soft leather.

The Helmet Plate

This most decorative helmet plate resembled that of Fife Mounted Rifles, but with some variations. It was comprised of a silvered/white metal four pointed hobnailed star, with the topmost point being displaced by a small silvered/white metal 'Victorian' crown similar in appearance to Type: Q[17]. Upon the star a ribbed St. Andrew's Cross in gilt metal, superimposed upon which was the 'Thane of Fife' as previously described for the Fife Mounted Rifles. The plate/badge was comprised of three separate pieces, these being the star, the cross, and the 'Thane of Fife'.

The Ear Rosettes and Chinchain

The ear rosettes were of white metal, and of the pattern illustrated in Fig: 9.J., with the silvered chinchain generally being of the one inch wide pattern backed with black leather, or alternatively of black velvet upon black leather.

The Plume and Rosette

A white horsehair 1871 pattern plume capped by a small silvered/white metal rosette of Type: 9.E., although some officers pattern plumes, were known to have been fitted with the medium sized rosette of Type: 9.C.

Other Ranks Helmet

The Skull, Plume Holder, Ear Rosettes, and Chinchain

The skull, plume holder and fittings were all of white metal, with the front inner peak only being lined with skiver. White metal ear rosettes of the same pattern as the officers, with a white metal, leather backed chinchain.

The Helmet Plate

The helmet plate was as for the officers pattern except that brass was substituted for gilt metal on the St. Andrews Cross, with the letters *'FLH'* being of similar metal.

The Plume and Rosette

A white horsehair plume with the standard pattern other ranks rosette in white metal.

Figure 53: Fife Light Horse officers pattern c. 1896-1901. Worn by Surgeon-Captain W. Stuart-Palm. Author's collection. Photo: Courtesy of the National Army Museum.

O.R.'s Full Dress Uniform c. 1896

A scarlet tunic with scarlet facings, the blue pantaloons having double scarlet stripes. Regimental Headquarters 1914: Kirkcaldy, Scotland.

The Queen's Own Royal Glasgow Yeomanry

This regiment can trace its origins back to 1797 when Troops were formed in the Glasgow area, the first Troop being accepted on 20th March 1797 (89), there being a connection with another Corps with the title The Royal Glasgow Light Horse that was raised c. 1796, and the Glasgow Sharpshooters. Disbandment occurred in 1802, with various corps then being re-raised, only to be disbanded in 1814 and 1828, although it appears that the Glasgow Troop was never officially disbanded (67).

In 1848, The Royal Glasgow and Lower Ward of Lanarkshire Yeomanry was raised, its official acceptance date being the 22nd July 1848 (89), with the honour of 'Queen's Own' being granted to the regiment in 1849. The full title of the regiment then changed to 'The Queen's Own Royal Glasgow Yeomanry', this title being retained until 1914.

During the war in South African, the regiment provided troops to form the 18th Company of the 6th Battalion Imperial Yeomanry (67).

Officers Helmet c. 1848/50

Whilst not the rarest of yeomanry helmets, that uniqueness possibly being shared by the trial pattern Essex Imperial Yeomanry helmet, and the trial pattern Imperial Yeomanry helmet, the Glasgow Yeomanry helmet is I consider one of the most attractive head-dresses. With its contrasting silver skull and gold coloured fittings, capped by a feather plume it would make a fine centrepiece for any helmet collection.

The Skull and Plume Holder
A silvered/white metal skull of the 'Albert' shape, with both peaks being decorated with gilt metal foliated strips, the peak edges being bound with gilt metal, and both inner peaks lined with skiver. The waist and rear seam bands, also in gilt metal, were of standard pattern Type: K. However the gilt metal plume holder was of special regimental pattern[18] for whilst the base was of the standard 'Albert' type, the socket although of similar style, comprised four tall 'thistles' with finials in place of the normal eight short leaf pattern finials. N.B. This pattern socket did **not sit within a short socket** having four large upright leaf finials, as on the plume holder of the Dragoon Guards and Dragoon regiments.

The Head Lining
The head lining was of quilted silk.

The Helmet Plate
This most attractive helmet plate was of a unique regimental pattern, consisting of a **wreath of thistles** surrounding a rococo shield, surmounted by a 'Victorian' crown of Type: M. all in gilt metal. Upon the shield *"The Star of the Order of the Thistle"*, which resembled the St. Andrew's Cross merged, with a four pointed rayed star in white metal. Upon the star was a gilt metal circlet bearing the motto of the Order of the Thistle, this being *"Nemo Me Impune Lacessit"*[19] within which was lion rampant. The plate/badge consisted of four separate pieces, these being the thistle wreath, the rococo shield, the star, and the circlet. N.B. There is an illustration of this helmet on page twenty-seven of W.Y. Carman's book on Yeomanry Head-Dress (63).

The Ear Rosettes and Chinchain
A large gilt metal ear rosette of the pattern illustrated in Fig: 9.G., with a one inch wide chinchain, being mounted upon black leather, and backed with black velvet.

The Plume and Rosette
For special occasions a dark green **cock's feather** plume was worn, (often referred to as being black), whilst for other orders of dress a black horsehair 'Albert' pattern plume was worn, both plumes being capped by a gilt metal rosette similar to that illustrated in Type: 9.C.

The officers of this regiment, appear to have continued to wear the 'Albert' helmet, long after most of the other yeomanry regiments had discontinued using this pattern of helmet in favour of the more modern 1871 model. The helmet appears to have remained virtually unchanged[20], the only modification seen by the author being on a helmet that sold in a Sussex auction salesroom in 1984. On this particular helmet the special pattern 'Albert' type plume holder was absent, in its place there being an 1871 pattern holder of Type: 25.A., complete with a cock's feather plume. However whilst the plume holder appeared to be contemporary with the remainder of the helmet, the feather plume did not 'sit correctly' within the plume socket.

Other Ranks Helmet

The Skull, Plume Holder, Ear Rosettes, and Chinchain
A white metal skull with brass decoration to the peaks etc. as for the officers helmet. A brass 'Albert' pattern plume holder was fitted to the helmet, although it is not known if the socket was of the unique 'thistle' pattern fitted to the officers helmet, or if it was of the standard pattern. Brass ear rosettes, with a brass seven eighths of an inch wide chinchain backed with leather.

The Helmet Plate
As for the officers pattern except that for gilt substitute brass. The composition of the helmet plate differed slightly there being only **three component parts,** these being the wreath/rococo shield/crown, the star, and the circlet.

The Plume and Rosette
A black horsehair plume having a small brass rosette of the pattern illustrated in Fig: 54. Whilst it is recorded that the regiment had a mounted band, the author has been unable to ascertain the colour of the musicians full dress plumes.

O.R.'s Full Dress Uniform c. 1911

A dark blue tunic with scarlet facings, the dark blue overalls having a single scarlet stripe. Regimental Headquarters 1914: Yorkhill Parade, Yorkhill, Glasgow, Scotland.

The Hampshire Yeomanry (Carabiniers)

The North Hampshire Yeomanry Cavalry was officially accepted on the 31st May 1794 (89), only like many other regiments at that period to be disbanded in 1828. The regiment was however re-raised in 1830, but without the 'North' in their title, being now known as the Hampshire Yeomanry Cavalry (67).

Two slightly differing dates are given for the year that the title 'Carabiniers' was conferred upon the regiment these being 1884 (67) and c. 1887 (70), this change of regimental title resulting in an alteration to the inscription on the strap on the helmet plate, of the full dress helmet.

Lieutenant Colonel H.G.L. Crichton[21] who commanded the regiment in 1884, having formerly served in the 10th and 21st Hussars (Lancers) is credited with replacing the small shako worn at that time with the Dragoon pattern helmet. This was shortly followed by the introduction of a tunic to replace the jacket worn previously (71), all of which must have improved the appearance of the troops and aided recruitment.

The strength of the regiment increased steadily, and by 1889 stood at some 189 of all ranks, rising to in excess of 200 by 1894, and having reached a strength of just over 400 by 1907. By 1914 the regiment was consisted of four squadrons[22] comprised of sixteen Troops (71).

During the war in South Africa the regiment formed the 41st Company of the 4th Battalion Imperial Yeomanry and the 50th Company of the 17th Battalion (67).

As there are **four, known differing versions** of this regiments full dress helmet, each pattern has been given a prefix letter of either A.B.C. or D., to aid identification.

The Hampshire Yeomanry c. 1884

Officers Helmet - Type: A

The Skull and Plume Holder
The skull was of best quality white metal, being thinner and lighter than the metal used on the other ranks helmet. The inner peaks were lined with skiver with the peak edges being bound in silvered/white metal. The standard pattern waist and rear seam bands being of Type: L., were also silvered, with the plume holder being of Type: C. in white metal.

The Head Lining
No information was available to the author as to the actual lining fitted to this particular pattern of helmet, although it is safe to assume that it was of the standard officers pattern of either quilted cloth or silk.

The Helmet Plate
A large silvered twelve pointed rayed star, upon which was a gilt metal elliptical strap bearing the title *"Hampshire Yeomanry"*, the strap being surmounted by a small silvered Victorian crown of the pattern referred to earlier as Type: Q. Within the strap a silvered metal 'Hampshire' rose upon a black leather ground (backing). The plate/badge was comprised of four separate pieces, these being the rayed star, the crowned strap, the leather backing, and the silvered rose.

The Ear Rosettes and Chinchain
The silvered chinchain was backed with black leather, or alternatively mounted upon black leather and backed with black velvet, and came in three different widths, these being five eighths of an inch, one inch, and a graduated width version. The medium sized, silvered metal ear rosettes were of the pattern illustrated in Fig: 9.I.

The Plume and Rosette
A white 1871 pattern horsehair plume[23] capped with a medium sized silvered rosette believed to have been similar to the pattern illustrated in Fig: 9.I., or Fig: 9.C., although it more likely that it was of the former pattern as this would match the ear rosettes.

Other Ranks Helmet

The Skull, Plume Holder, Ear Rosettes, and Chinchain
Skull of white metal, the waistband and rear seam band of Type: L, the plume holder of Type: 25C., with the ear rosettes being of Type: 9I., all in white metal, with a white metal graduated link chinchain backed with black leather.

The Helmet Plate
A white metal twelve pointed rayed star upon which was a brass/gilding metal crowned elliptical strap inscribed *"Hampshire Yeomanry"*, and within the strap a white metal rose on a black leather backing. The plate/badge was comprised four separate pieces as per the officers version.

The Plume and Rosette
An 1871 white horsehair plume, with the standard other ranks pattern rosette in white metal. The musicians in the mounted band wore red horsehair plumes from 1894 (62).

The Hampshire Carabiniers c. 1887-1901

Officer Helmet Type: B. (See Fig: 54.)

The skull, peak binding, waist band, rear seam band, plume holder, ear rosettes, chinchain, head lining, plume and rosette etc. were all as previously described. The only known difference being that the title on the gilt metal elliptical strap changed to **'Hampshire Carabiniers'**.

Officers Helmet Type: C. (See Fig: 54A.)

By giving this pattern of helmet the prefix letter C., it is not intended to imply that this variation of the helmet was worn at a later period than the helmet described as Type: B. It is my unconfirmed theory, that each of these two variations of the helmet were being worn by members of a Troop who were stationed in a different part of the county from the other.

The Skull and Plume Holder
Again a skull of silvered, or best quality white metal, but, with the peak edges being bound with **gilt metal**, the inner peaks being lined with skiver. The standard pattern front waist and rear seam bands of Type: L., were in **gilt metal** (often in frosted gilt), with the plume holder now being of the pattern illustrated in **Fig: 25.D.**, also in gilt metal, but of the type known as dead gilt.

Figure 54: Hampshire Carabiniers officers pattern c. 1887-1901. (Type: B.) Note that the chinchain has been shortened and that the plume is an other ranks pattern having the standard other ranks rosette, as used for the plumes of the rank and file in the Dragoon Guards and 1st and 6th Dragoon regiments. Author's collection. Photo: Courtesy of the National Army Museum.

The Head Lining

The lining was usually of beige quilted cloth, or alternatively of quilted silk.

The Helmet Plate

A twelve pointed rayed star in **gilt metal**, upon which was a **silvered**, crowned (Type: Q.) elliptical strap bearing the title *"Hampshire Carabiniers"*, within the strap on a black leather ground, the rose of 'Hampshire' in **gilt metal**. The number of component parts comprising the plate/badge being as described previously for the helmet Type: A.

The Ear Rosettes and Chinchain

The **gilt metal** ear rosettes were of Type: 9.I., with a **gilt metal**, **one inch wide** graduated link chinchain, backed with black leather, although it is reasonable to presume that black velvet mounted on black leather was also used.

The Plume and Rosette

A white 1871 pattern horsehair plume, capped with a medium sized **gilt metal** rosette thought to have been of Type: 9.I.

Officers Helmet - Type: D. Post 1902

The Skull and Plume Holder

The skull, waist band, rear seam band, plume holder and fittings etc., were all as listed above for the helmet Type: B. (c. 1887-1901).

The Head Lining

The lining appears to have been changed to **soft tan leather** (two and three quarter inches in depth) **with a scarlet silk** upper section.

The Helmet Plate

Gilt metal rayed star, with a silvered strap bearing the title *"Hampshire Carabiniers"*[24] surmounted by a silvered 'King's' crown similar to Type: R.

Ear Rosettes and Chinchain

Gilt metal ear rosettes of Type: 9.I., with a gilt metal chinchain being five eighths of an inch wide, mounted on black leather and backed with **black velvet.**

The Plume and Rosette

A photograph in the archives of the National Army Museum of a post 1902 pattern officers helmet, shows the plume rosette to be of Type: I. However on the only example of a post 1902 officers head-dress of this regiment examined by the author (which was a very late version) the plume fitted to the helmet was a troopers pattern in horsehair, with the other ranks pattern plume rosette having been **gilded.** N.B. The plume looked to be contemporary with the helmet.

Figure 54a: Hampshire Carabiniers officers pattern c. 1887-1901. (Type: C.). The red and white plume is incorrect for this regiment. Compare the pattern of plume holder fitted to this helmet with the one fitted to the helmet illustrated in Fig: 54. Author's collection. Photo: Author.

O.R.'s Full Dress Uniform c. 1897

A blue tunic with white facings, the pantaloons having a double white stripe. Regimental Headquarters 1914: Hyde Close, Winchester.

1st Hertfordshire Light Horse Volunteers

There was little confirmed information available to the author at the time of writing, relating to this corps/regiments history, other than the information contained in the excellent book on the Hertfordshire Yeomanry by J.D. Sainsbury (73) on which the following brief history is based.

In November 1862 a Troop of mounted volunteers designated the 1st Hertfordshire Light Horse Volunteers was formed at Bishop's Stortford. It became a Squadron when in October 1864 the establishment of the Corps was increased to two Troops, and continued to serve with good reports. Regrettably however *'it failed to survive the bankruptcy of its commanding officer, although all debts in the unit's name were cleared by the officers and members'* of the Corps, and was disbanded in June 1879 (73).

Officers Helmet c. 1862-69

The Skull and Plume Mount

A **German silver** skull (73), having the peak edges bound in gilt metal, with the waist and rear seam bands being of Type: K., also in gilt metal. Covering the **front seam joint** was a short gilt metal three quarters of an inch wide leaf and scroll band, that extended from below the base of the plume mount down beneath the top of the crown. The gilt metal plume holder[24a] was of the pattern illustrated in Fig: 25.E.

The Head Lining

The lining fitted to this helmet was of dark brown quilted cloth.

The Helmet Plate

A rococo shield surmounted by a large 'Victorian' crown of Type: M, all in gilt metal. Upon the shield a twelve pointed star of special pattern having **sharp-cut ends**, also in gilt metal. To the centre of the star a die-stamped elliptical strap bearing the title *"Herts Light Horse"*, and within the strap an intertwined 'V.R.' Royal Cypher all in **frosted silver**. It is thought that the plate/badge consisted of three separate pieces, these being the crowned rococo shield, the star, and the strap/centre device, although this has not been confirmed.

The Ear Rosettes and Chinchain

The ear rosettes were in gilt metal, and of the pattern illustrated in Fig: 9.G., with the gilt metal one inch wide chinchain being mounted upon black leather and backed with black velvet.

The Plume and Rosette

The helmet was surmounted by a most impressive red **feather plume**, capped by a medium sized gilt metal rosette.

Staff Officers Head-Dress

The following description of the cocked hat is taken from J.D. Sainsbury's excellent book on the Hertfordshire Yeomanry (73). *'The cocked hat with regimental looping and tassels was worn by the Quartermaster (white feather plume), Surgeon and Assistant Surgeon (Black feather plume), and Veterinary Officer (red feather plume)'* (73).

Other Ranks Helmet

The Skull, Plume Holder, Ear Rosettes, and Chinchain

A German silver skull (73), the plume holder being as for the officers helmet but in brass. The ear rosettes were of the 'Albert' pattern in brass, with a leather backed, brass chinchain.

The Helmet Plate

A crowned rococo shield as for the officers pattern, however, there was **not a twelve pointed star** to the centre of the shield, there merely being the die-struck centre device. This consisted of an elliptical strap, with title and cypher as for the officers pattern, but being in white metal, in place of frosted silver. The plate/badge; was comprised of two separate pieces, these being the crowned shield, and the centre device.

The Plume and Rosette

A red horsehair plume[25] of the 1871 pattern, capped with the standard other ranks rosette, thought to have been of brass.

O.R.'s Full Dress Uniform c. 1862-79

A blue tunic having scarlet facings, with the overalls being dark blue with a single broad scarlet stripe (73).

The Hertfordshire Yeomanry

Five independent Troops were formed in 1794 within the County of Hertfordshire with the first formed being accepted on the 8th June 1794 (89), all of which however were, one by one disbanded between the years 1807 to 1824. In c. 1830/31 seven new Troops of volunteer cavalry were raised, four of which were grouped together, being known as the *South Hertfordshire Corps.* Of the three remaining separate Troops only the North Hertfordshire Troop survived, and they in turn amalgamated with the South Hertfordshire Corps in 1871 to become the *Hertfordshire Yeomanry Cavalry*.

The regiment provided troops to fight in the war in South Africa by forming the 42nd (Hertfordshire) Company of the 12th Battalion Imperial Yeomanry (67).

Officers Helmet Pre 1880

The Skull

A silvered/white metal skull, the shape of which resembled the 1871 pattern, with the peak edges being bound with gilt metal, and both inner peaks being lined with green skiver. Covering the front seam band was a gilt metal three quarter inch wide leaf and scroll band as described above for the Herts Light Horse, with the waist and rear seam also in gilt metal, and being of Type: K. N.B. This skull appears to have been a 'mix and match' item, having the shape and appearance of the 1871 pattern, but being fitted with the earlier 'Albert' pattern waist band which completely encircled the waist.

The Spike

The plume was not worn with the helmet when it was first adopted, and therefore in place of the more usual plume holder was a gilt metal spike of the pattern illustrated in Fig: 25.G. This spike which was not capable of accepting the stem of a plume was affixed to the skull of the helmet by means of four short threaded studs positioned at north, south, east and west which passed through corresponding holes in the skull, then on through similar holes in a 'oval' shaped metal inner supporting plate, where brass washers and brass nuts were put in place to secure the spike. N.B. Although the inner plate had a centre hole and was surrounded by six smaller holes, the skull of the helmet did not have a hole at its crown. Therefore it was not possible to wear a plume with this helmet by exchanging the spike for a plume holder, without serious modification to the crown of the skull.

The Head Lining

The lining was of either beige quilted cloth, or of silk.

The Helmet Plate

A rococo pattern shield surmounted by a medium sized 'Victorian' crown similar in appearance to Type: M. all in gilt metal. Upon the shield a silvered 'Hart' (stag) trippant in a ford (stream), having flowers beneath the ford, these flowers being in a mixture of gilt and silvered metal. The plate/badge consisted of two separate pieces, these being the shield/crown, and the hart/ford/flowers.

The Ear Rosettes and Chinchain

The large, gilt metal ear rosettes were of the type illustrated in Fig: 9.G., usually having the proud centre, although it is not uncommon to also find the pattern illustrated in Fig: 9.F. fitted to the helmet. The gilt metal chinchain measured fifteen sixteenths of a inch in width and was mounted upon black leather, being backed with black velvet.

Officers Helmet c. 1880-1901 (See Fig: 55.)

The Skull, Plume Holder, and Lining

The skull was as described above, the spike however had now been **replaced with a gilt metal plume holder of the pattern illustrated in Fig: 25.E.**, which was again a mixture of the 'Albert' pattern base, with the socket[26] being a variation of the 1871 pattern. N.B. This unusual pattern plume holder was attached to the skull by means of three short threaded studs positioned at south-west, south-east, and north which passed through the crown of the skull, and on through a thin metal **triangular shaped** supporting plate where brass washers and nuts secured this fitment. With regard to the head lining, it is known that a beige quilted lining was fitted, and that on some officers pattern helmets, a **dark brown quilted head** lining was fitted.

Figure 55: Hertfordshire Yeomanry officers pattern pre 1902. Note the most interesting pattern plume holder. G. Frost collection. Photo: Courtesy of Geoff Frost.

The Helmet Plate

The only evident change to the helmet plate, was to the gilt metal crown that surmounted the rococo shield, which at some period in time changed from the medium sized crown to the large 'Victorian' pattern of Type: M.

The Ear Rosettes and Chinchain

The ear rosettes were as described above, the chinchain however appears to have increased in width to one inch, and was backed with either black or brown velvet.

The Plume and Rosette

A black horsehair 1871 pattern plume capped by a medium sized gilt metal rosette of the pattern illustrated in Fig: 9.C.

Other Ranks Helmet c. 1880-1901

The Skull, Plume and Holder, Ear Rosettes, and Chinchain

A white metal skull with the peak edges being bound in brass, with the front inner peak lined with skiver. The waist band, rear seam band, and plume holder were all as for the officers pattern helmet but in brass. Standard pattern head band with a leather liner. The brass ear rosettes appear to have been of the pattern illustrated in Fig: 9.I., although the author has seen a helmet fitted with the large 'Albert' pattern rosettes. A brass chinchain being backed with leather, with the plume being of black horsehair with the standard, other ranks pattern rosette in brass.

The Helmet Plate

On the other ranks helmet it appears that the smaller version 'Victorian' crown similar to Type: M. was retained, with the rococo shield being in brass, with the hart, the ford, and flowers being in white metal.

Helmet Post 1902

The only apparent change was to the helmet plate on which the crown was changed to a medium sized 'King's pattern crown[27].

The O.R.'s Full Dress Uniform c. 1897

A scarlet tunic with white facings. Pantaloons of dark blue with a double scarlet stripe. Regimental Headquarters 1914: Hertford.

The Imperial Yeomanry

Following the setting up of a Yeomanry Committee by the War Office in January 1901, *'the conclusions of which formed part of the Militia Forces Act of April 1901, the name of the force was changed from Yeomanry Cavalry to Imperial Yeomanry'. It's enhanced status can be judged by the fact that eighteen new regiments were added to its strength between the years 1901 to 1903'* (53). N.B. Some of these newly formed regiments adopted the dragoon style of dress.

Many readers will not be aware that an Imperial Yeomanry helmet was even considered, let alone actually produced, and therefore on behalf of collectors of military head-dress worldwide, and those having a general interest in this subject, I express my thanks to W.Y. Carman for searching out and including a photograph of this most rare of helmets in his book on Yeomanry Head-dress (63). For, without the inclusion of this photograph in his book, the details of this helmet would, I am sure have remained unknown to most collectors. In respect of this helmet I can do no better that to quote Bill who when referring to his illustration of this head-dress said *'The helmet in plate 40 shows that a full dress head dress was considered'*, and went on to say *'The conversion of old existing regiments and the creation of new ones seems to have obviated the need for a separate Imperial Yeomanry regiment'.*

This trial pattern head-dress is probably the most unique, and is certainly one of the rarest pattern Yeomanry officers[28] helmets ever made, for to my knowledge only two examples exist. One was recently on display at the Aldershot Military Museum, Aldershot, Hampshire, the other example being in the collection of a private owner, known to the author for some twenty-five years or more, to whom I am grateful, for providing many of the details given below.

Officers Helmet c. 1901

The Skull and Plume Holder

A gilt metal 1871 pattern skull, with peak edges being bound with gilt metal, with the waistband and rear seam bands being of the 1871 pattern and in like metal. The plume holder was of the pattern illustrated in Fig: 25.A., again in gilt metal.

The Head Lining

The head lining fitted to this helmet was of soft leather with a red silk upper section.

The Helmet Plate

The most elaborate helmet plate consisted of The Royal Arms (The House of Windsor), which comprised the shield, being quartered as follows, one and four: England, two: Scotland, three: Ireland (74). Surrounding the shield, the Garter bearing the motto *"Honi Soit Qui Mal Y Pense"* surmounted by a small 'King's' pattern crown which is itself surmounted by a small crowned lion. The supporters are dexter, a lion guardant, or crowned proper, and sinister, a unicorn guardant armed and unguled (75). The lion stands upon flowers and a scroll inscribed *"Dieu Et"*, whilst the unicorn, also stands above flowers and a scroll, which is inscribed *"Mon Droit"*. There are a spray of leaves positioned to the outer side of each of the Supporters, and beneath the supporters/scrolls is a double scroll bearing the title *"Imperial Yeomanry"*, the whole in **frosted (matt) silver** metal with burnished highlights. The plate/badge was a one piece[29] fitment.

The Ear Rosettes and Chinchain

Gilt metal ear rosettes of the pattern illustrated in Fig: 9.K[30], with the gilt metal chinchain being mounted upon leather, and backed with red velvet.

The Plume and Rosette

A white horsehair plume of the 1871 pattern, however no information was available as to the pattern of rosette fitted.

1st Lancashire Mounted Rifle Volunteers

This is another regiment who although not strictly cavalry in the true sense of the word, did when in full dress uniform wear a helmet of dragoon pattern, the details of which I hope be of interest to collectors of military head-dress. Regrettably information on this short lived regiment is somewhat scarce, and I have been unable to trace any regimental history, other than that the Corps was raised in early 1860, its headquarters being in Manchester, with three officers being gazetted on the 22nd March 1860. It became known as the 1st Lancashire Light Horse Volunteers' in 1861, and was last recorded as being in existence in 1873 (58).

Officers Helmet c. 1860

The Skull and Plume Mount

A silver plated 'Albert' pattern skull, the peak edges being bound in silver coloured metal, the front and back peaks being decorated with silvered foliated strips, with the waist and seam bands being in like metal. To the crown of the skull, a silvered plume holder of the 'Albert' pattern complete with finials.

The Head Lining
The head lining fitted to the helmet was of red leather.

The Helmet Plate
In silvered metal, the standard 'Albert' pattern crowned (Type: M.) wreath and rococo shield, upon which was mounted an eight pointed **silvered hobnailed** star. Upon the star, the centre device, this being an elliptical strap bearing the title *"Mounted Rifle Volunteers"*[31], and within the strap "The Arms of the County Palatine of Lancaster" being three lions passant guardant, all of which was in silvered metal. The plate/badge consisted of three separate pieces, these being the crowned shield/wreath, the hobnailed star, and centre device.

The Ear Rosettes and Chinchain
Medium sized, silvered ear rosettes of the pattern illustrated in Fig: 9.I., with a silvered chinchain measuring approximately one inch in width, being backed with red leather.

The Plume and Rosette
Of 'Albert' pattern, comprised of a red horsehair 'brush' supporting a falling white over red horsehair plume, capped by a medium sized **gilt** metal rosette (58).

1st Lancashire Light Horse Volunteers c. 1861-73

In 1861 the title of the 1st Lancashire Mounted Rifles Volunteers changed to the title given above, which resulted in the inscription on the strap of the centre device, being changed to *"1st Lancashire Lt.* Horse Voluntrs" (as spelt on the strap), with the star now being of **gilded** metal, and having 42 rays instead of the former 34 (58).

Other Ranks Helmet c. 1861-73

The Skull, Plume Holder, Ear Rosettes, and Chinchain
An 'Albert' pattern skull with all fitting as for the officers pattern, but in white metal. On the helmet examined by the author the plume holder was of Type: J., being **without finials**, however this may not have been the original holder for the helmet concerned. Large sized, white metal ear rosettes of Type: H or I, with the white metal chinchain being backed with brown leather. N.B. On an other ranks pattern helmet offered for sale by auction early in 1999, although appearing to be of the 'Albert' pattern, the peaks edges were not decorated with foliated strips.

The Helmet Plate
In white metal, the standard 'Albert' pattern wreath and rococo shield, however the 'Victorian' crown surmounting the shield was **smaller** than on the officers pattern helmet plate. A further variation was that, upon the shield was a **gilding metal hobnailed star**. To the centre of the star was a white metal strap bearing the post 1861 regimental title as described above.

The Plume and Rosette
On the helmet examined by the author, the plume comprised a **white** horsehair 'brush' supporting a falling white horsehair plume, capped by a large white metal rosette of similar pattern to the ear rosettes, however this plume may not have been the one originally fitted to the helmet.

O.R.'s Full Dress Uniform
A scarlet tunic having blue velvet facings, with **white breeches** being worn in place of pantaloons.

The Lothians and Berwickshire Yeomanry Cavalry

Berwickshire Yeomanry
In 1801 a Troop was raised in the Eagle district adding to the two Troops formed earlier in the Dunn district in 1797, whose official acceptance dates from the 7th May 1797 (89). A fourth Troop was raised in Coldstream in 1804, however in 1827 all these volunteer Troops were disbanded. It was to be a further twenty-one years before a new Troop was formed in 1848, they being named the 3rd or Berwickshire Troop, and being joined with the East Lothian Yeomanry(67).

East Lothian Yeomanry
Three Troops of volunteer cavalry were raised within the area in 1797, with a Corps being formed in Haddington in 1828. By the year 1838 none of these Troops existed, and it was not until 1848 that the East Lothian Yeomanry was re-raised (67).

Midlothian Yeomanry
Formed in 1800 as the Royal Midlothian Yeomanry Cavalry, disbanded in 1828, only to be raised again in 1888 (67).

West Lothian Corps
A Troop of volunteer cavalry was formed in Linlithgow[32] in 1803 which served until 1827. Sometime during the 1870s a Corps was again raised in this area (67).

Amalgamations

In 1888 the Midlothian Yeomanry merged with the East Lothians, and in 1892 they in turn amalgamated with the West Lothian Corps to form the Lothians and Berwickshire Yeomanry Cavalry (67).

Officers Helmet c. 1888-1902

The Skull and Plume Holder
An 1871 pattern skull of silvered/white metal, the peak edges being bound with gilt metal, with the inner peaks being lined with green skiver. The rear seam band was of the standard pattern Type: L in gilt metal, there was however **no front waist band** as such due to the composition of the helmet plate, which is described below. The plume holder[33] was of the pattern illustrated in Fig: 25.B., and was in gilt metal.

The Head Lining
Of beige quilted cloth, or alternatively being of soft leather with a red silk upper section.

The Helmet Plate
This helmet plate was yet another magnificent example of a Scottish yeomanry regiments helmet plate, being of the highest quality, and profusely decorated in gilt and silvered metals.

The design of the plate was closely based on the helmet plates worn on the leather helmet of the former Royal Midlothian Yeomanry Cavalry[34] and the East Lothian Yeomanry Cavalry[35] c. 1860-1888. It comprised a wreath of thistles surmounted by a small early pattern, 'Victorian' crown having prominent pearls upon its depressed arches, all of which was in gilt metal. Within/upon the wreath a silvered circular Garter bearing the motto *"Honi.Soit.Qui.Mal.Y.Pense"*, and within the Garter the 'Order of the Thistle' in gilt metal, this being a three ribbed St. Andrew's Cross, joined with a four-pointed rayed star, upon which was a circular strap bearing the motto *"Nemo.Me.Impune.Lacessit"*[19], and within the Garter the intertwined Royal Cypher of "V.R." also in gilt metal.

Positioned below, but detached from the wreath/garter, was a further spray of thistles in gilt metal, which extended completely across the waist of the skull terminating adjacent to each ear rosette socket, **thereby negating the need for a leaf pattern waist band**. Upon this lower wreath were mounted four separate scrolls in silvered/white metal, they being inscribed as follows when reading from left to right. 'Lothians' (upper left), Berwickshire' (upper right), 'Yeomanry' (lower left), and 'Cavalry' (lower right). The plate/badge was comprised of two separate units, the upper unit consisting of the thistle patterned wreath with crown, the garter, and the cross and cypher, the lower unit comprised of the wreath and the four scrolls.

The Ear Rosettes and Chinchain

Medium sized gilt metal rosettes of the pattern illustrated in Fig: 9.I., with a gilt metal chinchain being approximately fifteen sixteenths of an inch wide and backed with black leather.

The Plume and Rosette

A white 1871 pattern horsehair plume capped by a gilt metal medium sized rosette, of similar pattern to the ear rosettes.

Other Ranks Helmet

The Skull, Plume Holder, Ear Rosettes, and Chinchain

An 1871 pattern skull in white metal, the peak edges being bound with brass, and the inner front peak lined **brown** skiver. The rear seam band, plume holder[36], and ear rosettes all in brass, and of similar pattern as on the officers helmet, with the brass link chinchain being backed with reddish brown leather.

The Helmet Plate

A two piece die-struck helmet plate, the upper section comprised of the crowned wreath, the garter, and the 'V.R.' cypher all in brass, the lower section being the ear-to-ear thistle wreath with the four scrolls, also in brass.

The Plume and Rosette

A white 1871 pattern horsehair plume capped with a rosette thought to have been similar to the officers pattern, but in brass. The musicians of the mounted band wore scarlet plumes (62).

O.R.'s Full Dress Uniform

A scarlet tunic with blue facings, the pantaloons being blue with a double scarlet stripe. Regimental Headquarters 1914: 7, Wemyss Place, Edinburgh, Scotland.

c. 1902 Change of Crown, Cypher and Title

Sometime after the accession to the throne by King Edward VII, the crown on the helmet plate changed to a medium sized 'King's' or Tudor (Imperial) pattern crown, with the gilt metal cypher at the centre of the 'Order of the Thistle' changing from 'V.R.' to 'E.R. VII'.

In a brief, but very informative regimental history (76) reference is made to a change to the regiments title in 1902 to the *"Lothians and Berwickshire Imperial Yeomanry"*, and it would be reasonable to assume that consideration might have been given to the title scrolls on the helmet plate being changed.[37]

The Lothians and Border Horse

In 1908 the Lothians and Berwickshire Imperial Yeomanry changed its title to the Lothians and Border Horse, with the wording on the scrolls being changed accordingly. Perhaps the most distinguished officer to have ever served in the regiment was V.A.J. Hope, the 2nd Marquis of Linlithgow who was commissioned into the regiment with the rank of 2nd Lieutenant on the 1st June 1908. N.B. Brief career details of this officer are given in endnote number nine, of chapter five.

Officers Helmet 1908 (See Fig: 56.)

All details are as listed for the 1902 helmet of the Lothians and Berwickshire Yeomanry Cavalry, with only the title scrolls being changed, both in the wording and their position on the lower wreath. The new inscription read, when facing the helmet. *Lothians*, (left), *And* (upper centre, between Lothians and Horse), *Border* (right), and *Horse* (lower centre), with all scrolls being of silvered/white metal. This new pattern of plate/badge was made up of two separate sections as described previously, with the four scrolls being a one-piece fitment and mounted upon the lower section wreath.

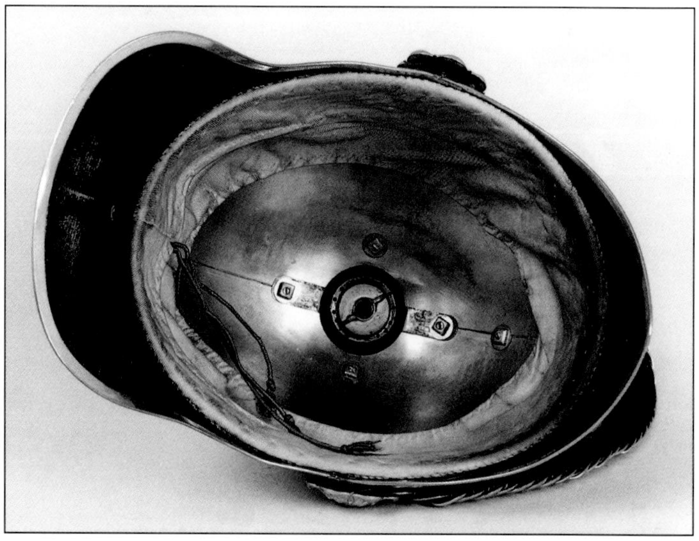

Figure 56a: Inside view of the Lothians and Border Horse helmet illustrated in Fig: 56. Note the collet and the securing nut for the plume holder situated at the centre of the skull. Author's collection. Photo: Courtesy of the National Army Museum.

Figure 56: Lothians and Border Horse officers pattern c. 1908. The former property of the 2nd Marquis of Linlithgow. Of particular interest is the use of thistles for the wreath in place of the more usual oak and laurel. Author's collection. Photo: Courtesy of the National Army Museum.

Montgomeryshire Yeomanry Cavalry

In 1803 there existed three Troops of volunteer cavalry, who together with twenty infantry companies were known collectively as the Montgomeryshire Volunteer Legion. The acceptance date of the first troop formed is given as the 9th September 1803, with the three cavalry Troops being stationed at Abermule, Newton, and Welshpool. The title Montgomeryshire Yeomanry Cavalry was apparently being used by c. 1804, and in 1813 a Berriew Troop was added, with further Troops being added in 1819 at both Llangedwyn and at Llanfyllin (77).

The year 1827 saw this regiment being disbanded, only to be re-raised in 1831, following serious riots that occurred in 1830, with an additional Troop being formed at Caersws, and another at Llanfyllin in 1862.

The regiment formed the 31st and 49th Companies of the 9th Battalion, and the 88th and 89th Companies for the conflict in South Africa (77).

Sometime after 1901 the regiments title changed to include the word 'Imperial', which resulted in a new strap being made for centre device on the full dress helmet plate, which was retained until the formation of the new Territorial Force in 1908. N.B. In 1909 a regimental history (78) co-written by Lieutenant Colonel R.W. Williams Wynn[38] was published, in which are several excellent colour illustrations of uniforms of the regiment, by the celebrated military artist Richard Simkin.

Officers Helmet c. 1856-1866

This pattern of helmet was a true 'mix n match' item of military head-dress, combining the then current 'Albert' pattern skull with a newly introduced pattern of plume holder, and utilising obsolete fittings dating back to the pre-1834 period. As limited information only has been available regarding this pattern of helmet, only particulars that have been confirmed as originating from a respected source have been given. No information however relating to the other ranks helmet has become available to the author, other than that it was similar in general appearance to the officers pattern (78).

The Skull

The skull was of black japanned metal of similar style to the 'Albert' pattern helmet, but having silvered metal **acanthus leaves applied to either side of the skull,** which in appearance is not unlike the decoration on the helmet worn by Dragoon Guards c. 1834-43, with the peak edges being bound with gilt metal or brass[39]. A plain silvered metal band having four 'ribs' extended across the front waist of the helmet from ear-to-ear with a silvered metal laurel leaf band covering the rear seam. There was also a narrow silvered leaf patterned band extending from below the plume base mount to beneath the top of the rayed plate to **conceal the front skull joint.**

The Plume Holder

The plume holder was a most interesting fitment being very similar, if not identical to the **plume holder fitted to the helmets of the Household Cavalry of the post 1871 period**[40]. It consisted of a four-sided fluted socket above a bulbous shaped ball, mounted upon an eight-pointed rayed star shaped base, the whole fitment in **silvered metal.**

The Head Lining

The head lining on this pattern helmet was of leather and padded cloth/silk.

The Helmet Plate

This most impressive helmet plate comprised a large silvered, rayed plate of the pattern worn on the helmet of the **Dragoon Guards from c. 1843 to 1847.** Upon the rayed plate a gilt metal, buckled strap bearing the motto *"Anorchfygol"*[41], and within the strap a gilt metal Welsh dragon (called the Red Dragon) with the silvered rays of the plate acting as a background for the dragon. Above the strap, gilt metal tri-partite scrolls bearing the title *'Montgomeryshire Yeomanry Cavalry'*. The plate/badge is thought to have been of either two, or three separate pieces, these being either the rayed plate, and the dragon/strap/scrolls, or the rayed plate, the scrolls, and the dragon/strap.

The Ear Rosettes and Chinchain

The 'ear rosettes', if that is what they may be called, were in the form of silvered lion's head bosses, being very similar to the pattern fitted to the long since obsolete Dragoon Guards helmets of the **pre-1834 period**. The chinchain however was of a later pattern, being of silvered **rope ringed** links mounted upon leather, and backed with black velvet.

The Plume and Rosette

The plume fitted to this pattern of helmet appears to have been very similar in appearance to the pattern of plume fitted to the Household Cavalry helmets of the post 1871 period. On a helmet of this pattern sold in a Sussex auction salesroom in 1979, and on a similar helmet sold at the same location in 1984, both plumes were of the 1871 pattern, being of horsehair, and very alike in appearance to the plumes of the aforementioned regiment, both plumes having the hair at the top arranged so as to fall over a circular mould. The former plume was **red in colour,** and was fitted with a **dark coloured 'screw-on ball'** similar in appearance to the gilt metal ball fitted to the stem of the Household Cavalry plumes. The rosette fitted to this particular plume was regrettably unidentifiable. The later plume was **black in colour** and also looked to have the aforementioned ball fitting, being capped by a medium sized rosette (not of Household Cavalry pattern). N.B. Both of these plumes looked to be contemporary with the helmet to which they were fitted.

Head-Dress c. 1866-1882

Sometime during 1866 the regiment appear to have moved away from the heavy cavalry Dragoon pattern helmet, to adopt the light cavalry form of head-dress with a busby being adopted. Although strictly not within the terms of reference of this book, the following is a brief description of the officers pattern busby worn by the regiment at this period, as described by W.Y. Carman in his book on Yeomanry Headdresses (63). *'The busby is said to have been introduced in 1866 and is described in the Records as with a scarlet bag, white lines (silver busby line), silver chinchains. A white boss*[42] *was worn below the plume but not on the bag. The bag had silver braid all round the edge but not down the centre. A white plume with a red base'.*

Officer Helmet c. 1882-1896 (See Fig: 57.)

The Skull and Socket

A silvered/white metal 1871 pattern skull, having the front and rear peak binding also in white metal, with both front and back inner peaks being lined with green skiver. Standard pattern waist and rear seam bands of Type: L, both in

Figure 57: Montgomeryshire Yeomanry officers pattern post 1896. A helmet that in the author's opinion has very little visual appeal, due to the fact that all the fittings (except for the plume) are silvered. Author's collection. Photo: Courtesy of the National Army Museum.

silvered metal. The socket at this period was of the pattern illustrated in Fig: 25.F., in white metal, which was not capable of accepting a plume stem.

The Head Lining

Head lining of quilted beige cloth, or alternatively of quilted silk.

The Helmet Plate

The plate for this pattern of helmet, retained none of the features of the earlier pattern helmet plate, with the exception of the figure of a dragon. It was comprised of a silvered eight pointed **hobnailed star** upon which was mounted the centre device, comprising a silvered strap bearing the title *'Montgomeryshire Yeomanry Cavalry'*, with a 'Welsh' dragon within the strap, on a silver coloured ground. The plate/badge consisted of four separate pieces, these being the star, the strap, the dragon, and the backing plate (ground).

The Ear Rosettes and Chinchain

Medium sized, silvered ear rosettes of the type illustrated in Fig: 9.C., with the silvered chinchain being either fifteen sixteenths of an inch wide, or one inch in width, and backed with black, or alternatively red leather.

Officers helmet c. 1897-1902

All details are as given for the helmet worn during the period c. 1882-1896, except for the following.

The Plume Holder and Plume

By about 1897, the spike previously worn atop the helmet had been replaced by a white metal plume holder of the type illustrated in Fig: 25.D., which was now capable of accepting a plume. The 1871 pattern white horsehair, or alternatively **shredded whalebone**, plume was capped with either a small **gilt** rosette of Type: 9.E., or a medium sized rosette of Type: 9.C.[43].

Officers Helmet c. 1902

All details as given for the 1897 pattern helmet, except that the title on the strap of the centre device, changed to *'Montgomeryshire Imperial Yeomanry'*.

Officers Helmet Post 1908

Some time after the formation of the Territorial Force in 1908, the title on the strap on the centre device reverted to the former title of *'Montgomeryshire Yeomanry Cavalry'*. N.B. The title on the strap of the centre device of a helmet, attributed to 2nd Lieutenant J.D. Frost of the c. 1910 period, bore the wording 'Montgomeryshire Yeomanry Cavalry' which confirms the use of this title on helmets worn after 1908. However this use of a regimental title at two differing periods in time, with a break of some six years in-between, does make it difficult to identify at what period, a helmet bearing this particular title was worn.

Other Ranks Helmet

The Skull, Plume Holder, Ear Rosettes, and Chinchain

A white metal 1871 pattern skull with all fittings in like metal. The **front seam joint** was covered by a narrow leaf patterned band that extended from below the front terminal of the plume holder base, down beneath the top ray of the helmet plate star. Only the front inner peak was lined with green skiver on the helmet of the rank and file. The helmet was fitted with a white metal spike/plume holder, dependent upon the period in time. The ear rosettes were in white metal, and of similar pattern to those fitted to the officers helmet, with a white metal chinchain, being backed with brown leather, crimson leather, or alternatively with maroon leather.

The Helmet Plate

The helmet plate was similar in appearance to the officers pattern, but differing in that the white metal eight pointed star was of the **rayed** pattern, and not hobnailed. The centre device also differed in quality, in that the 'Welsh' dragon and the titled strap consisted of a one piece die-struck item. The plate/badge was comprised of two separate pieces, these being the rayed star, and the strap/dragon/backing.

The Plume and Rosette

An 1871 pattern white horsehair plume capped by the standard pattern other ranks plume rosette in brass[43]. No information was available to the author regarding the colour of plumes worn by the members of the band.

O.R.s Full Dress Uniform

A scarlet tunic with black facings, with dark blue pantaloons having a broad single scarlet stripe. c. 1899.[44] Regimental Headquarters 1914: Welshpool, Wales.

The King's Own Royal Regiment of Norfolk Imperial Yeomanry

Possibly, the counties earliest Corps of volunteer cavalry can be traced back to a report that appeared on the 14th September 1782 in the *Norwich Mercury*, which stated that *'On Sunday morning, a very respectable body of gentlemen, farmers, and tradesmen, waited on his Lordship (*Lord Viscount Townshend*) as volunteers to serve in a corps (styled the Norfolk Rangers)'* (56).

In 1794 the Norfolk Rangers were enrolled as Yeomanry, with many other bodies of volunteer cavalry being raised within the County of Norfolk, amongst them being The Norfolk Fencible Cavalry 1794-1800, the Provisional Cavalry of Norfolk c. 1797-1800, and The Suffolk and Norfolk Border Yeomanry Cavalry c. 1833-1850. The year 1861 saw the formation of the Norfolk (Norwich) Mounted Rifle Volunteer Corps, later retitled the Norfolk (Norwich) Light Horse Volunteers, however with their disbandment in 1867 it was to be over thirty years before the County once more possessed its own corps of volunteer cavalry (56).

In 1901 at the direction of King Edward VII[45], and under Army Order 138/1901 the *Norfolk (King's Own) Imperial Yeomanry*[46] was raised with their acceptance date being given as 14th May 1901 (89). The regiment had no less a personage than the King as its Honorary Colonel, this being by no means the sole royal connection for the regiment, as 'A' Squadron[47] was commanded by Major, His Highness Prince Frederick Duleep Singh. A further royal connection occurred, when on 11th June 1902 it was announced in the *London Gazette*, that H.R.H. Prince Frederick Charles of Denmark[48] had been appointed to be Honorary Lieutenant Colonel of the regiment (56).

Officers Head-Dress 1901-1904

The regiments first full dress head-dress, consisted of a cork bodied helmet of the 'Colonial' pattern, which was covered in a light shade of cotton drill in six seams, bound with pale leather. At the top of the skull, a 'dead' gilt, metal spike, similar in appearance to the plume holder illustrated in Fig: 25.H, but not being capable of accepting a plume stem. To the side of the helmet, a gilt metal hook onto which the gilt metal chinchain could be attached, when not required to be worn under the chin. Around the waist of the helmet was a royal blue silk puggree having seven evenly spaced gold braid retainer loops. To the front of the helmet a gilt metal badge in the form of an intertwined ER VII Royal Cypher surmounted by a 'King's' crown. N.B. when not in review order, the gilt metal spike was replaced by a drab coloured ventilator button.

Other Ranks Head-Dress

Similar in appearance to the officers pattern, but having a plain brass spike, with the puggree being of plain drab. A brass chinchain was worn when in review order, with a leather strap being worn when in other orders of dress.

Regimental Order 1905

Notification that a new form of head-dress was to be adopted was given in the above order, which included the following *'In continuance of Regimental Order No 5 of October 1904, it is notified for General Information that a new helmet*[49] *for the Regiment has been approved by His Majesty and will shortly be issued'* (56).

Officers Helmet 1905

The Skull and Plume Holder

The appearance of the skull was 'more Germanic' than 'Albert' shaped, and was of black japanned **aluminum**, with the peak edges being bound in gilt metal. The waist and rear seam bands were also in gilt metal and of Type: L., with the plume holder being of the pattern illustrated in Fig: 25.D., in like metal.

The Head Lining

The head lining fitted to this pattern of helmet, was of beige quilted cloth, or alternatively of silk.

The Helmet Plate

A gilt metal eight pointed rayed star, within a wreath of gilt metal, laurel leaves. Upon the rayed star the Royal Cypher of Edward VII, being an intertwined E.R.VII in silver/white metal, and positioned slightly above the cypher a medium sized 'King's' crown similar in appearance to Type: R., also in silver/white metal. Upon the lower sections of the laurel wreath a silver/white metal tripartite scroll bearing the title *'King's Own Norfolk Impl: Yeomy* (as spelt on scrolls). The plate/badge consisted of four separate pieces, these being the wreath/rayed star, the crown, the cypher, and the tripartite scroll.

The Ear Rosettes and Chinchain

Medium sized ear rosettes as illustrated in Fig: 9.I. in gilt metal, with the chinchain being one inch wide, with gilt metal links, and backed with black leather, or being of the tapering version with gilt metal links, with a black leather backing.

The Plume and Rosette

The horsehair plume was of the 1871 pattern and was unique in being **saffron yellow in colour**, also referred to as canary yellow, capped by a medium sized gilt metal rosette, thought to have been of the type illustrated in Fig: 9.C., 9.D., or 9.E.

Other Ranks Helmet

The Skull, Plume Holder, Ear Rosettes, and Chinchain

The skull was similar in overall appearance to that of the officers pattern, but being of **black boiled leather** instead of japanned aluminium. The peak binding, front waist and rear seam bands were all in brass, as was the plume holder which was identical in appearance to the type fitted to the officers helmet. The ear rosettes appear to have been of the pattern illustrated in Fig: 9.K., in brass metal, with the brass link chinchain being backed with leather.

The Helmet Plate

The helmet plate for the rank and file was similar to that of the officers, but differed in that there was no **rayed star** onto which to surmount the crown and cypher. Additionally unlike on the officers pattern helmet, the crown and cypher were joined together and formed a part of the wreath, the cypher having only the leather of the skull as a backing. On the only example of an other ranks plate examined by the author, the wreath was soldered to the crown, which in turn was soldered to the cypher, with the scrolls being soldered to the wreath, making in effect a one-piece plate/badge.

The Plume and Rosette

A horsehair plume of similar colour to the officers having the standard other ranks non-detachable small brass rosette[50] Having carefully examined a photograph of a dismounted trumpeter taken c. 1914 (56), it would appear that the plume of the band was of the same colour as for the rest of the regiment.

Officers Helmet c. 1911

All details as for the 1905 pattern helmet, except that the Royal Cypher changed to that of the newly crowned King, being GRV[51] in silver/white metal. N.B. All post 1911 pattern officers helmet plates seen by the author, had the scroll bearing the word *Impl.* which does not appear to have ever been deleted from the title scrolls.

O.R.'s Full Dress Uniform c. 1905

A dark blue tunic with yellow facings, with the pantaloons also being of dark blue, and having a single yellow stripe[52]. Regimental Headquarters 1914: Cattle Market Street, Norwich, Norfolk.

Northamptonshire Imperial Yeomanry

The Earl Spencer formed a regiment within the county in 1794 which was officially accepted on the 3rd May 1794, and served for some thirty-four years, until being disbanded in 1828. Various independent Troops were raised in 1830, all of which were gradually disbanded, the last remaining corps being the Royal Kettering Troop which existed until 1873 (67). N.B. The Earl Spencer family connection with the regiment has continued over the years.

In 1902 a new regiment was raised with the title *'Northamptonshire Imperial Yeomanry'*, its acceptance date being given as the 7th February 1902 (89). N.B. As with several regiments formed in 1902, the word *Imperial'* was deleted from this regiments title sometime after 1908.

Royal Kettering Corps of Yeomanry Cavalry

No information was available to the author on the officers head-dress of this corps, however the following is a brief description of the other ranks helmet. A skull of dark blue cloth, being not dissimilar in appearance to an English police officers helmet, but having the front peak bound with brass. The helmet plate comprised a brass eight pointed star having sharp-cut ends, to the centre of which was a cypher within a strap (details unknown), and mounted separately, and slightly above the star a small 'Victorian' crown. A brass 'Albert' pattern plume holder of Type: I., supported a red horsehair plume, having a small brass rosette, the rose pattern ear rosettes, supporting a brass leather backed chinchain (80).

Officers Helmet c. 1907

The Skull and Plume Holder

A silvered/white metal[53] 1871 pattern skull, the peak edges being bound in gilt metal, with both inner peaks being lined with skiver. The front waist band and rear seam bands were both of Type: L. in gilt metal, with the plume holder, which was of the pattern illustrated in Fig: 25.B., also being in gilt metal.[54]

The Head Lining

The head lining fitted to this helmet, was usually of beige quilted cloth.

The Helmet Plate

The most decorative helmet plate consisted of a twelve pointed silvered rayed star[55], upon which was mounted gilt metal tripartite scrolls formed to give the appearance of a circular/oval strap. The upper of the three scrolls extended from the top of the lower left scroll over to the top of the lower right scroll, with the lower left being joined to the lower right at the centre of the 'strap'. The scrolls bore the regimental title in the following order, upper scroll *'Northamptonshire',* lower left scroll *'Imperial'*, and lower right scroll *'Yeomanry'*. Within the strap/scrolls, the centre device, being a prancing 'White Horse of Hanover' in silvered/white metal, above gilt metal 'union flowers', comprising a spray of rose, thistle, and shamrock, all on a gilt metal ground. The plate/badge was comprised of four separate pieces, these being the rayed star, the scrolls, the prancing horse/flowers, and the gilt metal ground. N.B. The horse/flowers of the centre device, was attached to the backing plate (ground) by five small bend over metal pins.

The Ear Rosettes and Chinchain

Two slightly different pattern of gilt metal ear rosettes appear to have been fitted to the helmets of this regiment, these being the patterns illustrated in Fig: 9.I., and Fig: 9.J. The chinchain was of gilt metal links, and was one inch in width, being backed with black leather.

The Plume and Rosette

A most unique and impressive plume, being of the 1871 pattern and having cornflower blue (pale blue) over white horsehair[56], capped with a gilt metal rosette of Type: 9.E., although it is possible that Type: 9.C. rosette was also fitted to this regiments plume.

Other Ranks Helmet

No information can be given regarding a full dress helmet for the rank and file of this regiment, as the author has neither seen, nor heard of the existence of such a helmet. N.B. It is extremely likely that the full dress helmet was not issued to the rank and file.[57]

O.R.'s Walking Out Uniform c. 1911

A dark blue tunic with cornflower blue facings, the overalls also being dark blue in colour, with two cornflower blue stripes. Regimental Headquarters 1914: Clare Street, Northampton.

The North Somerset Yeomanry

The North Somerset can trace its origins back to the Frome Troop of Cavalry, raised within the county in 1798, and being officially accepted on the 20th June 1798 (89). During this same period Troops of volunteer cavalry were being formed at Bath, Beckington, Mells, Road, and Woolverton, however in common with volunteer Corps raised in other counties at this period, by 1802 all these Troops had been disbanded (57).

In 1803 the Frome Volunteers were re-raised as the Frome Selwood Troop of Volunteer Cavalry, and within a year they had united with the East Mendip Cavalry, to become the Frome and East Mendip Regiment of Volunteer Cavalry. This new title was to last for some ten years, before they then became the North Somerset Yeomanry Cavalry (57).

Between 1814 and 1817 several further Troops were added, increasing the overall regimental strength, and bringing the number of men to a total 661, and by 1819 it was decided to divide the regiment into two divisions, one being known as the Bath Division, the other the Frome Division.[58]

During the war in South Africa the regiment provided officers and men to serve in the 48th Company of the 7th Battalion Imperial Yeomanry (67).

Officers Helmet c. 1851

The Skull and Plume Holder

The 'Albert' pattern skull was silver plated, or alternatively of best quality white metal, with both peaks being decorated with gilt metal foliated strips. The peak edges were also bound with like metal, with the inner peaks being lined with skiver. The scroll and leaf pattern band which encircled the waist and the rear seam band were in gilt metal, as was the 'Albert' pattern plume holder of Type: I., which was complete with finials.

The Head Lining

The head lining was of leather and silk, or alternatively of quilted silk, although it is quite likely that quilted beige cloth was also used.

The Helmet Plate

In gilt metal, the standard 'Albert' pattern wreath and rococo shield surmounted by a large 'Victorian' crown of Type: M. To the centre of the shield a diamond-cut silver star having eight points, mounted upon which was the die-struck centre device, being an elliptical strap bearing the title *'The North Somerset'*. Within the strap was an intertwined 'V.R'. Royal Cypher all in gilt metal[59]. The plate/badge consisted of three separate pieces, these being the wreath/shield/crown, the star, and the centre device.

The Ear Rosettes and Chinchain

Two differing pattern of gilt metal ear 'rosettes' appear to have been fitted to the officers pattern helmet, one type being the standard 'Albert' pattern as illustrated in Fig: 9.G. The other type of rosette was a special pattern, **lion's head boss**,[60] not dissimilar to the ear bosses fitted to British Lancers chapka's (caps) of the post 1816 period. The chinchain was of gilt metal backed with red leather, or alternatively mounted on leather and backed with black velvet.

The Plume and Rosette

An 'Albert' pattern horsehair[61] plume being black in colour was worn up until c. 1856, when the colour was change to white. The gilt metal plume rosette was of the pattern illustrated in Fig: 9.C.

Other Ranks Helmet

The Skull, Plume Holder, Ear Rosettes, and Chinchain

An 'Albert' pattern skull in white metal, with all fittings including the plume holder, ear rosettes and leather backed chinchain being in brass.

The Helmet Plate

The standard 'Albert' pattern wreath, shield and crown in gilding metal or brass, rather than in gilt metal as on the officers pattern helmet. The eight pointed star also differed in that it was in white metal, and of the **hobnailed** pattern. The die-struck centre device was as for the officers, but in brass. N.B. There was a pair of flat blades to the reverse of the crown.

The Plume and Rosette

A black 'Albert' pattern horsehair plume was worn up until c. 1855-56, the colour then being changed to white. The plume is thought to have had the smaller sized, other ranks non-removable brass rosette. The musicians in the band appear to have worn an 'Albert' pattern white over red hanging horsehair plume (57), with the horsehair brush beneath the falling plume, probably being red in colour.[62]

Officers Helmet Post 1902

The only obvious change appears to have been to the helmet plate, with the crown changing to a large version 'King's' crown, and the Royal Cypher changing to an intertwined 'E.R. VII[63], the helmet being worn up until c. 1914 (57).

O.R.'s Full Dress Uniform c. 1888

A dark blue tunic with white facings, with the pantaloons also being dark blue in colour, with a double white stripe. Regimental Headquarters 1914: Bath, Somerset.

Shropshire Yeomanry

It is recorded that in 1795, two Troops of volunteer cavalry were formed, these being at Market Drayton, and at Wellington, the acceptance date of the first Troop formed being given as the 11th January 1795 (89). Also on record is that at one time there were no less than eleven Corps within the County of Shropshire, included amongst this number being Corps with such names as the Hales Owen Cavalry, the Oswestry Rangers, and the Pimhill Light Horse.

The Corps existing in 1814 were regimented to become known as the Shropshire, Shrewsbury, and the North Shropshire Yeomanry, and in 1828 the Shropshire Yeomanry Cavalry and the Shrewsbury Yeomanry Cavalry merged to form the South Salopian Yeomanry Cavalry, with the 'North Shropshire' changing its name to the North Salopian Cavalry.

In 1872 the Shropshire Yeomanry Cavalry was formed, when the North Salopian Yeomanry Cavalry, and South Salopian Yeomanry Cavalry were amalgamated. The regiments title changed to the Shropshire Imperial Yeomanry in 1901, when the regiment provided officers and men for the 13th Company of the 5th Battalion Imperial Yeomanry (67). N.B. The title *'Shropshire Imperial Yeomanry'* was taken into use from the 17th April 1901 until the 1st April 1908 when the title changed to *'Shropshire Yeomanry'* (91).

North Salopian Yeomanry

The type of helmets worn by this regiment, prior to its amalgamation with the South Salopian Yeomanry Cavalry is outside the scope of this book, however the following is a brief description of the officers helmets of periods c. 1825 and c. 1855.

Officers Helmet c. 1825 (63)

A 'Roman' pattern helmet similar in appearance to the type worn by the seven regiments of Dragoon Guards c. 1818-1834, having a steel skull, with gilt metal laurel sprays either side of the rear of the skull, with the peaks being bound with gilt metal. A high steel comb surmounted the skull, with to the front, a gilt metal ornamented finial, in the shape of a lion's head with paws outstretched. To the rear centre of the skull, just below the base of the comb, a small oval gilt metal plaque bearing *'NSY'*. The gilt metal helmet plate, comprised a large rayed plate with square-ends, bearing the Royal Arms within the Garter on Prince of Wales's feathers, with lion and unicorn supporters, together with motto scrolls below. The helmet was completed by having gilt metal lion-head bosses, and gilt metal chinscales (53). Head lining of black leather with a drawstring.

Officer Helmet c. 1855

A black leather helmet was adopted c. 1855, having silvered/white metal fittings, including a thin silver band at the waist of the skull. The helmet plate comprising an eight-pointed, rayed, silvered star, the uppermost point being displaced by a 'Victorian' crown, which was not dissimilar in appearance to the crown referred to previously as Type: Q. To the centre of the star a strap bearing the title 'North Salopian Yeomanry', and within the strap an intertwined 'V.R.' Royal Cypher. A special pattern, silvered ball and socket plume holder, supported a white over red horsehair plume. Regrettably no information was available to the author regarding the ear rosettes, chinchain, or lining.

South Salopian Yeomanry

Prior to the introduction of the 'Albert' pattern helmet this regiment also wore a helmet of the 'Roman' pattern, similar to that worn by the North Salopian Yeomanry, but having the initials *'SSY'* on the small oval plaque situated at the rear centre of the skull.

Officers Helmet c. 1853-1872 (91)

The Skull and Plume Holder

A silvered/white metal 'Albert' pattern skull having both peaks decorated with gilt metal foliated strips, the peak edges being bound with gilt metal, with the inner peaks being lined with skiver. The waist and rear seam bands were in gilt metal and of Type: K., with the plume holder, which was also of the 'Albert' pattern being Type: I., and having finials, being in like metal.

The Head Lining

On the only example of an officers pattern helmet of this period examined by the author, the skull was fitted with a head lining of brown quilted silk. However when taking into account the apparent overall restoration on this particular helmet it may have been that this lining was a replacement.

The Helmet Plate

In gilt metal, and based on the standard 'Albert' pattern wreath and rococo shield, but having **olive/laurel leaves**[64] **both left and right of the shield,** and being surmounted by a Victorian' crown similar to Type: M. Upon the shield an eight pointed silvered hobnailed star, to the middle of which was the centre device. This consisted of a gilt metal strap, bearing the title *'South Salopian Yeomanry'*, and within the strap *'The Arms of Shrewsbury'* being three leopard's faces/heads[65] on a gilt metal ground. The plate/badge consisted of three separate pieces, these being the wreath/crown/shield, the star, and the centre device.

The Ear Rosettes and Chinchain

The gilt metal ear rosettes were of the pattern illustrated in Fig: 9.G., with the gilt metal chinchain being backed with either black leather, or mounted upon leather and backed with black velvet.

Figure 57a: South Salopian Yeomanry senior N.C.O.'s pattern pre 1872. Note. Although the plume is of the correct pattern, the colour is incorrect as it should be black. Author's collection. Photo: Author.

The Plume and Rosette

A black 'Albert' pattern falling horsehair plume complete with a black horsehair 'brush', capped by a medium sized gilt metal rosette of the type illustrated in Fig: 9.C.

Other Ranks Helmet Pre 1872 (See Fig: 57A.)

The following details are taken from a helmet examined by the author which though of a high grade, was not of officers quality, and may therefore have been a senior N.C.O.'s helmet.

The Skull, Plume Holder, Ear Rosettes, and Chinchain

The skull was as for the officers pattern, but with all fittings being in brass, the front peak being lined with skiver. The brass plume holder was of Type: J., this being a variation of Type: I., but **being without finials.** Why the officers should have the plume holder with finials, whilst the rank and file had the pattern without, is a mystery. The brass ear rosettes were of medium size, and of the pattern illustrated in Fig: 9.J. or alternatively the larger pattern of Type: 9.G., with the brass chinchain being **graduated**, and backed with black velvet.[66] N.B. The chin chain for troopers/privates would have been backed with leather.

The Helmet Plate

All details as for the officers helmet plate, but in brass. However close examination of the reverse of this particular plate showed signs of it having either once have been gilded, or have been of gilding metal.

The Plume and Rosette

A black horsehair plume as for the officers helmet, but with a brass rosette. N.B. The author has also seen two other ranks pattern helmets, fitted with plumes of white horsehair capped by a medium sized brass rosette, each of these plumes appearing to be contemporary with its helmet. My unconfirmed theory, is that these helmets may have been worn by trumpeters of the regiment.

Shropshire Yeomanry Cavalry

Officer Helmet Post 1872

The skull and fittings were as described for the South Salopian Cavalry helmet, the only apparent differences being as follows. The title on the helmet plate changed to *'Shropshire Yeomanry Cavalry'*, with the ear rosettes changing to the pattern illustrated in Fig: 9.I.[67] The plume holder changed to the 'Albert' pattern Type: J., this being the version **without finials**, and the plume, whilst remaining of the 'Albert' pattern changed from a black 'brush' beneath a falling black horsehair plume to a **red 'brush' beneath a white over red falling horsehair plume,** the plume rosette remaining unchanged.[68]

Officers Helmet Pre 1901

The Skull and Plume Holder

A silvered/white metal 1871 pattern skull, the peak edges being bound in gilt metal with the inner peaks being lined with green skiver. The front waist and rear seam bands were of Type: L., in gilt metal, as was the plume holder which was of the ball and socket pattern as illustrated in Fig: 25.B. N.B. The regimental histories do not record in which year the 1871 pattern skull was taken into wear, what is known however, is that the 'Albert' pattern skull was still being worn c. 1887[68] and that known examples of officers helmets having the later 1871 pattern skull and bearing the 'Victorian' crown on the helmet plate (dating them as pre 1901) do still exist.

The Head Lining

No information was available to the author regarding the type of head lining fitted to this helmet, however it is reasonable to assume that it would have been of either quilted cloth or quilted silk.

The Helmet Plate

The helmet plate comprised a rococo shield surmounted by a large 'Victorian' crown of Type: M., all in gilt metal. Within the shield, a diamond-cut silver star having eight points upon which was mounted the centre device. This consisted of a gilt metal strap bearing the title *'Shropshire Yeomanry'*, with the Arms of Shrewsbury as described previously, within the strap on a gilt ground. The plate/badge was made up of three separate pieces, these being the shield/crown, the star, and the centre device.

The Ear Rosettes and Chinchain

Gilt metal ear rosettes of the pattern illustrated in Fig: 9.H., with the gilt metal one-inch wide chinchain being backed with either black leather, or mounted upon leather and backed with black velvet.

The Plume and Rosette

A white over red 1871 pattern horsehair plume capped with a gilt metal rosette (pattern unknown).

Other Ranks Helmet Pre 1901

The Skull, Plume Holder, Ear Rosettes, and Chinchain

An 1871 pattern skull in white metal with all fittings including the waist leaves and rear seam bands being in brass. The brass plume holder differed from the officers version in that it did **not have the ball beneath its socket**, being of the pattern illustrated in Fig: 25.A. The brass ear rosettes appear to have been the standard other ranks pattern, (Type: 9.K.) with the brass chinchain being backed with leather.

The Helmet Plate

The other ranks helmet plate is thought to have been similar to the officers pattern, but with the shield/ crown, and centre device in gilding metal and the star white metal.

The Plume and Rosette

An 1871 white over red horsehair plume with standard other ranks rosette in brass. Although this regiment is known to have had a band, no information was available to the author as to the colour of the musicians plumes.

Officers and Other Ranks Helmet c. 1901-1908

All details as given above, the only apparent changes being to the helmet plate where the crown changed from 'Victorian' to a 'King's' (Tudor) version, with the title on the strap being changed to read *'Shropshire Imperial Yeomanry'*.

Officer Helmet Post 1908

Again all details as for the c. 1901-08 helmet with the exception of the following. The title on the strap of the centre device reverted to *'Shropshire Yeomanry'*, and the ear rosettes appear to have changed to a **slightly smaller version** as illustrated in Fig: 9.I., with the chinchain now being backed with **red leather.**

O.R.'s Full Dress Uniform c. 1911

A blue tunic with scarlet facings, the pantaloons also being blue with a single scarlet stripe. Regimental Headquarters 1914: Shrewsbury, Shropshire.

Staffordshire Yeomanry

The *'Staffordshire Volunteer Cavalry'* was raised on the 4th July 1794, being one of the few Corps raised as a Regiment from its inception. The regiment was comprised of five 'Divisions', these being the Leek, the Lichfield, the Newcastle, the Stafford and the Walsall Division.

Over the next six years, several other Troops of volunteer cavalry were raised within the County, amongst them being the Loyal Handsworth Volunteer Cavalry, The Stone and Eccleshall Volunteer Cavalry, the Tamworth Troop, the Uttoxeter Cavalry and the **Royal Pottery Troop** commanded by Captain **Josiah Spode.** However following regulations introduced in 1813, whereby single Troops of volunteer cavalry were either to transfer to existing regiments, or to amalgamate to form larger Corps, the Stone and Eccleshall, the Tamworth Troop, and the Uttoxeter Troop joined the Staffordshire Volunteer Cavalry, leaving the Loyal Handsworth Volunteer Cavalry as the only independent Troop in the County, until their disbandment in 1827.

Following the Coronation of Queen Victoria in June 1838, Her Majesty graciously bestowed upon the regiment the honour of the title *'Royal'* the regiments new title becoming *'The Queen's Own Royal Regiment of Staffordshire Yeomanry Cavalry'*.

Amongst the many officers who have served in the regiment over the years were several of high and noble birth, many of who commanded the regiment at some period. Amongst them were such names as Lord Paget 1840, Lord Bagot 1871, The Marquis of Angelsey 1884, The Earl of Shrewsbury 1885, and The (4th) Duke of Sunderland 1894, to name but a few (59).[87]

Following the reorganisation of the Yeomanry in 1893 the regiment was brigaded with the Warwickshire Yeomanry to form the 8th Yeomanry Brigade, and during the war in South Africa, the regiment provided officers and men for the 6th (Staffordshire) and 106th (Staffordshire) Companies of the 4th Battalion Imperial Yeomanry (67).

Officers Helmet c. 1850

The Skull and Plume Holder

An 'Albert' pattern **skull of black patent leather,** the peaks being decorated with silvered foliated metal strips, with the peak edges bound with silvered metal. The waist and rear seam bands were of Type: K., and were also in silvered metal, as was the plume holder, which was Type: J., being the 'Albert' pattern **without finials**[70].

The Head Lining
The head lining was of cotton, or alternatively of brown quilted cloth, although as red leather was used on the chinchain it is possible that similar leather may have been used for the head lining.

The Helmet Plate
The standard 'Albert' pattern wreath and rococo shield, surmounted by a 'Victorian' crown of Type: P., the whole in silvered metal. To the centre of the shield an eight pointed **hobnailed** silvered star, mounted upon which was a pierced gilt metal strap bearing the title *'The Queen's Own Royal Yeomanry'* on a dark ground. Within the strap a gilt metal *'Stafford'* knot also on a dark coloured ground[69]. The plate/badge consisted of five separate pieces, these being the wreath/shield/crown, the star, the strap, the 'Stafford' knot, and the ground (backing plate to the knot). N.B. The 'Stafford' knot was a personal cognisance of the Earls of Stafford in the 15th century.

The Ear Rosettes and Chinchain
Medium sized silvered metal ear rosettes, of the pattern illustrated in Fig: 9.I., with the last link of one end of the chinchain, being attached to a small 'ring' that was affixed to the lower petals of the right hand rosette. The left hand rosette had a small silvered hook, which hung down from, and was secured behind its lower petals, onto which to attach the last link of the 'loose' end, of the chinchain. The links of the chinchain were of silvered metal, being backed with red leather.

The Plume and Rosette
A black 'Albert' pattern flowing horsehair plume complete with a black horsehair 'brush'. The plume was capped by a most distinctive and unique pattern finial, being **in the shape of a silvered acorn** on a black 'disc'.

Other Ranks Helmet

The Skull, Plume Holder, Ear Rosettes, and Chinchain
The skull was similar in appearance to the officers helmet, as was the plume holder, with all fittings being of white metal, including the ear rosettes, and the leather backed chinchain.

The Helmet Plate
As for the officers pattern, except that the plate was die-struck in white metal, and of one piece.

The Ear Rosettes and Chinchain
The ear rosettes were of similar pattern to those on the officers helmets, but in white metal, as was the leather backed chinchain.

The Plume and Rosette
A black horsehair 'Albert' pattern plume, capped by a similar style of acorn finial, to that fitted to the officers pattern plume.

Officer Helmet c. 1860 (See: Fig: 58.)
The second 'Albert' pattern helmet, was adopted sometime around 1860, and had the following notable changes.

The 'Albert' pattern skull was now of **black japanned metal**, with the peaks being decorated with silvered metal foliated strips. The peak edges were bound with silvered metal, with the inner peaks lined with green skiver. The silvered metal, plume holder however, remained unchanged.

Figure 58: Queen's Own Royal Staffordshire Yeomanry officers pattern c. 1860-93. Of interest is the unusual shape of the crown surmounting the helmet plate. Author's collection. Photo: Courtesy of the National Army Museum.

The Head Lining
The head lining was of **dark brown leather, with a red silk** upper section.

The Helmet Plate
The helmet plate appears to have remained unchanged, being as described for the c. 1850 pattern plate. N.B. On the many helmet plates of this period seen by the author, including the example in the author's collection, both the pierced strap and the 'Stafford' knot were **on a silvered ground.**

The Ear Rosettes, and Chinchain
The ear rosettes were as previously described, however the chinchain was now three quarters of an inch wide, being backed with **black leather,** or alternatively mounted upon leather and backed with **black velvet**.

The Plume and Rosette
The horsehair plume remained black until c. 1870, when it changed to a white falling plume over a white 'brush', with the 'acorn' finial gradually being replaced, by a silvered metal **rosette.** Photographs of helmets sold in auction, show that the helmets appear to have been fitted with rosettes of the pattern illustrated in both Fig: 9.E., and Type: 9.C. N.B. White **shredded whalebone**, is also known to have been used for the officers plumes, in place of horsehair.

Figure 58a: Queen's Own Royal Staffordshire Yeomanry officers pattern pre 1893. Compare the 1871 pattern plume holder on this late pattern helmet with the one illustrated in Fig: 58. F. Mitchell Collection. Photo: Author.

Other Ranks Helmet c. 1860

The Skull, Plume Holder, Ear Rosettes, and Chinchain
A black metal japanned skull with all fittings, including the plume holder which remained unchanged, being in white metal. On some examples of this helmet examined by the author, whilst the front peak was lined with green skiver, the inner rear peak was **painted in a like shade of green**, whilst on other helmets seen, both the front and rear inner peaks were painted green. N.B. This painting to the inner peaks appeared to be contemporary with the rest of the helmet. The chinchain was of white metal links, backed with leather. N.B. On a helmet examined by the author, and thought to have belonged to a senior Non Commissioned Officer, the lining was of **beige quilted cloth**, in place of the standard pattern, leather head lining, normally fitted to other ranks helmets.

The Helmet Plate
Of similar appearance to the officers plate, but being die-struck of white metal, and a one-piece component. The plate/badge was a one piece item. N.B. On the senior N.C.O.'s helmet seen by the author, whilst the wreath/shield/crown/star/strap was a die-stuck one piece item, the 'Stafford' knot was in **gilt metal**, being a separate piece superimposed onto the ground within the strap.

The Plume and Rosette
A black 'Albert' pattern horsehair plume, the acorn finial gradually being replaced by a white metal **rosette**, similar to the pattern illustrated in Fig: 9.C., or Fig: 9.D. N.B. Although it is recorded that this regiment did have a band, regrettable there was no information available to the author, regarding the colour of plume worn by the musicians in this band.

Changes Prior to c. 1893/94
By the late 1890s, the helmet had remained almost unchanged since the adoption of the black japanned skull in c. 1860, however, about 1890 the officers helmet was given a 'face lift', making its appearance closer to the 1871 pattern, the modifications being as follows.

The Skull and Plume Holder

The silvered foliated metal strips to the front and rear peaks were gradually omitted, with the scroll and leaf pattern band that encircled the waist, being replaced by a spray of laurel leaves (left), and oak leaves (right), being similar in appearance to the fitment on the Household Cavalry officers helmet[71].The head lining also appears to have changed to one of silk. The silvered metal plume holder, changed to the pattern illustrated in Fig: 25.E., with the 'Albert' pattern base being retained, but having the later, **1871 pattern plume socket** fitted (See Fig: 58A.).

The Helmet Plate, Ear Rosettes, and Chinchain

The helmet plate appears to have remained unchanged, however, the silvered ear rosettes no longer had the 'ring' and 'hook' as described for the 1860 pattern ear rosette. The chinchain was now backed with either black, or red leather, and secured to the helmet by being attached to the ear rosette sockets, as described for the Dragoon Guards pattern helmet.

The Plume and Rosette

The modification to the plume socket, necessitated a change to the type of plume to be fitted, and therefore a white horsehair 1871 pattern plume with silvered rosette was adopted.

The 1893 Trial Pattern Helmet

The following description is based on a black and white illustration of the 1893 trial pattern helmet, that appeared on page seventy-one, of W.Y. Carman's book on Yeomanry Headdresses (63), in which Bill Carman advises that *'Round about 1893 thoughts of a new head-dress were considered, for although such a pattern exists, evidence of its wear is lacking'.* The helmet concerned is not identified in the text as being either an officers helmet, or an other ranks pattern, although from the illustration it is evident that the helmet is of the latter version. As stated above, the illustration is in black and white and therefore, the colours of the metals given below, may not be entirely accurate. N.B. In the photograph concerned, no plume was fitted to the helmet.

The Skull, Plume Holder, Ear Rosettes, and Chinchain

The standard pattern 1871 skull, front waist band and rear seam bands, complete with the pattern of plume holder illustrated in Fig: 25.A., all apparently in white metal. The ear rosettes were the standard other ranks pattern of Type: 9.K., with the white metal chinchain, being backed with leather, having metal tags at either end of the chain.

The Helmet Plate

A twelve pointed rayed star in white metal, upon which was a gilding metal strap, bearing a title, that **appears to read** *'The Queen's Own Royal Yeomanry'.* Within the strap, on **what appears to be** a black leather ground, the 'Stafford' knot in gilding metal. The plate/badge appears to have been made up of four separate pieces, these being the rayed star, the strap, the leather ground, and the 'Stafford' knot.

O.R.'s Full Dress c. 1890

A dark blue tunic with scarlet facings, the pantaloons also being dark blue, with double scarlet stripes[72] Regimental Headquarters 1914: Barley Street, Stafford.

The Suffolk Yeomanry

The Regiment appear to claim that their origins can be traced back to the year 1793, although the official date of their being accepted is given as 4th May 1794. Nine units were raised during this period, however by 1828 the last of these Troops had been disbanded. In 1831 the Bury St. Edmond's Troop was formed, and some thirty seven years later, they joined with the Long Melford Troop, to become known as the *'West Suffolk Yeomanry'.*

By 1876 the West Suffolk Yeomanry had changed its title to become the *'Suffolk Yeomanry Cavalry'*, with a further change of title occurring in 1885, when the regiment was granted the title 'Loyal Suffolk Hussars'. In August 1894 there was a further addition with the title *'Duke of York's Own'* being granted, the regiment having by this time the honour of having The Duke of York as its Honorary Colonel[73]. The new title of the regiment now became the *'Duke of York's Own Loyal Suffolk Hussars'*, with the distinction of Imperial Yeomanry being carried from 1901 to 1908 (63).

The regiment has throughout its long history had several changes to its style of dress, they being dressed in the uniform of **Dragoons** prior to 1828, when titled the *1st Regiment of Suffolk Yeomanry Cavalry,* dressed as **Lancers**, in c. 1846 when known as the *'Long Melford Troop'*, as **Heavy Dragoons** in 1876, when titled the *'Suffolk Yeomanry Cavalry'*, and as **Hussars** in 1885, when they became the *'Loyal Suffolk Hussars'.*[72]

During the war in South Africa, the regiment raised the 43rd and 44th Companies of the 12th Battalion Imperial Yeomanry (67).

Head-Dress c. 1828 and c. 1862

Sometime prior 1828 a leather helmet of the pre 1812 Light Dragoon pattern was worn (63), and c. 1865 a differing pattern of leather helmet was worn, this being before the adoption of the metal 'Albert' pattern helmet. The following is a brief description of the officers version of each of these pattern of helmet, regrettably however, there was no information available to the author regarding the other ranks version of either of these two pattern of helmets.

Officers Helmet Pre 1828

The Skull and Crest Holder

A black leather skull of Light Dragoon pattern, the peak edges being bound with **silver plated** metal. A **silver plated** metal high ornamental crest having a *Medusa's* head finial (facing forward) to the front of the crest, with a hole in the top of the crest to accommodate a plume. Across the front of the waist a scroll bearing the title *'1st Regiment Suffolk/Yeo. Cavalry'* (as spelt on scroll) (63), with just above the scroll, a black pleated silk turban with chains, having a rear rosette bearing a silver bullion tassel (83).

The Helmet Plate

An eight pointed rayed star, to the centre of which was a garter bearing the motto *'Honi.Soit.Qui.Mal.Y.Pense'*, and within the garter an intertwined 'G.R.' Royal Cypher all in silvered metal. The plate/badge appeared to be a one piece, die-struck item.

The Ear Rosettes, Chinscales, and Plume

Silvered quatrefoil 'ear bosses', being totally dissimilar to any previously referred to pattern of ear boss/rosette, having four flat scalloped 'terminals' of similar appearance to the scalloped scales on the chinscales, they being of silvered metal, backed with velvet (83). A falling red and white plume completed the helmet (63).

Officers Helmet c. 1862

The Skull and Plume Mount, and Lining
A black patent leather skull being similar in overall appearance to the 'Albert' pattern, the peak edges being bound with gilt metal. At either side of the skull was a thin gilt metal band, that ran from beneath the side terminal of the plume holder, and extended downwards behind the 'ear boss', to terminate under the outer edge of the peak binding. To the front of the skull was a similar band extending from beneath the front plume base terminal, down behind the crown that surmounted the escutcheon of the helmet plate.

The gilt metal plume holder was not of a standard pattern, being comprised of what appeared to be four flat terminals above which was a vented 'collar'. Upon the collar a small round ball surmounted by a flat sided fluted plume socket similar in appearance to the socket fitted to the plume holder illustrated in Fig: 25.H. No information was available to the author, regarding the type of head lining fitted to this helmet (84).

The Helmet Plate
In gilt metal, an escutcheon surmounted by a 'Victorian' crown being similar in general appearance to Type: Q crown. Upon the escutcheon an intertwined Royal Cypher of 'V.R.' with a single scroll beneath the cypher bearing the title '*Suffolk*'. The plate/badge appeared to be of one piece (84).

The Ear Rosettes and Chinchain
Gilt metal 'lions head' ear bosses, with the gilt metal chinchain being mounted upon leather, and backed with velvet.

The Plume
A red horsehair plume being similar in appearance to the post 1871 Household Cavalry pattern, complete with the small gilt screw-on ball. No information was available to the author, regarding the pattern of plume rosette fitted.

Officers Helmet c. 1876-1883

The Skull and Plume Mount
A gilt metal 'Albert' pattern skull having the front waist and rear seam bands of Type: K., with both peak edges being bound with gilt metal, the inner peaks being lined with skiver. What was unusual about this helmet, is that both peaks were **without the foliated gilt metal strips** normally associated with this pattern of skull. The gilt metal plume holder was of Type: I., having seven finials. N.B. It is of interest that this pattern of helmet was adopted by the regiment, when in the regular cavalry this style of helmet was now obsolete.

The Head Lining
The head lining was of leather with a silk upper section.

The Helmet Plate
The standard 'Albert' pattern wreath, and rococo shield surmounted by a large crown of Type: M., all in gilt metal. To the centre of the shield, was a silvered, eight pointed hobnailed star, upon which was mounted the die-struck centre device. This consisted of a gilt metal strap, bearing the title '*Suffolk Yeomanry Cavalry*', with an intertwined 'V.R.' Royal Cypher within the strap. The plate/badge was made up of three separate pieces, these being the wreath/shield/crown, the star, and the centre device.

The Ear Rosettes and Chinchain
Large, gilt metal, 'Albert' pattern ear rosettes of the type illustrated in Fig: 9.G., with the one-inch wide gilt metal chinchain being backed with black or red leather.

The Plume and Rosette
A white horsehair 'Albert' pattern plume, complete with white horsehair 'brush', capped by a medium sized gilt metal rosette of the pattern illustrated in Fig: 9.C.[74]

Other Ranks Helmet c. 1876-1883

The Skull, Plume Holder, Ear Rosettes, and Chinchain
As for the officers helmet, being a brass, standard pattern 'Albert' skull, and like the officers pattern helmet, being **without the foliated metal strips to the peaks.** All other fittings, including the plume holder (with finials), the large sized ear rosettes, and the leather backed chinchain being in brass.

The Helmet Plate, and The Plume
The helmet plate was as for the officers helmet, except substitute brass for gilt metal, and white metal for silvered metal. The plume was as for the officers pattern, with a medium sized brass rosette. No information was available to the author, regarding the colour of plumes fitted to the helmets of the musicians in the regimental band. N.B. There was a pair of flat blades to the reverse of the crown of the helmet plate.

O.R.'s Full Dress Uniform c. 1883

A dark green tunic having scarlet facings, the pantaloons also being dark green with a double yellow stripe. N.B. In Ron Harris's booklet on Yeomanry Drum Banners and Mounted Bands (62), he refers to 'a glorious green and gold uniform, a reminder of the ten years 1868-1878, when the regiment had a **green dragoon** uniform'. Regimental Headquarters 1914: Bury St. Edmunds, Suffolk.

The 1st Sussex Light Horse Volunteers

Very little is known of this Troop of volunteer light horse that was raised in August 1871, having its headquarters at Brighton, Sussex. It is however recorded that the Corps were present at the Grand Volunteer Review, held near Brighton on Easter Monday, the 1st of April 1872, the Corps being under the command of Captain F.S. Shenstone, where they formed part of the cavalry of the Lewes Force together with a squadron of the 19th Hussars. Whilst they are described as wearing blue uniforms at this review, no other uniform information appears to have been recorded. This short lived Troop was disbanded in June 1875 (85). N.B. An authoritative and respected source on the light horse volunteers states that the tunic was in fact red, with dark blue facings (100).

The following limited information relating the head-dress of this Corps, is based on a photograph of a helmet, and an actual example seen by the author in a private collection. However, as neither the example in the photograph, nor the helmet in the private collection, was identified as being either an officers or an other ranks pattern helmet, the description given is based on the assumption that the helmets concerned were of officers quality.

Helmet c. 1871-1875 (See Fig: 59.)

The Skull and Plume Holder
The silvered/white metal skull was similar in appearance to that of the 1871 pattern, **but having the 'Albert' pattern leaf and scroll band round the waist** in gilt metal, with a gilt metal oak-leaf band covering the rear seam. The peak edges were also bound with gilt metal. The plume holder was most distinctive consisting of a **six-sided tapering fluted socket above a floriated base** of the 'Albert' pattern all in gilt metal, and similar to the pattern illustrated in Fig: 25. H.

The Head Lining
No information was available on the type of head lining fitted to this particular helmet.

The Helmet Plate
The pattern of helmet plate fitted to this helmet was quite unique, being an eight pointed rayed star, having **predominantly flat rays**, the uppermost point being displaced by a medium sized 'Victorian' crown, being similar, but not identical to crown previously referred to as Type: Q. Upon the rayed star, a strap bearing the motto *'Per Saxa Per Igness'*, and within the strap, an intertwined monogram of *'SLH*, the whole in gilt metal. No information was available to the author on the number of component parts that made up this particular helmet plate. N.B. This particular pattern of star with its flat rays, coupled with the style of crown, was very similar to that fitted to the blue cloth helmet of infantry officers c. 1900.

The Ear Rosettes and Chinchain
Medium sized gilt metal rosettes (pattern not identified), with the right hand rosette having a hook, which hung down from, and was secured behind its lowest petal, onto which to secure the 'loose' end of the gilt metal chinchain.

The Plume and Rosette
The plume appeared to be of 1871 pattern in white horsehair, being capped with a medium sized gilt metal rosette, similar to the ear rosette illustrated in Fig: 9.I., this being the pattern of rosette fitted to the officers plumes, of the 7th Dragoon Guards, of the post 1871 period.

The Sussex Yeomanry

On the 4th June 1901 His Majesty, King Edward VII gave his approval for a regiment of yeomanry to be formed within the county, the name of this regiment to be the *'Regiment of Sussex Imperial Yeomanry'*, they being officially accepted on the 11th June 1901. The regiment was gazetted ten days later with Lieutenant Colonel Lord Leconfield, late of the First Life Guards being appointed as its

Figure 59: Sussex Light Horse helmet c. 1871-75. Of particular interest is the most unusual pattern of plume holder, and the style of the helmet plate. Note: The original of this photograph has been reproduced in reverse order. Photo: Courtesy of R.G. Harris.

commanding officer, with the headquarters of the newly formed regiment being established at No. 10 Great College Street, Brighton, Sussex.[74a]

Recruiting for the newly formed regiment commenced at the Regimental Headquarters on 1st October 1901, and in just over six months 69 men had joined, and had been sent South Africa to join the various Yeomanry Companies serving there (85), including the 69th Company of the 7th Battalion Imperial Yeomanry. N.B. The word 'Imperial' was dropped from the regiments title in 1908 (63).

This newly formed regiment, was by no means the first corps of volunteer cavalry to be raised within the County of Sussex, there having been four Troops raised as early as 1794, under the combined title of the *'Sussex Troops of Gentlemen and Yeomanry'*, the acceptance date being given as 23rd June 1794 (89).

In 1802 most of the volunteer corps in the County were disbanded, but upon war breaking out in 1803 the disbanded corps were revived, with several new ones being raised, and by 1805 there were no less than ten Troops within the County. However as in most other counties, disbandment frequently occurred, and by 1817 only the Lewes Troop, and the Midhurst Troop still existed.

The year 1831 saw the Arundel and Bramber Yeomanry Cavalry being raised, the members of this troop wearing a uniform that comprised a shako with hair plume, a blue coloured Light Dragoon style jacket, and white overalls. This Troop existed for some seventeen years before being disbanded in 1848 (85).

With regard to this regiments head-dress of the post 1901 period, the author has no knowledge of the existence of an other ranks pattern, full dress helmet, nor of such a helmet ever being issued to the other ranks, the form of head-dress normally worn by the rank and file when in full dress, being the slouch hat with a feather plume. It would therefore appear, that this pattern of full dress head-dress was only worn by the officers of the regiment on special occasion such as the 1937 Coronation, and at levees etc.[75]

The following description of this most impressive officers pattern helmet, is based on two fine photographs that appear in the Ogilby Trust booklet on this regiment (85), on an illustration of this helmet in W.Y. Carman's book on Yeomanry Headdress (63), and on an actual example seen by the author at an auction house salesroom in 1984.

Officers Helmet c. 1909-1937

The Skull and Plume Holder

A silvered metal 1871 pattern skull, the peak edges being bound with gilt metal, the inner peaks being lined with skiver. The front waist band, and rear seam band were of Type: L., and were also in gilt metal. The plume holder was the pattern as fitted to the officers helmet of the 2nd Dragoon Guards, as illustrated in Fig: 25.B., having a medium sized oval shaped ball beneath the fluted socket all in gilt metal.[76]

The Head Lining

On the only example of this helmet seen by the author, the head lining was of brown quilted cloth.

The Helmet Plate

This impressive helmet plate, was comprised of a gilt metal twelve pointed rayed star, upon which was an elliptical shaped band, also in gilt metal. The band bore the title *'Sussex Yeomanry'*, and within the band on a gilt ground, *'The County Arms of Sussex'*, in frosted silver, this being a shield bearing six martlets, with the shield being surmounted by a small 'King's' crown of Type: R. The plate/badge was comprised of four separate pieces, these being the rayed star, the elliptical band, the gilt ground, and the shield/crown.

The Ear Rosettes and Chinchain

On the example of this helmet seen by the author, the ear rosettes were of the other ranks pattern (Type: 9.K.), and had been gilded, with the chinchain having gilt metal links, and being backed with leather. N.B. This particular chinchain appeared to be a replacement item.

The Plume and Rosette

The plume colour was unique to the regiment, being of the 1871 pattern with yellow over dark blue horsehair,[77] capped by a gilt metal rosette (type unknown). N.B. Although c. 1912 the regiment did have a band, they appear not to have worn the full dress helmet (85).

O.R.'s Full Dress Uniform c. 1909

A dark blue tunic with dark blue facings, the overalls also being dark blue with a single yellow stripe. Regimental Headquarters 1914: The Drill Hall, Church Street, Brighton, Sussex.

The Westminster Dragoons

Following the several military reversals experienced by the British Army during the early stages of the war in South Africa, the British Government decided to raise a body of volunteer mounted marksmen, who could 'ride and shoot', to combat the guerilla war tactics employed by the Boers, and to in effect 'beat them at their own game'.

This decision resulted in the creation of several new yeomanry regiments, amongst which were three from the London area, they being titled the City of London Yeomanry (Rough Riders), whose full dress uniform was that of a Lancer regiment, the 3rd County of London (Sharpshooters) Imperial Yeomanry, who were styled as Hussars, and the 2nd County of London Imperial Yeomanry (Westminster Dragoons), whose full dress was basically a Dragoon uniform. N.B. All of three of these London regiments were officially accepted on the 18th July 1901 (89).

The first Commanding Officer of the newly formed Westminster Dragoons was Lieutenant Colonel Charles Rosedew Burn, late of the 1st (Royal) Dragoons, with his second in command being Major J.M. Rogers, also late of the 'Royals'. In view of this connection with the 1st Dragoons, it is hardly surprising that when the time came to consider what pattern of full dress was to be adopted by the new regiment, that the style chosen closely resembled that worn by Lieutenant Colonel Burn's former regiment.

Although not raised until 1901, the regiment provided men for the 35th, 38th, and 39th Battalions of Imperial Yeomanry' who saw service during the Boer War, the regiment being granted the battle honour *'South Africa 1902'* (86).

Officers Helmet c. 1902

The Skull and Plume Holder

A silver plated, or alternatively best quality white metal 1871 pattern skull, the peak edges being bound with gilt metal, with the inner peaks being lined with green skiver. The front waist, and rear seam bands were of Type: L., both being in **frosted** gilt metal. The plume holder was of the pattern illustrated in Fig: 25.A., and was in burnished (bright) gilt metal.

The Head Lining

The head lining was of quilted beige cloth, although it is known that soft leather was also used.

The Helmet Plate

A burnished, gilt metal twelve pointed rayed star, upon which was the centre device, consisting of a white metal garter bearing the motto *'Honi Soit Qui Mal Y Pense'*, being surmounted by a small white metal 'King's' crown of Type: R. Within the garter the 'Prince of Wales's' feathers in gilt metal on a white metal ground. To the lower left of the garter a white metal label bearing *'2nd County'*, and to the lower right of the garter a similar label bearing *'of London'*. The plate/badge was comprised of three separate pieces, these being the rayed plate, the garter/crown/labels/ground, and the Prince of Wales's feathers. N.B. It is not recorded if the gilt letters 'I.Y.' as described below for the post 1903 pattern plate were fitted to the c. 1902 example, which incidentally is one of the most rare pattern of helmet plate.

The Ear Rosettes and Chinchain

Medium sized, gilt metal ear rosettes of the type illustrated in Fig: 9.J., with a three quarters of an inch wide, gilt metal chinchain mounted upon leather, being backed with black velvet.

The Plume and Rosette

A **purple** 1871 pattern horsehair plume, capped with a small gilt metal rosette of Type: 9.E.

Other Ranks Helmet c. 1902

The Skull, Plume Holder, Ear Rosettes, and Chinchain

A white metal 1871 pattern skull, with all fittings including the plume holder which was of Type: 25.A., being in brass. On the other ranks helmet only the front inner peak was lined with skiver. Brass ear rosettes of the same pattern as for the officers helmet, with the brass chinchain being backed with **black leather.**

The Helmet Plate and Plume

As for the officers pattern except, substitute brass for gilt metal. A purple 1871 pattern horsehair plume, with the standard other ranks pattern rosette in brass.

Officers and Other Ranks Helmet Post 1903-1911

All details as for the c. 1902 pattern helmet, the only noticeable change being to the helmet plate, where the 'Prince of Wales's' feathers were replaced by a gilt metal numeral ***'2'***, (brass for the other ranks). Additionally, mounted upon the rayed star, and positioned immediately below, and between the inner ends of each of the white metal labels, the letters *'I.Y.'* in gilt metal, (again brass for the other ranks). The plate/badge consisted of four separate pieces, these being the rayed star, the garter/crown/labels/ground, the numeral '2', and the letters 'I.Y.'. See Fig: 60. for an illustration of the other ranks pattern helmet.

Plume - All Ranks c. 1911

In 1911 the purple plume, which had a tendency to fade and lose its colour was replaced by a white one.[78] N.B. On an officers pattern plume in the author's collection the plume stem is stamped '2CL' (2nd County London).

O.R.'s Full Dress Uniform c. 1903

A scarlet tunic with purple facings, the pantaloons being dark blue with a single yellow stripe[79]. Regimental Headquarters 1914: Elverton Street, Westminster, S.W. London.

Figure 60: Westminster Dragoons other ranks pattern c. 1903-1911. Note the unique purple coloured plume, and the letters I.Y. attached to the labels on the helmet plate. Author's collection. Photo: Author.

Figure 60a: A sergeant of the Westminster Dragoons in mounted review order. Note the post 1911 white horsehair plume fitted to the helmet. Photo: Courtesy of R.G. Harris.

1st West Yorkshire Yeomanry Cavalry

The 1st West Yorkshire Yeomanry Cavalry, later to be titled the **Yorkshire Dragoons** can trace their ancestry back to the *'1st or Southern Regiment of West Riding Yeomanry '* formed in 1794, and officially accepted on the 13th August 1794 (89). However following the Peace of Amiens in 1802, disbandment of the regiment occurred, only for them to be re-raised some seventeen months later on the 15th August 1803. By the year 1821 the regiment was known as *'The Southern Regiment of West York Yeomanry'*, this title being retained until 1844, when the regiment adopted the title *'The 1st West Yorkshire Yeomanry Cavalry'* (54).

A further change of title occurred in 1889 when under 'Army Order 184 of April 1889', the title of the regiment became the *'Yorkshire Dragoons Regiment of Yeomanry Cavalry'*, approval for the new title having been given by Her Majesty Queen Victoria. It was at this period that the regiments full dress uniform changed to closely resemble that of the 6th Dragoon Guards (Carabiniers), the tunic being dark blue in colour with white facings, with the overalls also being dark blue, and having a double white stripe. N.B. The most noticeable difference between these two regiments was probably the colour of the metal used for the full dress helmet.

Following their escort duty to Queen Victoria when she visited the City of Sheffield in 1897, the regiment's title was again changed, this time to ***'The Yorkshire Dragoons (Queen's Own) Yeomanry Cavalry'***, this being under Army Order 94 of the 1st July 1897 (54).

During the war in South Africa the regiment provided officers and men for the 11th, 66th, and 109th Companies of the Imperial Yeomanry (54).

N.B. Of particular interest, is the fact that this regiment had the unique distinction of having a **commissioned officer** holding the post of Field (or Commanding Officers) Trumpeter[80] (62).

Officers Helmet c. 1876-1889

The Skull and Plume Mount

A **silver plated** skull, or alternatively one of best quality white metal, in the style of the 1871 pattern helmet with the peak edges bound with like metal, with both inner peaks being lined with green skiver. The waist band was similar to the 'Albert' pattern band as it completely encircled the waist, it differed however, in that it was of a **unique** regimental pattern of silvered **rose-leaves**. The band covering the rear seam was also of special pattern, being one inch in width and of also of **rose-leaf** pattern. The silvered metal plume holder was of Type: J., being the pattern without finials. N.B. The peaks on this pattern of helmet did **not have the foliated metal strips.**

The Head Lining

The head lining was of either of ribbed pattern quilted cloth, being beige in colour, and having a single tying cord, of quilted cotton and silk, or entirely of quilted silk.

The Helmet Plate

The helmet plate was of a unique regimental pattern consisting of a silvered metal wreath comprised **entirely of rose-leaves**, being surmounted by a small sized silvered 'Victorian' crown of Type: Q. To the centre of the wreath, a silvered eight pointed **hobnailed** star upon which was mounted an oval strap bearing the title *'1st West Yorkshire'*. Also upon the star, and surrounding the lower half of the strap, were two semi-circular labels, the left label bearing the word *'Yeomanry'*, with the right label bearing the word *'Cavalry'*, the whole in gilt metal. To the centre of the oval strap, a silvered 'Yorkshire' rose on a gilt metal ground. The plate/badge was comprised of four separate pieces, these being the wreath/crown, the star, the strap/labels/ground, and the silvered rose. N.B. The wreath/crown was most unusual, in that it was a **cast item**, being much heavier, and more solid than the 'Albert' pattern die-struck wreath/crown/shield, and therefore less prone to accidental damage when being cleaned.

The Ear Rosettes and Chinchain

The silvered metal ear rosettes were of the pattern illustrated in Fig: 9.K. with burnished highlights, with one rosette having a small silvered 'ring' secured to its lower petals, onto which was attached the last link of one end of the chinchain. The opposite rosette had a small silvered hook which hung down, and was secured beneath its lower petals, onto which would be attached the 'loose' end of the chinchain.[81] The chinchain itself was of silvered metal, being three quarters of an inch wide mounted upon leather, and backed with black velvet.

The Plume and Rosette

A white falling horsehair plume supported by a white horsehair 'brush' of the 'Albert' pattern, capped with a silvered metal rosette (pattern unknown).

Other Ranks Helmet c. 1876-1889

As for the officers pattern, but substitute white metal for silver, and brass for gilt, with the head lining being of leather, with the **narrow width** silvered chinchain also being leather backed. N.B. In an illustration of a dismounted sergeant in review order, that appeared in the Ogilby Trust booklet on this regiment (54), both the brush and the base of the flowing 'Albert' pattern plume appear to be bound around the centre.

O.R.'s Full Dress Uniform c. 1876

A dark blue tunic without facings, the dark blue overalls having double white stripes[82] (54).

2nd West Yorkshire Yeomanry Cavalry

In his article on the Yorkshire Yeomanry, W.Y. Carman records that *'The 2nd West Yorkshire Yeomanry (Prince of Wales's Own)'* might claim the troop raised in May 1798 as its ancestor', and further advises that 'a Troop was raised in the same month at Huddersfield, but both were disbanded in 1802' (93). N.B. In 1817 the Huddersfield squadron was re-raised, only to be disbanded again in 1826.

A Troop was raised in 1843 at Morley, with another being formed at Agbrigg, with the title *'2nd West Yorkshire Yeomanry Cavalry'* being adopted in 1844. The distinction of *'Prince of Wales's Own'* was added to the regimental title in 1884 (93).

The regiment was finally disbanded in 1894 when a fourth 'D' squadron of the **Yorkshire Dragoons** was formed, consisting of three Troops based at the following locations. 'A' Troop at Huddersfield, 'B' Troop at Halifax, and 'C' Troop at Bradford (54).

Officers Helmet c. 1853/54-1889 (63)

The Skull and Plume Holder
A **silver plated** metal skull of the 'Albert' pattern, having both peak edges decorated with gilt metal foliated strips, the inner peaks being lined with green skiver. The waist and rear seam bands were also in gilt metal and of Type: K. The gilt metal plume holder was of the 'Albert' pattern Type: I. complete with finials.

The Head Lining
The head lining was of beige quilted cloth, or alternatively of silk.

The Helmet Plate
In gilt metal, the standard pattern 'Albert' wreath and rococo shield surmounted by a crown of Type: M. To the centre of the wreath a silvered eight pointed **hobnailed** star, upon which was mounted a gilt metal circular strap bearing the title '2nd West Yorkshire Yeomanry'. Within the strap, a silver plated metal 'Yorkshire' rose. The plate/badge consisted of four separate pieces, these being the wreath/shield/crown, the star, the circular strap, and the rose.

The Ear Rosettes and Chinchain
The helmet was fitted with special pattern gilt metal **lion's head** bosses, being not dissimilar to the type fitted to British Lancer caps, and being similar, if not identical to the bosses fitted to some of the officers pattern helmets of the North Somerset Yeomanry. A gilt metal, one-inch wide chinchain backed with black leather, or alternatively mounted upon black leather, and backed with black velvet.

The Plume and Rosette
A black 'Albert' pattern hanging horsehair plume surmounting a black horsehair 'brush', being capped by a medium sized gilt metal rosette, similar to that illustrated in Fig: 9.C., or alternatively Type: 9.I[83]. N.B. Late pattern helmets appear to have been fitted with **white** 'Albert' pattern horsehair plumes.

Other Ranks Helmet

All details as described for the officers pattern, except that the skull was of steel/white metal, and all fittings were in brass. The helmet plate was of brass/copper and white metal. The helmet was fitted with a leather head lining, and a leather backed brass chinchain. Plume as per officers, but with standard other ranks pattern brass rosette.

O.R.'s Full Dress Uniform c. 1889

A dark blue tunic, with the facings thought to have been white. Dark blue pantaloons with a double white stripe.

Yorkshire Dragoons

Officers Helmet c. 1889-1904 (See Fig: 61.)

All details as previously given for the 1st West Yorkshire Yeomanry except for the following highlighted changes.

The Helmet Plate (See Fig: 61A.)
A silvered metal wreath comprised of rose leaves surmounted by a small 'Victorian' crown of Type: Q. To the centre of the wreath a silvered eight pointed **diamond-cut** star upon which was mounted a gilt metal **garter bearing the motto *'Honi Soit Qui Mal Y Pense'*.** Also upon the star, and surrounding the lower half of the strap, two semi-circular labels, the left bearing **Yorkshire'**, with the right label bearing ***'Dragoons'***, all in gilt metal. Within the garter a silvered 'Yorkshire' rose. The plate/badge was as for the 1st West Yorkshire helmet plate.

The Ear Rosettes (See Fig: 61C.)
The pattern of ear rosettes remained unchanged except that the 'ring' and hook were discontinued, with the chinchain now being attached to the ear rosette socket.

Other Ranks Helmet c. 1899-1904
The following details have been compiled from information gathered by examining illustrations of helmets contained in auction sale catalogues.

The Skull and Plume Holder
White metal skull of 1871 pattern, having the rose pattern front waist band and rear seam band, **or alternatively having the laurel-leaf pattern front waist band, and the oak-leaf rear seam band** previously referred to as Type: L. in white metal. Sometime after 1899 the white metal plume holder changed to one of the 1871 pattern as illustrated in Fig: 25.A,[84] with the plume changing to one of the same pattern. Musicians of the band wore the same colour plume as the rest of the regiment.

The Helmet Plate
A crowned white metal wreath as for the 1st West Yorkshire Yeomanry. To the centre of the wreath a white metal eight pointed hobnailed star upon which was mounted a brass strap bearing the title 'Yorkshire Dragoons', and within the strap on a brass ground a white metal rose[85]. Plate/badge: as for 1st West Yorks. N.B. Although not confirmed, it is possible that the centre device consisting of the strap/rose/backing on the other ranks helmet plate was a one piece die-struck fitment.

Officers Helmet c. 1904

In 1904, the 1871 pattern plume holder replaced the earlier 'Albert' version, with the plume also changing to the later' pattern, with the silvered metal plume rosette being either Type: 9.C., or alternatively of Type: 9.E. The crown that surmounted the wreath on the helmet plate also changed from the 'Victorian' crown to a 'medium sized King's' crown.[86] N.B. The alteration to the crown was achieved at a much slower rate that the change of plume holder as illustrated in Fig: 61., which shows the helmet having the 1871 pattern plume holder, but retaining the 'Victorian' pattern crown. Indeed in the booklet by L. Barlow and R.J. Smith (54) it states 'It is doubtful whether the updating of the inscription on the plates was completed throughout the Regiment before 1914'.

The following additional minor changes were also noted by the author when examining actual examples of officers Post 1904 period helmets: the rose

Figure 61: Yorkshire Dragoons officers pattern helmet with officers pattern plume c. 1897-1904. It is of particular interest that although having the 1871 pattern plume holder adopted c. 1904, the helmet plate still has the 'Victorian' pattern crown. Author's collection. Photo: R. Biondi

HONI SOIT QUI MAL Y PENSE
YORKSHIRE DRAGOONS

Opposite, Figure 61a: Close up view of the helmet plate in which can be seen the unique rose pattern wreath surrounding the centre device.

Figure 61b: Offset view of the helmet in which can be seen the rose pattern waist band.

Figure 61c: Side view of helmet showing the silvered ear rosette. This pattern of rosette, but in brass, is the version fitted to the other ranks helmets of both the Dragoon Guards and the 1st and 6th Dragoons.

Figure 61d: Rear view of helmet showing the regimental pattern rear seam band consisting of rose leaves.

pattern front waist band, and the similar pattern rear seam band were both in frosted silver, although it is likely that this was the case on earlier pattern skulls, and that the frosting effect had become worn with age. The head lining was now of brown quilted cloth, with the chinchain being backed with black leather.

O.R.'s Full Dress Uniform c. 1902

A dark blue tunic having white facings, the pantaloons also being dark blue with a double white stripe. Regimental Headquarters 1914: Doncaster, Yorkshire.

NOTES

[1] In 1794 Abingdon was within the borders of the Royal County of Berkshire, but of recent years following a review of, and change to certain county boundaries, it is now within the County of Oxfordshire.

[2] Apparently from 1860 to 1864 a corps/regiment named the Derbyshire Mounted Volunteers existed. I have no knowledge of their history or their uniforms, I do however have details of their full dress helmet plate which consisted of the 'Albert' pattern oak and olive wreath surrounding a rococo shield surmounted by a crown of Type: M. Upon the shield a hobnailed star, with the centre device being an oval strap bearing the title *"Derbyshire Mounted Volunteers"*, and within the strap an unusual shaped 'shield' with a sideways-on triangular shape to its centre.

[3] These large pattern ear rosettes were the version with the proud (raised) centre.

[4] It has been recorded that on an early pattern plume the 'brush' was white in colour instead of the more usual red, and it is known that there also exists another early version, having a full red, beneath a falling white plume without the 'brush' normally associated with the 'Albert' pattern plume.

[5] A known supplier of the other ranks helmet during the late Victorian period was Harry Lyons Contractor, 12 Ritter Street, Woolwich, London.

[6] It is reasonable to expect that upon King Edward VII's accession to the throne, that the Royal Cypher on the helmet would have changed to ER VII, however I could find no record, either photographic or written of this change having ever taken place on either the officers or the other ranks helmets.

[7] The Staffordshire Yeomanry are known to have worn an 'Albert' pattern helmet having a leather skull c. 1850.

[8] This pattern helmet did not have the foliated metal strips to the edges of the front and rear peaks, that was usually to be found on an 'Albert' pattern helmet.

[9] On all officers pattern helmets of this regiment examined by the author, the plume was of an other ranks pattern. However in the booklet of this regiment produced by the Ogilby Trust (58) there is on page 12, a copy photograph of two seated officers of the regiment holding their helmets, and the plume rosette shown in this photograph appears to be of the pattern illustrated in Fig: 9.C., or possibly similar to the ear rosette Type: 9.I.

[10] On an other ranks helmet sold in a Buckinghamshire salesroom in 1995 the right hand ear rosette had a hook onto which to hang the 'loose' end of the chinchain.

[11] A photograph of the officers of the West Essex Yeomanry taken in 1874 shows that this regiment had adopted the full dress uniform of a hussar regiment.

[12] *"Audacter et sincere"* - translation: Boldly and truly.

[13] The author is of the opinion that this helmet was a trial pattern for a senior N.C.O. as whilst the skull, lining, and plume were of other ranks quality, the centre device was not of one piece (die-struck), but had the shield in white metal being applied to the strap/ground being similar in appearance to the centre device on the officers pattern helmet plate c. 1911.

[14] Another known supplier of the other ranks helmet prior to the outbreak of the First World War was Messr J. Compton and Sons Limited.

[15] *"Decus et tutamen"* - translation: An ornament and a safeguard.

[16] *"Pro aris et focis"* - translation: For hearth and home.

[17] A photograph taken of a group of officers attending the 1911 Coronation (69), includes an officer of the Fife and Forfar Yeomanry, which clearly shows him wearing the helmet of the former Fife Light Horse.

[18] For undress, wear a gilt metal, leaf pattern top-spike was worn by the officers, the spike being secured to the helmet in a similar manner as for the hair, or feather plume.

[19] *"Nemo me impune lacessit"* - translation: No one invokes me with impunity (75).

[20] The 'Albert' pattern helmet appears to have been the last pattern of full dress head-dress for the officers of this regiment, and was worn up until the abolition of the full dress uniform. However the author has neither seen, nor heard of the existence of an officers helmet plate bearing the 'King's' crown.

[21] Lieutenant Colonel the Hon H.G.L. Crichton commanded the regiment from the 16th January 1884, and died in 1922. His full dress helmet was sold at a Sussex auction salesroom in January 1984 (100 years after he assumed command of his regiment).

[22] In 1914 the four squadrons were based as follows. A: Portsmouth. Isle of Wight. Petersfield and Tichfield Troops. B: Winchester and Alton. Aldershot and Farnborough. Basingstoke and Bishop Waltham Troops. C: 1st Southampton. 2nd Southampton. Romsey. Andover and Eastleigh Troops. D: 1st Bournemouth. 2nd Bournemouth. Burley (Ringwood). Highcliffe. Stuckton (Ford) and Beaulieu Troops (71).

[23] The noted author R.G. Harris in his book on the Yeomanry Regiments (72) states *'White horsehair plumes had been authorised in 1894'*. In view of this statement it is quite possible that the plume holder was not fitted prior to 1894, and that a spike of Type: 25.F. was worn in its place, although this has not been confirmed.

[24] In his article (70) on this regiment Ron Harris states that 'Although the Carabiniers designation replaced the word Yeomanry in the regimental title, it was quite common to find the old wording on helmets up to as late as 1914'.

[24a] The 'wings' of the plume socket on this version of holder were narrower, than on the standard pattern plume holder that is illustrated in Fig: 25.A.

[25] In his excellent book on the Hertfordshire Yeomanry (73) J.D. Sainsbury mentions that a white over red feather plume was worn by the rank and file, although the wearing of this plume was unauthorised.

[26] The plume socket had a 'key' at the base of its stem and was secured by the method described in chapter five. Whilst this socket was very similar to the standard 1871 pattern as illustrated in Fig: 25.A., the pronounced lip was absent from its lowest part, where it joined the plume base. (See Fig: 55.) N.B. There was more than one version of this socket fitted to the helmet.

[27] The only example of a Post 1902 pattern helmet of this regiment seen by the author is on a photograph in the archives of the National Army Museum where the 'King's' crown was not joined to the rococo shield, but was a separate piece mounted just above the top of the shield.

[28] Both the examples of this particular pattern helmet known to the author are officers pattern helmets.

[29] This helmet plate is similar in appearance to the plate once worn on the blue cloth helmet of the Royal Artillery, being minus their gun, but with the addition of the Imperial Yeomanry scrolls.

[30] On the helmet displayed at the Aldershot Military Museum the gilt metal ear rosettes were of the pattern illustrated in Fig: 9.I.

[31] A helmet plate of this regiment also exists with the title *"Lancashire Mounted Rifle Volunteers" (58)*.

[32] The name Hope/Hopetoun has been associated with the West Lothian area for many generations, with V.A.J. Hope (the 2nd Marquis of Linlithgow) having served in the Lothians and Border Horse c. 1908. See Fig: 56. for an illustration of his helmet.

[33] On an officers pattern helmet sold at a Sussex auction house salesroom in 1979 the plume holder fitted was not as described above, but was of the pattern illustrated in Fig: 25.A. It is not known whether this plume holder was a replacement fitment or not.

[34] The title on the helmet plate of this regiment was inscribed on four scrolls as follows: Royal (upper left). Midlothian (upper right). Yeomanry (lower left). Cavalry (lower right), the scrolls being superimposed upon the lower ends of the thistle wreath that surrounded the *"Order of the Thistle"*.

[35] The title on this regiments helmet plate was also on four scrolls reading as follows: East (upper left). Lothian (upper right). Yeomanry (lower left). Cavalry (lower right) the scrolls being mounted as described above.

[36] On an other ranks helmet examined by the author (thought to have been a warrant officers pattern), the plume socket had a square base which passed through a ventilated collet that was permanently secured to the inner crown of the skull, where a bend over tab at the base of the 'square' socket was flattened against the collet to secure this fitment in place.

[37] With regard to the scrolls on the helmet plate, the author has neither seen, nor heard of the existence of a helmet plate bearing the word *'Imperial'* within its title, and therefore concludes that the scrolls remained unchanged until c. 1908.

[38] The Williams Wynn family connection with command of the regiment can be traced back many generations, with Charles W. Williams Wynn handing over command to Sir Watkin Williams Wynn Bt in 1844, who in turn handed over to Charles Watkin Williams Wynn in 1877. There was a then a short break in the family command in 1878 for some eleven years, before Sir H.L. Watkin Williams Bt, C.B., took command in 1889, he being succeeded by his brother R.W. Williams Wynn, D.S.O. in 1906, who commanded the regiment until 1916 (77) .

[39] This particular helmet did not have the foliated strips to the front and rear peaks as was usual on most helmets of this pattern.

[40] That this pattern of plume holder was fitted to a helmet worn c. 1856-66 raises the questions, is it possible that the yeomanry adopted a new pattern fitment before the regular cavalry ?, or is the date 1871 which is generally accepted as being the year when the Household Cavalry adopted the last pattern helmet inaccurate by a few years ?. These are interesting questions, which must regrettably for the present, remain unanswered.

[41] *"Anorchfygol"* - translation: Unconquerable.

[42] With regard to the white boss on the front of the busby, Philip J. Haythornthwaite when referring to this boss records that *'It is evident from photographs of Lieut. Sir William Grenville Williams Bt., and Lieut. Thomas W. Gill, apparently taken at the annual training in October 1868, that the boss was not present on officers busbies' (77)*.

[43] It would seem reasonable to assume that as the skull and all fittings on this helmet were either **silvered or in white metal**, that the plume rosette would have been in the same colour metal. However on all the helmets of this regiment seen by the author, including one in my own collection, the plume rosette was of **gilt metal** for the officers, and of brass for the other ranks.

[44] The adoption of a Dragoon style of full dress uniform is apparently due to the one time Adjutant, Captain A.G. Fife. This officer who was serving with the 6th Dragoon Guards at the time, was appointed Adjutant to the Montgomeryshire Yeomanry on May 6th 1882, and carried out much needed reform in the uniforms *'which at that time was neither Hussar nor Dragoon'. 'Under the sanction of the War Office **a white metal dragoon helmet, with a spike** modeled on that of Captain Fife's Regiment, the Carabiniers, was introduced, but no plume was worn' (78)*.

[45] An interesting tale regarding this regiments helmet was told to me many years ago by a friend which is worthy of repeating here. Apparently, although the Great War was brewing, *'The Kaiser was a regular guest of Edward VII at Sandringham* (Norfolk), and *both monarchs being keen on sailing they raced against each other off the Norfolk coast'. 'One evening after dinner, the Kaiser suggested that King Edward should form a troop of Yeomanry from the male employees on the Sandringham estate. When the King agreed to do so the Kaiser sketched out a Germanic design for the helmets of this* (proposed) *Troop on the tablecloth, and based on this design they were duly made and issued'. The tablecloth drawing is believed to still exist* (79).

[46] The regimental title changed to *'The King's Own Royal Regiment, Norfolk Imperial Yeomanry'* during the closing stages of 1905, and King Edward VII became its **Colonel-in-Chief** (56).

[47] As at the 26th July 1901 the squadrons were based at the following locations. A Squadron: Norwich and district. B Squadron: North-east Norfolk. C Squadron: West Norfolk. D Squadron: South Norfolk. (56)

[48] Upon his accession to the Norwegian throne, H.R.H. Prince Frederick assumed the title King Haakon VII of Norway and was subsequently appointed Honorary Colonel of the Regiment. N.B. He had been previously been Honorary Lieutenant Colonel (56).

[49] Early in 1905 sample helmets of the basic 'Albert' pattern were made up by Messrs Hawkes & Co, Piccadilly, London, and in May 1905, 22 officers pattern and 525 other ranks pattern helmets were supplied to the regiment (56).

[50] On a sergeants helmet that sold in a Sussex auction salesroom in 1980, the helmet was fitted with a plume having a medium sized rosette being similar in appearance to the rosette fitted to the officers plume.

[51] In the Ogilby Trust booklet (56) it states that: *'examples of officers helmets bearing GRV cypher badges, dating them c. 1911-14 both with and* ***without*** *the title scrolls are known'*. It also states that *'the author is not aware of any* ***O.R.*** *pattern helmets with the GR cypher'*.

[52] It is recorded that in 1906, included in the cost of an other ranks full dress uniform were the following items:

Helmet with furniture	£1.0.0.
Helmet, spike and chains sets	£0.4.0.
Helmet, plume	£0.4.0.
Dress frock, lined	£0.16.6.
Overalls with yellow stripes	£0.17.6
Breeches	£1.2.6.(56).

[53] A helmet seen by the author in the collection of a well known English collector, had a **skull of gilt** metal. On either side of the waist leaves on this helmet, was evidence of a small hole having been expertly filled and then gilded, and it is my opinion that this helmet at one time had been fitted with a single scroll of the type to be seen on a 1st Dragoon Guards, or an Essex Yeomanry helmet and that possibly, this 'Northamptonshire Yeomanry' helmet was a 'made-up' item.

[54] In R.G. Harris's book on yeomanry uniforms (72) there is an excellent colour illustration by the well known military artist E.A. Campbell, of an officer c. 1905, in dismounted review order wearing his helmet. Regrettably however the artist has depicted the plume mount, waist leaves, and chinchain all as being silver in colour which I respectfully suggest is incorrect for this regiment, and may be artist's licence.

[55] The rayed star was very similar, if not identical to the pattern fitted the last version helmet of the 6th Dragoon Guards (Carabiniers).

[56] In the booklet 'The Yeomanry Force at the 1911 Coronation' (69) there is an illustration by the well respected modern day military artist R.J. Marrion, in which the plume is depicted as being white over blue as opposed to blue over white. These plume colours may just be artist's licence, however it is always possible that the colours on some officers plumes may for whatever reason have been reversed, although this has not been confirmed.

[57] Regarding the apparent non-provision of a full dress helmet for the other ranks of this regiment, it is conceivable that due to the impending phasing out of full dress uniforms for the yeomanry regiments, that only the officers of the regiment possessed a full dress helmet, and that its wear was restricted to special occasions such as levees, etc. The Northamptonshire Yeomanry was not alone in this situation, as it is known that in several other regiments raised after 1901, that the other ranks were not issued with a full dress head-dress, the Bedfordshire, East Riding, Lincolnshire, and Sussex Yeomanry being but a few of these regiments.

[58] In 1819 the regiment was divided into the following Divisions:

Bath Division	Frome Division
A: Bath	G and H: Frome
B: Stoneaston	I and K: Mells
C: Keynsham	L: Shepton
D and E: East Harptree	M: Batcombe
F: Bedminster (57).	

N.B. For some unknown reason the letter J does not appear to have been used as a Troop designation.

[59] Whilst on all the officers helmets seen by the author the centre device was a die-struck item, it is possible that an alternative version existed having the 'V.R.' superimposed upon the centre ground of the strap as on some helmet plates, on the officers pattern helmet of the 5th Dragoon Guards, although this has not been confirmed.

[60] See W.Y. Carman, *Head-Dresses of the British Army - Cavalry*, Plate No. 29 (23rd Lancers 1816-17) for an illustration of similar ear boss.

[61] Prior to 1856 a black feather plume with a *'natural greenish tinge'* (57) was also worn, assumedly for special occasions.

[62] Ogilby Trust Booklet No. 2, *North Somerset Yeomanry*, has a photograph of a kettle-drummer wearing a white over red plume, on page 10 of booklet.

[63] On the post 1902 helmet plate the Royal Cypher of E.R. VII appears to have been a separate superimposed device and not die-struck as on the 'Victorian' helmet plates.

[64] For some unknown reason the wreath was comprised of olive/laurel leaves only, as opposed to the recognised 'Albert' pattern wreath of oak leaves (left), and olive/laurel leaves (right).

[65] The three leopard's heads were facing to the front and positioned with two heads being above a single head.

[66] Although the chinchain on the helmet concerned appeared to be contemporary with the remainder of the helmet, it is always possible that it may have been a replacement fitment.

[67] A photograph in the archives of the National Army Museum illustrates an other ranks helmet that has the same pattern ear rosettes as on the officers helmet, but having in addition on the right hand rosette, a small 'ring' secured to its lower petals (as previously described for the Berkshire Yeomanry), onto which is secured the end link of the chinchain (81).

[68] The information given on the Post 1872 officers 'Albert' pattern, is based on a helmet supplied to 2nd Lieutenant H.R. Williams, by Messrs Hawkes & Co, 14 Piccadilly, London. N.B. 2nd Lt Williams was commissioned in 1887 (82).

[69] With regard to the backing to the pierced strap and the 'Stafford' knot, several years ago on a helmet that sold at a London salesroom, both the strap and garter appeared to be on a dark coloured ground, possibly dark blue enamel. However on a similar pattern helmet sold at a Sussex salesroom, whilst the strap was backed with enamel, the knot was on a silvered metal ground. The author has also seen a similar version, where the pierced strap was backed with pale blue enamel.

[70] A known maker and supplier to the regiment of this pattern of helmet was Messrs *'Andrews' 9 Pall Mall, London,* helmet maker to Her Majesty, Queen Victoria.

[71] The change to the pattern of helmet, that did not have the foliated strips to the peaks, or the encircling waist band appears to have been achieved gradually, as the author has seen examples of helmets exactly as described for the c. 1860 pattern complete with the peak decoration, but having the 1871 pattern plume socket in place of the 'Albert' pattern.

[72] Right up until c. 1893/94 the full dress uniform of this regiment was a complete hybrid, with the head-dress being the heavy cavalry 'Dragoon' helmet, being worn with a light cavalry 'Hussar' style tunic (59). However, in 1894 the helmet was replaced by a busby, and the transformation to a Hussar regiment was completed.

[73] H.R.H. George F.E.A., Prince of Wales. and Duke of Cornwall and York (later King George V) was appointed Honorary Colonel of the regiment on the 30th July 1892 (6).

[74] For special occasions such as parades etc., a white **feather** plume, capped by a medium sized gilt rosette was worn by the officers of the regiment.

[74a] Four squadrons were established as follows: A Squadron: Hove. C Squadron: Chichester. B Squadron: Lewes. D Squadron: Hastings.

[75] It is recorded that the full dress helmet was worn by the Commanding Officer, and at least three other officers at the Coronation of King George VI in 1937 (85).

[76] On a helmet that sold in an auction salesroom in 1984 the shape and size of the ball beneath the socket was of a different pattern, being more round than oval, with the stem beneath the ball also being noticeably taller.

[77] With regard to the colour of this regiments plume, there is mention of a differing colour plume having been considered at one period. In the Ogilby Trust booklet on the Sussex Yeomanry (85), reference is made to sketches by the celebrated military artist Harry Payne, commissioned in 1906 by Messrs Hobson and Sons, Military Tailors, in which a watercolour painting was submitted by the artist to Hobson and Sons showing a white metal helmet of Dragoon pattern with gilt metal fittings, but having a **scarlet plume**.

[78] As mentioned previously, upon the introduction of the full dress helmet, the plumes were purple, however as this colour was not fast, and the dye tended to run when the helmet were worn in the rain, the plume colour was changed to white after a few years. The last time that the purple plumes were worn, was at the funeral of King Edward VII in 1910, the regiment having been chosen to undertake cortege duty, with the first occasion that the white plumes were worn, being at the Coronation of King George V in 1911, when the regiment provided part of the guard lining the procession route (87). N.B. It is recorded that upon seeing the troopers in their scarlet tunics and helmets with white plumes, they were referred to as 'Life Guards' by some onlookers. For those troopers within earshot of this remark, it must surely have filled their hearts with pride to have been mistaken for members of such a prestigious regiment.

[79] The colours of the officers pattern tunic of scarlet (material) gold (lace) and purple (facings) were those of the royal racing colours of King Edward VII, they being purple, scarlet, and gold.

[80] Samuel Suckley was born on the 31st October 1845 in the town of Sheffield. He joined the 1st West Yorkshire Yeomanry Cavalry as a Kettle-drummer in October 1856, and by 1874 had risen through the ranks to become the regiment's Bandmaster. On the 23rd July 1892, at the age of 46 he was commissioned 2nd Lieutenant. He held the post of Commanding Officers Trumpeter until 1898, and remained on the Active Army List until January 1911, when his name appeared under the section headed 'Officers Retired from the Imperial Yeomanry', although it is believed he continued in the post of Bandmaster until 1914 (92).

[81] On an officers helmet seen by the author, the chinchain had three 'loose' links at one end, thus by selecting a particular 'loose' link, the wearer would be able to adjust the chain for a more comfortable fit.

[82] Although in 1876 the 'heavy cavalry' Dragoon pattern helmet had been adopted by the regiment, they continued to wear the 'light cavalry' Lancer style tunic (complete with plastron) taken into wear c. 1864/65 for many more years.

[83] On a rosette fitted to a plume of the 2nd West Yorks Yeomanry examined by the author, in place of the normal short threaded socket was a threaded stud fixing, and to the top of the plume stem was a nut onto which was screwed the plume rosette.

[84] There are known examples of other ranks helmet having the 1871 pattern plume holder, which were previously fitted with the 'Albert' pattern plume holder. On these helmets the original holes at the crown of the skull which corresponded with the position of the plume base studs of the earlier pattern holder, were either filled with brazing metal, or covered by a thin metal cone. Additionally whilst it is known that the plume holder Type: 25.A. was fitted to the helmet of the rank and file, the author has also seen a photograph of a helmet fitted with a plume holder similar to Type: 25.D., and another having a plume holder fitted with a socket having several flat sides. N.B. These plume holders may have been replacement fitments.

[85] Helmets described as being of **officer pattern** have been sold at auction having this pattern of helmet plate fitted. Whilst it has not been confirmed, it is just possible that two differing pattern of helmet plate were fitted to the officers helmet, although it is more likely that those with the 'Yorkshire Dragoons' title were senior N.C.O.'s helmets.

[86] There is in existence at least one pattern of officers helmet plate of the post 1902 period, where the old cast metal plate of the '1st West Yorkshire Yeomanry Cavalry' was used, having the 'Victorian' crown replaced by a 'King's' crown, with the original title of the 1st West Yorks being hidden from view by the garter bearing 'Honi Soit Mal Y Pense', with the two new title straps (Yorkshire Dragoons) being superimposed upon the original title (Yeomanry Cavalry). (88).

[87] Towards the end of the nineteenth century it was by no means unusual to find men of high birth serving as officers in yeomanry regiments, as the following interesting information published in 1896 clearly shows. Currently serving, and holding commissions in the various regiments of Yeomanry Cavalry in Great Britain are the following: Four Princes, four Dukes, six Marquises, twenty-three Earls, twelve Viscounts, twenty-one Lords, twenty-nine Honourables, and thirty Baronets.(99)

8

Purchasing a Helmet

Choosing a Theme

How the collector new to militaria decides what helmets to collect is obviously a matter of personal choice, however, once a theme has been decided upon I would strongly advise that the chosen topic is adhered to as it can be extremely costly changing from one to another, and there is always the possibility that difficulties may be experienced, when attempting to 'sell off' the original items purchased, without a financial loss being incurred.

The theme itself can take the form of a particular type of head-dress such as the busby, lance cap, shako, or helmet etc., or be concentrated on a particular period in time such as the early or late Victorian period. It may take the form of the various differing patterns of head-dress worn by a particular regiment, from its formation to the withdrawal of full dress, or the helmets worn by the particular regiment during a given period of time. In the case of the yeomanry cavalry the theme might be based on the head-dress worn by the regiments of a particular county, such as London, Lancashire or Yorkshire, each of which had more than one regiment of yeomanry, albeit that this would entail collecting varying types of cavalry head-dress such as a busby, a lance cap, and the metal helmet.

If deciding to collect yeomanry helmets, a suitable regiment that offers a varied choice is the Hampshire Yeomanry/Carabiniers who, to my knowledge, wore at varying times during the period c. 1884-1915 at least four slightly differing patterns of helmet. N.B. Although not confirmed, it is my theory that the reason why there were some many differing patterns of helmet was that due to the large area covered by the county, with the squadrons of this regiment being based in different regions of the county. It is therefore conceivable that each squadron purchased their head-dress from a military outfitter within their immediate area, hence the slight differences to the helmet.

Seeking Advice

Having decided upon a theme, it should may then be decided whether the first helmet to be purchased is to be an officers or an other ranks pattern helmet, this choice possibly being influenced by the capital available with which to purchase the helmet. Before proceeding further a brief word of caution, it is not my place to preach to collectors new to this field of militaria, nor to established militaria collectors who might be considering the purchase of a full dress helmet to complement a cavalry tunic with overalls/pantaloons that are already in their collection. I do however offer the following words of advise which I sincerely hope will be of some assistance in this respect.

As with the purchase of a motor vehicle or any other expensive article/item, if the intending purchaser has little, or no knowledge regarding the subject concerned, they should attempt to recruit the assistance of an established collector or a friend who hopefully will be able to offer constructive advise. If such a person is not already known to the prospective buyer, a good way to meet people with a similar interest is by joining a militaria collectors society, always provided that such an organisation exists within your city/town. If however this avenue is not available, if may be worth while finding out if there is a Model Soldier Collection Society in your locality as collectors of model soldiers often also collect militaria. A look at the classified advertisement section of a militaria magazine such as Classic Arms & Militaria, Military Illustrated, Military Modelling and 'Regiment' may well provide the names of some reputable militaria dealers who may be approached for advise. N.B. It is worth remembering that a dealers who sells a variety of militaria, and whose stock may range from cap badges to complete uniforms may not necessarily be knowledgeable on all aspects of this hobby, and therefore may only be able to offer a considered opinion on a particular item.

Theatrical/Tattoo Head-Dress

It goes without saying that all helmets under consideration should be examined very carefully before parting with any hard earned cash. Over the years many items of head-dress have been adapted for theatrical use, and therefore may have had parts removed or added to alter the helmets appearance to suit the wardrobe managers requirements. Additionally items of head-dress become available for purchase that have either been modified to resemble earlier pattern helmets, or have been specially produced for use at military tattoos, albeit that genuine replacement parts may have been fitted, and this makes it difficult to authenticate such items.

Let the Buyer Beware

As already stated, the serious collector should beware of theatrical or military tattoo items, or 'made up' helmets. As we all know, unscrupulous people will stop at nothing to 'make a fast buck', and the following are a few examples seen by the author which when first seen appeared to be collectable items of militaria, however closer inspection of these items revealed that they were not what at first sight they had appeared to be.

Household Cavalry: As far back as 1991 it was rumoured that 'fake' troopers helmets bearing the King's crown to the helmet plate, and in unissued condition were being offered for sale at a North of England Arms Fair (95). On a suspect example recently seen by the author the head lining was of **black** leather, the chinchain backing was of a **pale coloured** leather, the skiver to the front peak was a **very pale** green in colour, and the fittings were attached to the skull by a dubious method.

Staffordshire Yeomanry: An officers helmet with an unmarked black japanned skull, revealed that in fact, dents to the skull had been removed by a panel beater, which had then been professionally spray painted at a car repair bodyshop.

Westminster Dragoons: What appeared to be a 'mint' condition other ranks helmet of this regiment, was in fact an unissued condition skull, onto which the helmet plate, chinchain, plume holder and plume etc. had been added to 'make up' a complete helmet.

5th (Royal Irish) Lancers: On a c. 1900 sergeants pattern lance cap the damaged gold lace that surrounded the waist of the cap had been removed and expertly replaced by modern gold lace.

15th Hussars: An officers sabretache purported to be the pre 1840 version with silver coloured wire embroidery, turned out upon being closely inspected with a jewellers eyeglass to have specs of gilt amongst the wire. The gilding to the wire had apparently been removed to give the appearance of it having silver wire embroidery, when in fact it was a c. 1880 pattern sabretache with gold embroidery with had far less value (95).

Northamptonshire Yeomanry: Finally I respectfully refer readers of my observations on an officers pattern helmet of this regiment as recorded under Chapter seven, endnote No.53.

Replacement Fittings

It is not unusual to find an item of head-dress that has at some time been fitted with either associated/replacement parts, or reproduction fittings, such as the plume, ear rosettes, chinchain, and even the head lining. As always it is a matter of personal choice as to whether or not to purchase a helmet fitted with 'associated' parts, my view on this matter being, that if as a whole the helmet is a collectable piece, then it is worth purchasing the item in the hope that the required genuine items may at some later date be acquired from either a fellow collector or a specialist militaria dealer.

Having taken account of the above, a prospective purchaser would be wise to take account of any replacement items fitted to the helmet concerned before agreeing a price and concluding the sale, as a item of head-dress with associated fittings is not as saleable as an untouched item. In view of this fact I offer the following information relating to damaged helmets, and the component parts, which are most likely to have been replaced with associated/replacement fittings, **all of which will effect the value of a helmet.**

The Skull

Dents or creases to the skull will have an obvious effect of the value of a helmet, as will areas of wear or rubbing on a gilt metal, or silver plated officers pattern helmet. As briefly mentioned in Chapter 9, it is sometimes possible to reduce the effect of minor dents by use of a wooden spoon, however to re-gilt or replate a silver plated skull will be extremely costly, and if carried out, the 'restored' helmet will have lost its 'appearance of age'. The inside of the helmet should be closely examined to establish if the holes cut into the skull to accept the studs on the helmet plate match up, for if there are any additional, crudely made holes visible this might possibly indicate that the helmet plate has been replaced at some time. This visual check is most important, for it is not unknown for unscrupulous dealers to remove a fairly common pattern of helmet plate, and to replace it with a rare version plate, thereby increasing the helmets value quite considerably, whilst at the same time destroying its authenticity.

In the case of an other ranks 1871 pattern helmet of one of the seven regiments of Dragoon Guard, or the two regiments of Dragoons, if the binding/rim of the back peak is stamped with regimental issue marks which do not correspond with the numeral on the helmet plate, this does not necessarily mean that the helmet has been 'made up', as troopers were occasionally transferred from their parent regiment to a similar one, as was the case with John Cusack M.M., as previously described in Chapter 2.

The Plume Holder

On the 'Albert' pattern helmet, it is worth removing the plume to check that the correct number of finials are present at the top of the tall inner socket of the plume holder, as often some of these finials are damaged or missing completely. Additionally, it is not unknown for a helmet of this pattern to be sold to an unsuspecting buyer with this inner socket completely missing, with the plume merely 'sitting' within the shorter socket that is attached to the base of the plume holder assembly.

Occasionally an officers 1871 pattern helmet is offered for sale, that has for whatever reason, has had the original plume socket replaced with one from an others ranks pattern helmet. It is therefore well worth looking inside the skull of the helmet to establish the method by which the socket is secured to the plume base. If possible, also check to see that the collet is in place, and that the stem of the socket has the 'key' as described in Chapter 5, and illustrated in Fig: 20A., the presence of which authenticates the fitting as being of officers pattern.

A final word of advice relating to the plume holder, concerns the ball beneath the socket pattern as illustrated in Fig: 25.B. Positioned immediately beneath the bulbous ball that supports the plume socket, there should be a short tube having a milled edge. If this tube is not evident, then it is highly likely that the plume holder has been damaged at this particular point, and has subsequently been repaired.

The Head Lining

On an officers pattern helmet, the quilted cloth head lining will frequently be in a stained condition, this should not usually affect the value of the helmet to a great extent, however torn, perished, or missing linings will reduce its value. If the head lining appears to be in unworn condition and it is possible the lining has been replaced, remove an ear rosette and it will then be possible to examine the small rivets that hold the ear rosette socket in place to see if they look contemporary with the rest of the helmet. N.B. The leather head lining on an other ranks pattern helmet should also carefully be examined for signs of the lining having been replaced.

The Helmet Plate

An 'Albert' pattern helmet plate should be examined to make sure that all the leaves on the wreath are present, for signs of age cracking, solder repairs, and that the tips of the star are undamaged. N.B. A similar visual check should be carried out on Household Cavalry helmet plates.

On the 1871 Dragoon Guards/Dragoons officers pattern helmet plate, the tips of the star should be carefully checked to ensure that they are all present, the enamel (where appropriate), examined for signs of damage, and the centre device carefully checked to ensure it is genuine.[1] On other ranks pattern plates of these regiments, the backing to the numeral should be carefully inspected to ensure that it is either of black leather, or of black japanned metal, for it is not uncommon to find that where a leather backing has rotted way, black paint has been applied to hide this damage.

The Ear Rosettes and Chinchain

Ear rosettes of the 1847 'Albert' pattern should be carefully examined as it is known that 'restrike' pattern ear rosettes have been produced using the original dies, that said, it is better to have such a rosette, than none at all. On an officers pattern helmet, particular attention should be paid to the type of rosettes fitted, to ensure that they are of the correct pattern for the regiment concerned, and that they are not from an other ranks helmet. To establish if the rosettes are contemporary with the helmet, unscrew one of the rosettes, and hold it against the waist leaves to compare the colour of the gilt or silver.

Chinchains are frequently either in a very worn condition, missing completely, or have had the backing replaced, again any one of which is better than no chain. Particular attention should be paid to a chinchain fitted to an officers pattern helmet, as often the chain fitted is of the other ranks pattern, or on occasions, of the type fitted to a blue cloth helmet as worn by infantry officers. If possible, check the length of the chinchain using a tape measure, the normal length being 17"-18", as several chinchains seen by the author had been shortened by having some of the links removed.

The Plume

On the rare occasions that an 1847 'Albert' pattern helmet is to be found in an auction house salesroom, or at a specialist militaria shop, the plume should be examined very closely as some helmets are fitted with modern day **reproduction** plumes. These plumes are generally of reasonably good quality, and are fitted with 'restrike' rosettes that have been made from the original rosette dies. As a possible means of identifying a reproduction plume, I would recommend that the colour and condition of the actual hair, together with the stem and binding be examined, to ascertain if their condition appears to be consistent with an item made well over a hundred years ago.

Officers 1871 pattern helmets are occasionally to be found fitted with plumes described as being 'associated'. This frequently means that the plume is of the correct colour for the regiment but is an other ranks pattern plume. To establish if the plume is in fact an officers pattern, try unscrewing the half cup located at the top of the stem, where the hair is bound to the stem. The plume rosette should also be able to be unscrewed, although this in itself does not confirm the quality or pattern of plume, as on modern day replacement plumes the rosette also unscrews, **although the half cup does not.** N.B. The unscrewing of the rosette and half cup does not always apply to yeomanry officer plumes.

NOTES

[1] On an officers pattern helmet of the 3rd Dragoon Guards seen by the author in a London militaria shop some years ago, the centre device (Prince of Wales's plume), backed with red enamel looked to be most suspect. Closer examination of the helmet plate revealed that the P.O.W.'s feathers were in fact a silver coloured **collar badge** of the type worn by the infantry.

9

Care, Preservation/Restoration of the Helmet

Regardless of whether a particular item of head-dress has been acquired to complete a full dress uniform, is the first helmet upon which a collection is to be built, or is a recent acquisition for an established collection, the proud owner will probably wish the item to look as near as possible to how it would have looked when worn by the soldier concerned. There are varying views of whether or not a helmet in a dirty, but untouched condition should be cleaned, repaired and restored to its former glory. Many collectors prefer to leave the head-dress in the condition it is in when acquired, and one must respect this view. However, there are several ways that the appearance of a helmet can be improved without actually undertaking any major restoration work, and the following advice is given in the hope that it will be of some assistance to both new and established collectors.

The Plume

When purchasing a helmet, it is often the plume that is in a dirty condition, white plumes frequently having become a dirty yellow in colour. Discoloured or dirty horsehair plumes may benefit from being washed with a proprietary brand of shampoo, of the type suitable for normal hair. In the case of an 1871 officers pattern plume it is advisable to first remove the rosette and the half cup located beneath the plume, at the top of the stem, this of course is not possible on the other ranks pattern plume. The plume should then be immersed in a bowl of lukewarm water, with the shampoo being gently massaged into the hairs of the plume. **Great care should be taken** to ensure that as far as is possible, the hairs do not become matted, as once the plume has dried, entangled hairs are difficult to brush and may be pulled loose by the hairbrush, thereby thinning the plume. The damp plume should be rinsed, and then gently massaged using a named brand of hair conditioner (also of the type suitable for normal hair), rinsed thoroughly in clean lukewarm water, then placed into a plume bag and hung in a natural position to dry. Once dry the plume may be **gently** brushed, and the rosette and half cup replaced. N.B. Information on how to make a simple plume bag are given in chapter eleven, these details having been loosely based on the plume bags issued to members of the mounted squadron of the Household Cavalry Regiment.

The Skull and Fittings

The cleaning of the skull and fittings is again very much a matter of personal choice, there being some collectors who prefer to see all items in their collection in a 'bright and shiny' condition, whilst other choose to leave the skull and fittings in an untouched condition, as this tends to give the helmet an air of age and authenticity.

If it is decided that the skull and fittings are to be cleaned, then this task should be carried out with **extreme caution and care**. If it is considered necessary to remove the helmet plate, or the plume holder from the skull, always unscrew any nuts very slowly, and if resistance is met, I would suggest that the attempt is abandoned, and the helmet cleaned with the fitments still in place.

Officers Helmets

Officers helmets having gilt metal skull and fittings may be cleaned by very gently washing the skull etc. with lukewarm soapy water, using a very soft cloth, care being taken to ensure that the head lining **does not become wet.** The skull/fittings may then be wiped with a **soft** cloth dipped in clean lukewarm water, wiped over with a **soft dry** cloth to remove any excess soapy water, and then dried using a hair dryer on a modest heat setting, which will force warm air into the seams, such as the peak binding, rear seam, and waist band. The skull and fittings may then lightly polished using a soft duster. Do not under any circumstances polish too vigorously, as the gilding on most helmet skull and fittings is extremely thin, and continued rubbing may well result in the gilding being worn away, with the result that the copper base shows through. The plume holder, ear rosettes and plume rosette may also be cleaned in a similar manner. The skiver lining the inside of both the front and rear peaks, may benefit from having lanolin cream gently massaged into the skiver, and then wiped over with a soft cloth.

Silver plated skulls, plume holders, ear and plume rosettes may be cleaned by using a long lasting proprietary brand of silver polish, such as 'Goddards Long Term Silver Polish', however care must be taken to ensure that the silver polish does not come into contact with any gilded metal fittings, as the very thin layer of gilding could be damaged/removed. The skiver lining the peaks on these helmets may be treated as described above. **It is worth remembering that continued polishing of a gilded/silver plated item is likely to remove a minute layer of gilding/silver.**

Creases/dents to the skull, are best left untouched unless they seriously affect the appearance of the helmet. It is sometimes possible to remove **some** creases/dents by laying the damaged side of the helmet onto a sock filled with soft sand, and then by gently rubbing the inside of the skull at the affected area, with a round nose **wooden** spoon. **Extreme caution should be exercised**

if attempting this remedial action, as over enthusiastic rubbing will make the damage worse.

For those officers pattern helmets having a soft leather head lining, the lining may be treated by gently massaging lanolin cream into the leather and then 'wiping' over with a soft clean duster. Helmets fitted with a combined leather/silk head lining may have the leather part treated as above, **I would not** however recommend any attempt at cleaning the silk section of these dual linings, nor the quilted cloth pattern of head lining, as fitted to the majority of officers pattern helmets.

The Helmet Plate

Most pattern of helmet plate may be cleaned by using lukewarm soapy water for the gilt parts, and silver polish for the silver plated parts. Once again **extreme care should be taken** if attempting to undo the brass nuts that hold the helmet plate in place, and if the plate is of the pattern that has the bend - over tabs, I would strongly recommend that they are left alone, and that the plate is cleaned whilst still attached to the skull of the helmet.

Helmet plates having worn gilding/silver plating may be have their appearance improved by having the worn part regilded/re-plated by a silversmith or goldsmith, however if this restoration work is carried out it is unlikely that the regilded/re-plated item will be exactly the same colour as any other gilded/plated fittings on the helmet which will have acquired their particular tone over a period probably in excess of a hundred years.

On the helmet plates of the 1st, 2nd, 3rd, and 4th Dragoon Guards, the enamel that backs the garter, and the Royal Cypher/Crest of England/Cross of St. Patrick is often found to be in a chipped condition, which will to some collectors detract from plates appearance. By contacting a goldsmith or silversmith it may be possible to obtain the name and address of an enameller who will be able to replace the damaged enamel. It is essential however that if this step is to be taken, that the collector emphasises to the enameller the importance of the replacement blue and red enamel matching the colour of the damaged enamel, as this craftsman will have access to a great many differing shades of blue and red enamel.

The Chinchain

Chinchains backed with velvet may benefit from the backing being brushed to improve their appearance, and chains having a leather backing may be treated with lanolin cream, as described in chapter eight. The stitching that holds the chain links onto the backing will often be found to have rotted away, with the result the leather hangs loose from the chain. It is possible to re-stitch the chain to the leather, however this is a most difficult task, and may take several hours to complete. Unless totally confident about re-stitching a chinchain, I would recommend that the item is taken to a leather specialist to be repaired. If however you are brave enough to attempt this task please remember, **you must not sew to tightly, or the end result will be a twisted chinchain**.

Other Ranks Helmets

The brass helmets and fittings of the Dragoon Guards, and the white metal helmets of the Dragoons, and Yeomanry regiments may safely be cleaned with a branded, good quality metal polish such as 'Brasso'. Information regarding the cleaning of other ranks pattern helmets has already been given, and may be found under the heading 'Cleaning can lead to damage' in chapter four. The skiver to the front peak, and the leather head harness/lining may safely be treated with lanolin cream as previously described. Should a collector possess a black, japanned metal helmet of the type worn by the Staffordshire Yeomanry, and the japanning be badly chipped, it may be worth visiting an automobile paint sprayer who may be prepared to respray the skull for you. If this option is to be considered seriously you should bear in mind that it will be necessary for the helmet plate, the plume holder, the chinchain and ear rosettes, and possibly the waist and rear seam bands to be removed, and replaced once the respraying has been completed. I personally would suggest that a skull having a few chips to the japanning, will look far more authentic than a 'bright and shiny' resprayed helmet, although this is of course a matter of personal choice.

10

Storage and Transportation of a Helmet

Occasions may arise when it will become necessary to transport a helmet from the collector's home, to another location. This may occur when the collector wishes to take a particular item of head-dress to show to a either a fellow collector, a friend, to display the item at a militaria society meeting, or perhaps to take the helmet to a militaria shop to sell, or part exchange. Regardless of the actual financial value of the helmet, the last thing a collector wishes to occur, is for the helmet to be damaged in transit. Whilst in 'Victorian' times, an officer would transport his helmet in a metal carrying tin specifically designed to carry the helmet, I would not however, recommend this method of transporting a valuable helmet, should a collector be fortunate enough to possess such a case in his collection. I do however offer the following information, which I hope may be of assistance in ensuring that an item of head-dress is not damaged in transit.

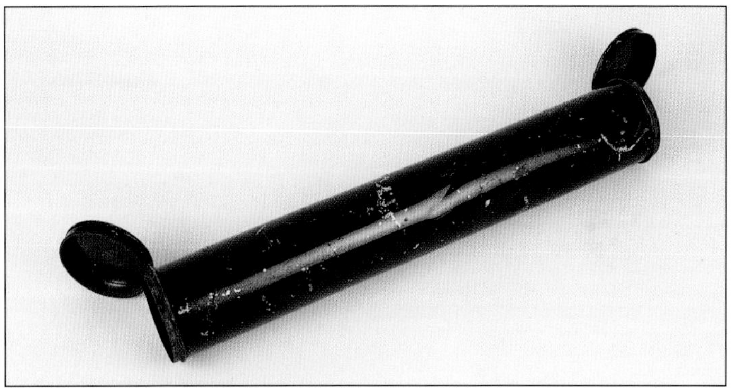

Figure 62: An officers plume tin (carrying case) of the 7th (Princess Royal's) Dragoon Guards. Author's collection. Photo: R. Biondi.

The Plume

The plume should be remove prior to packing the actual helmet, and may be wrapped in a suitable cloth item such as a pillow case or a towel. Alternatively the plume may be placed within a **plume bag**, of the type used by the Household Cavalry Regiment. Such a bag may easily be made, by obtaining a suitable piece of plain or white cotton cloth measuring some four and a half inches in width, by twenty inches in length. Taking one of the narrow ends of the material, a hem should be sewn, through which a drawstring may be passed. The two longer sides of the material should then be hemmed and sewn together to achieve a 'tube' effect. A suitable drawstring, such as a cotton 'bootlace' should then be passed through the narrow hemmed end (top) of the bag, which is then complete. The top of the plume is then gathered in the palm of the hand, and gentle pushed into the bottom of the bag until the rosette may be seen at the top end, when the drawstring is drawn together and tied. If a collector is fortunate enough to have an officers metal plume case/tin in his collection, then using such a case/tin is an ideal means of safely transporting a plume. See Figs: 8. and 62. for two examples of an officers plume case/tin. N.B. If using a plume bag to store or transport an 'Albert' pattern plume, extreme care should be used when pushing the plume into the bag to ensure that the hairs of the 'brush' are not pushed downwards.

The Plume Socket

As most collectors will be aware, the finials on the plume socket of the 1847 'Albert' pattern helmet can easily be bent, or broken off completely if not treated with extreme care. It may therefore be considered prudent to remove the complete plume holder assembly from the skull of the helmet before it is packed away. **Extreme care** should be taken if attempting to remove the small brass nuts that are affixed to the studs of the plume holder base, as these nuts may well have remained unmoved for over a hundred years, and may therefore have 'seized' onto the studs. If **resistance is met** when attempting to undo a nut, it is probably best to leave the complete plume holder in place, as undue pressure may result in the stud becoming detached from the base of the plume holder base. If, in view of the above the plume holder assembly is to remain on the helmet, then a suitably thick piece of foam rubber, with a hole cut into its centre, and then placed over the socket, should help protect it from accidental damage. With regard to the 1871 pattern helmet, the plume socket can easily be bent, or even fractured at its base if not treated with extreme care, and I would therefore suggest that the socket is removed prior to the actual skull being packed away. Removal of the socket from the officers 1871 pattern helmet is achieved by unscrewing the brass circular 'nut' located at the base of the plume stem, and on the other ranks pattern helmet, by unscrewing the brass lock 'nut'. The plume socket can then be wrapped in a soft cloth, and placed into a padded postal bag, or something similar for safe keeping.

The Helmet Plate

When transporting an officers pattern helmet, consideration should be given to the possibility of damage occurring to a helmet plate having an enamel backing to the garter etc., such as on the 1st, 2nd, 3rd, and 4th Dragoon Guards hel-

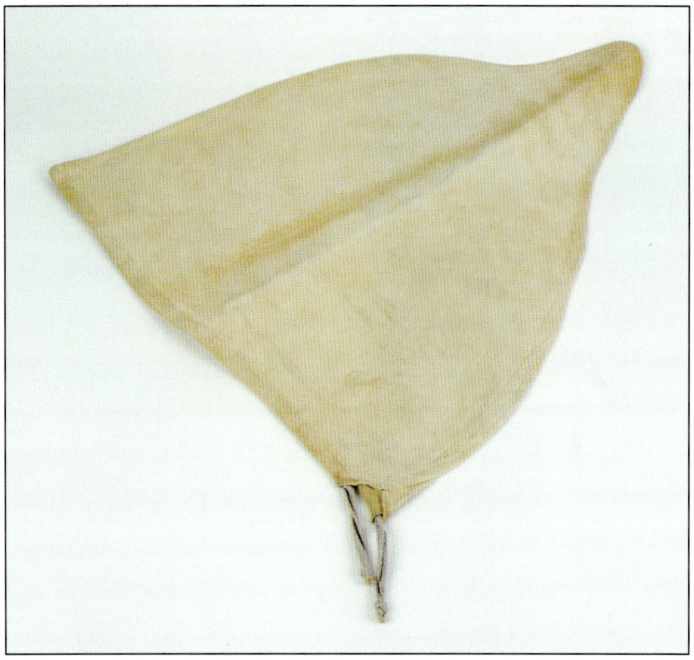

Figure 63: An officers chamois leather helmet bag of the 4th (Royal Irish) Dragoon Guards c. 1922. Authors collection. Photo: R. Biondi.

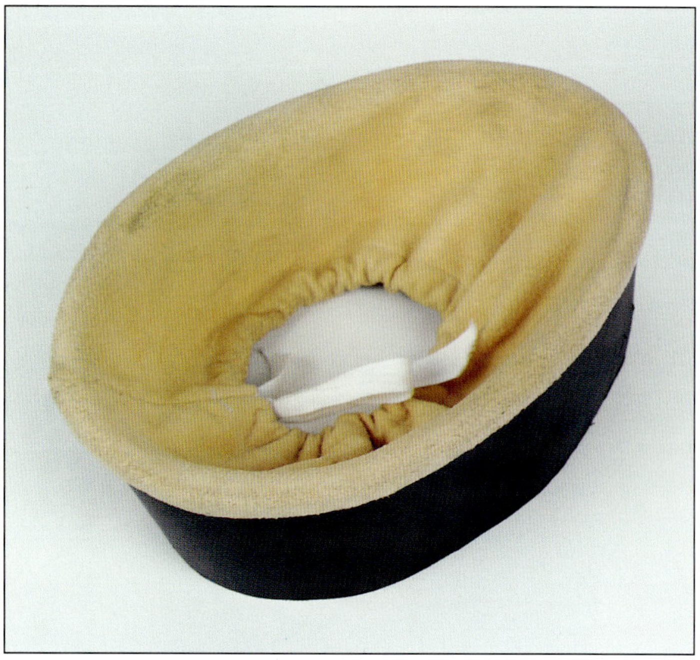

Figure 64: A chamois leather head lining as fitted to a present day, Household Cavalry officers helmet. Author's collection. Photo: R. Biondi.

mets. It may be considered advisable to remove the complete helmet plate from the skull of the helmet, and to wrap the plate in a suitable soft cloth, or place it into a suitable sized padded postal bag. **N.B. extreme caution should be exercised** if the helmet plate is the type fitted with bend-over two pronged tab, as the metal that these tabs are made of could be brittle, and they may fracture and break off if pried open.

The Chinchain and Ear Rosettes

Whilst it is not essential that the chinchain be removed, doing so will ensure that the metal links do not come into contact with the skull, or the enamel on the helmet plate, if this component part has not already been removed. If it has been decided to remove the chinchain from the helmet, it might then be a sensible idea to pay attention to the backing of the chinchain. For an officers velvet backed chain, **gently brushing** the velvet lining with a soft brush should remove any fluff etc. that might have adhered to the material, and for a leather backed chinchain the gentle application of lanolin cream will feed the leather, and help to prevent it drying out and cracking. Shortly after the lanolin cream has been applied the leather should be wiped gently with a soft dry cloth.

Packing the Skull and Fittings

When transporting a helmet, a chamois leather helmet bag of the type used by some officers, (See Fig: 63.). is ideal for this purpose. However if a collector does not posses such a bag, then an old pillow case to which a 'drawstring' has been attached makes an ideal 'helmet bag' in which to transport the helmet. The author has also seen an example of a wooden 'helmet tree', which was fitted inside the skull of an officers helmet. The purpose of this 'tree' was to maintain the shape of the skull of the helmet when the item of head-dress was not being worn. It might also possibly have been used by an officer, when transporting his helmet from one cavalry station to another, although this has not been confirmed.

For those of us whose collection does not include a helmet tree, then the skull and fittings etc., may be placed into a suitably sized, **strongly constructed** cardboard box/carton, the base of which should be lined with either foam rubber, or 'bubble pack'. The gap between the walls of the box/carton and the actual helmet may lined with a similar protective material, as should the top of the box/carton. N.B. When taking a helmet out of your home for whatever reason, it is advisable to notify the company that insures the contents of your flat/house, to enquire if the company is prepared to issue a temporary cover note in respect of accidental damage to the helmet, or possibly even theft of the head-dress, whilst the item is away from your home.

11

Displaying the Helmet

Regardless of whether a collector has only one helmet amongst a collection of uniforms, swords etc., or an entire collection of military head-dress, good condition other ranks metal helmets are expensive, and the cost of officers pattern helmets even more so. It therefore makes sound sense to ensure that the head-dress is cared for and protected from dust, atmospheric pollution, and attack by moth, all of which can have disastrous effects on the plume, the skull of the helmet, its chinchain and the head lining etc.

Display Cabinets

A glass fronted cabinet is ideal for displaying items of head-dress, whilst at the same time helping to protect valuable helmets from becoming tarnished, which is particularly important in the case of a silver plated skull, where after a period of time a patina occurs, with the result that the silver plate becomes almost black in colour. A suitable cabinet will also help protect the horsehair plumes from the effects of tobacco smoke (where applicable), as smoke from a cigarette, cigar, or pipe may discolour a light coloured plume.

In the case of an officers pattern helmet, the cabinet will also help to protect the quilted cloth head lining, the skiver lining the inside of the peaks, and the velvet backing to the chinchain from attack by moth, as the larvae of these insects feed on cloth, fur, and leather etc. One has only to see the top of a lancer officers chapka, or a busby bag that has been attacked by moth to see the irreparable damage that occurs if the head-dress is not suitably protected.

Finding a suitable cabinet in which to display a collection of military head-dress may prove to be no easy task, for antique display cases, both genuine and reproduction, whilst being ideally suitable in that they would complement the helmets, are usually extremely expensive to purchase. Also suitable for displaying a collection are purpose built display cabinets, however these items are also very expensive to purchase, and are probably beyond the financial means of most collectors. Ready made display cabinets may be purchased from large furniture outlets/stores, however the majority of cabinets seen by the author appear to be intended for displaying glassware and china ornaments etc., and have been unsuitable for displaying items of head-dress in the face forwards position, due to their lack of depth. Suitable display cases may however sometimes be obtained from one of the suppliers of second hand business equipment and furniture, that are to be found in most cities and major towns, where perhaps an open fronted bookcase may be found, to which may be added runners and glass sliding doors, thereby turning the bookcase into a display cabinet.

For the purposes of exhibiting a single item of head-dress, the oval shaped glass domes having fitted wooden bases, that were popular in Victorian times to exhibit stuffed animals and birds, of which both antique and reproduction examples may be found in antique shops etc., are, if of the correct dimensions ideal for this purpose.

There are several methods of actually displaying an item of head-dress that is contained within a display cabinet, with probably the cheapest and simplest way being to place the helmet onto a piece of dark coloured material such as velvet, with the chinchain placed either outside or within the front peak. N.B. If using this method to display more than one helmet, the items of head-dress should be spaced a reasonable distance apart to prevent damage, should the cabinet accidental be moved or rocked, which might cause the helmets within to rock from side to side and come into contact with each other, and possibly cause damage.

Supporting the Helmet

An alternative method of exhibiting a helmet within a display cabinet, is for the head-dress to be supported by a simple wire frame which can easily be made by a collector, or for a more realistic effect, the use of a polystyrene model head of the type used to display wigs may be used. Alternatively for those collectors whose pocket can bear the cost, a professionally made studio head as used by window dressers, makes an ideal mode of display. N.B. If either a polystyrene, or studio head is to be used to support a helmet, I would strongly recommend, that should the helmet to be displayed be of the officers pattern, **that the draw-strings are loosened** to permit the skull of the helmet to sit upon the upper part of the supporting 'head'. This will ensure that the weight of the helmet is not being totally borne by the lining, which due to its age, might possibly being in a fragile condition and tear under the strain.

The Display Stand (See Fig: 65.)

A further alternative method of displaying a helmet is by means of a purpose made wooden stand. A cheap, but effective stand can easily be constructed using a suitable wooden base measuring approximately 7 inches x 7 inches x 3/4 inches, at the centre of which is positioned a piece of wooden dowelling having an approximate diameter of 1 1/2 inches, and being some 10 inches in height. N.B. An old wooden broom or mop handle is ideal for this purpose.

The wooden dowelling is first glued into place, and then further secured by a steel screw for added strength. A circular piece of either hardboard or plywood having an approximate diameter of 4 inches is affixed to the top of the dowelling by means of a screw. Onto the circular hardboard/plywood base is then placed a suitable sized and shaped piece of foam rubber, which is then covered by piece of strong cloth material, sufficient in size, to not only cover the foam, but to also hang down some 5 inches below the circular base. The material is then pulled down below the circular base to form a dome shape, where the loose ends of the material are gathered together beneath the base, and held in place by means of string, or by two or three strong elastic bands. The string/elastic bands are then covered with PVC insulating tape, and the 'loose' ends of the material trimmed with a sharp knife to 'tidy up' this part of the stand. At the centre of the dome, a small hole is cut into both the cloth material and the foam rubber, being of a sufficient size and depth to permit the plume 'wing' nut to sink into the foam, when the helmet is placed upon the 'head' of the stand, which assists in stabilizing the helmet.

The wooden parts of the stand may then be stained and varnished, with the overall appearance of the display stand being enhanced by affixing either a collar badge, or a cap badge (a 'restrike' badge is most suitable for this purpose) to the centre front of the wooden base. If a collar/cap badge is to be affixed to the front of the stand it should obviously be of the same regiment as the helmet being displayed. N.B. If an officers pattern helmet is to be displayed upon this type of stand, the drawstring/s should be loosened for the reason given above.

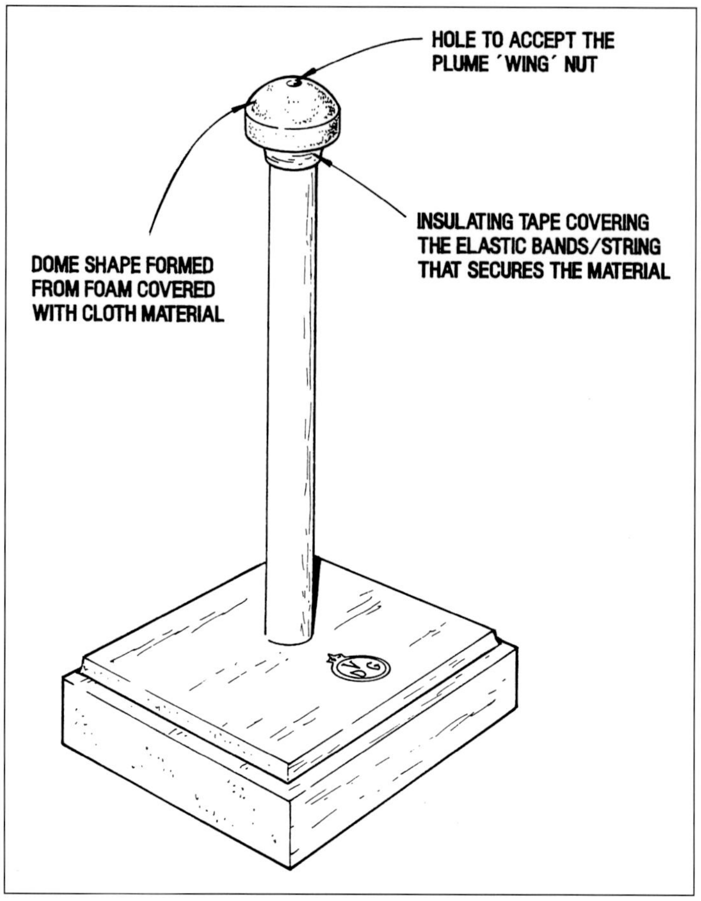

Figure 65: A Simple Display Stand. Author.

Appendices

Appendix I

Appreciation of Helmet Prices

As with almost all collectable antique items, the price one might reasonable expect to pay for a metal cavalry helmet, whether officers, or other ranks pattern has risen consistently over a period of many years, and it has been observed by the author that many of the better condition, rarer and more desirable helmet sold in auction house salesrooms and in specialist militaria shops are being purchased by overseas buyers.

Placing a Value on a Helmet.

Just how one places a value on a particular helmet will depend on whether the item of head-dress is seen from the vendor's viewpoint, or the purchasers. Many readers will have experienced how the value of a motor vehicle is often seen as a "nice condition car, in a nice colour, with low mileage" when seen from the vendors view, however when offered for sale at a used car salesroom, and seen from a car salesman's view it becomes a "car in only reasonable condition, with the colour being a bad selling point, and the particular model unpopular and hard to sell".

Condition of the Helmet

The condition of a helmet is to many, but not all collectors, a most important factor that will influence the decision whether or not to buy a particular item. Helmets, like all items of a soldier's uniform were meant to be worn as daily wear, as full dress for parades etc., and often in battle, and therefore it is reasonable to expect a certain amount of wear and tear (commonly known as service wear). Just how much the condition of a particular item of head-dress will influence the prospective purchaser, will obviously be a matter of personal choice. A helmet that has slight unrepaired damage, or a contemporary professional repair may be considered still collectable, whilst a similar helmet that has a crude modern day repair may not. As mentioned previously many helmets are fitted with replacement items and this factor may well influence the decision whether to purchase or not.

Gone forever are the days when one could visit a specialist militaria shop where you would find a helmet of almost any period, of any regiment in almost mint condition complete with all original fittings. In those days these items were so plentiful that you could almost choose which particular regiment's helmet you wished to purchase in advance of your visit to the militaria shop.

Auction House Salesrooms

From the vendors point of view, the price a particular helmet is expected to sell for if sold through an auction house salesroom is often based on the price originally paid for the item by the vendor, and of course a profit margin, for we all like to make a profit when we sell an item. The expected sale price is therefor often far higher than the actual price realised in the sale.

Many factors will effect the price realised, such as the description given in the auction catalogue, the condition of the item, its rarity, the current market value of similar condition helmets, and the number of collectors willing to bid for the helmet.

For the prospective purchaser, there are various factors that will influence how much a collector is prepared to pay for a particular item of head-dress, included in which may be the helmet's rarity, whether or not the item is required to complement a uniform etc., and how long the collector has been seeking the particular item. Other considerations will include what other avenues of supply are open to him, such as militaria fairs, or specialist militaria shops, and last, but not least, how much can be afforded, although an impulse buy will often cause the purchaser to disregard the later. N.B. It is worth bearing in mind that the price a particular helmet realises in an auction sale may not be a benchmark for similar pattern helmets, as often the selling price reflects how much a determined bidder was prepared to pay for the helmet **on that day.**

Helmets that often realise a far higher price than is normal will include those that were only worn for a short period of time by a particular regiment, and those formerly owned by an officer who achieved fame, or high rank, or both, examples of which are given later in this chapter.

Condition/Grade

The following is my personal system of grading the condition of a particular item of head-dress, and will almost certainly be at variance with the grades used by militaria dealers, and those given in auction salesroom catalogues.

For the purposes of grading the condition of a helmet, I have based my grades on an officers 1871 pattern helmet of the Dragoon Guards, and therefore for an other ranks pattern helmet, brass replaces gilt metal, white metal replaces silver plated, and leather is substituted for quilted cloth.

Excellent Condition

A helmet that has hardly been worn, being in almost untouched condition, with all fittings, including the plume being original to the helmet. The plume to be of officers quality and fitted with the correct pattern rosette for the regiment. The skull should be in an unmarked condition, with the gilt bright, or the silver plate unblemished, as should the plating on the ear rosettes, plume holder and fittings etc. The star of the helmet plate to have all tips present, the gilt to the centre device bright, with the enamel backing (where appropriate) to be in undamaged condition. The lining to be undamaged with little or no staining, with the stitching on both the lining, and the chinchain to be in good condition.

Very Good Condition
The correct pattern plume with rosette. The skull and plume holder having minor marks, or rubbing to the gilt and silver plate that does not effect the overall appearance of the helmet. Minor service wear to the helmet plate, but having all star tips present, and the enamel undamaged. Minor staining and signs of age wear to both the lining and the chinchain backing.

Good Condition
A correct or associated plume. The skull with either small creases or dents, the gilt/silver plate rubbed in places, particularly on the plume socket. One or two tips to star either bent or missing, the enamel lightly chipped. Medium/heavy staining to the head lining, with some damage to the cloth/ silk. The chinchain leather/velvet backing present, but with stitching faults.

Quite Good Condition
As for good condition, but with more serious damage to the helmet plate. The plume socket damaged, with perhaps the peak binding cracked in several places, with the chinchain or ear rosettes missing. Not a helmet for the serious collector.

Appreciation of Prices

The following compilation of helmet prices is composed of information assembled from auction salesroom catalogues, dealers lists, specialist militaria shops, and interviews with collectors covering the period 1960 to 1999 inclusive and gives an indication of how helmet prices have risen over the past thirty-nine years. Included within this compilation are a few helmets previously owned by famous cavalry officers, such as Field Marshal Allenby, Captain Oates, the Marquis of Linlithgow, and others. N.B. The descriptions taken from auction catalogues have been reproduced below using the actual terminology used in the relevant catalogue, however, these descriptions have where practical, been abbreviated to reduce unnecessary preamble and repetition. Additionally, where appropriate, the authors observations and opinion on the condition of a particular item have been given in bold text.

Sources Consulted

Blunderbuss Antiques (Central London), Bosley Militaria Auctioneers (Marlow, Buckinghamshire), Christie's Auctioneers (South Kensington, London) Military Antiques (Islington, London), Phillips Auctioneers (Central London), Regimentals Militaria (Islington, London), Spink's Auctioneers (Central London), Tradition (Central London), Geoff White Militaria (Bristol), and Wallis and Wallis Auctioneers (Lewes, Sussex), and various militaria fairs.

Grade Abbreviations

EXC: Excellent Condition. VGC: Very Good Condition. GC: Good Condition. QGC: Quite Good Condition. Illus: Indicates that the particular helmet concerned, was illustrated in the salesroom catalogue from which the written description given below has been taken.

Household Cavalry 1842 Pattern

Year Month	Source	Price
1984 May	Wallis & Wallis	£1000.

Life Guards. A rare Albert pattern **officers** silvered helmet of the Life Guards. Falling white horsehair plume supported by a short upright white plume, in acanthus holder. Large gilt badge, the central device in gilt, silver and enamel. Leather backed gilt ring chinchain. GC. (no lining, minor dents to skull, minor wear to gilt). This pattern helmet is difficult to obtain in any condition. Illus. **The enamel on the helmet plate did not look correct, otherwise a very nice helmet.**

1995 Nov — Regimentals — £2100.
A **Life Guards.** A very rare early 1840's period Life Guards **Troopers** helmet, having an excellent undented skull. Very large Life Guards plate at front. Tall white horsehair plume. Portions of original leather troopers liner remaining with makers name engraved to rear neck guard of helmet. Illus. **Despite the condition of the head lining, this helmet was in VGC for its age. An <u>extremely rare helmet,</u> the Household Cavalry Museum at Windsor does not even possess an example of this pattern of other ranks helmet in its collection.** N.B. See Fig: 2. for an illustration of the helmet.

1996 April — Blunderbuss — £4500.
Royal Horse Guards. An **officers** helmet complete with plume. **EXC condition, gilt very crisp, complete with chinchain and rosettes. Either an unworn, or a restored example.** N.B. see Fig: 1. for an example of a similar helmet.

Household Cavalry 1871 Pattern

1962 Nov — Wallis & Wallis — £42.
Royal Horse Guards. An **officers** German silver helmet. KC. Complete with its scarlet plume & scaled chinstrap in VGC. Illus. **Plume appeared to be other ranks pattern, ear rosettes of Life Guards pattern.**

1984 May — Wallis & Wallis — £1700.
Life Guards. A very fine and desirable post-1902 **officers** helmet. Gilt fittings with leather backed gilt brass chinchain and large bosses, large gilt helmet plate, falling white horsehair plume capped by domed gilt button. Grey silk lining. Old tailor's label inside reads "25/6/25 Lord Allenby 7.3/8 full". VGC. Illus. (silk lining worn in parts). Note: The Auctioneers feels satisfied that this helmet is indeed that of **Field Marshal Sir Edmund Allenby**, Colonel of the 1st Life Guards. **This helmet was in EXC condition for its age.** N.B. See Fig: 10. for an example of a similar helmet.

1992 May — Wallis & Wallis — £2300.
Royal Horse Guards. A good Victorian **officers** silver plated helmet. Gilt, silver and enamel helmet plate, leather backed chinchain, scarlet **yak hair** plume with large gilt rosette, padded silk lining. In tin case with nameplate **"Lord Herbert".** VGC. (chinchain stitching loose, very minor gilt rubbing). Illus. **Lord Herbert (15th Earl of Pembroke) commissioned 1899.**

1992 May Wallis & Wallis £900.
The Life Guards. A good Victorian **troopers** white metal helmet. Brass ornaments, leather backed graduated link chinchain and ear rosettes. Brass and white metal helmet plate, and white hair plume with small rosette. Leather liner. VGC. It is unusual to find other ranks Victorian items in this condition, evidently never issued for service. Illus. N.B. See Fig: 11. for an example of a similar helmet.

1995 March Spinks £2700.
Royal Horse Guards. an **officers** helmet of **white metal** with gilt fittings. QC helmet plate of gilt and enamel, together with a white horsehair plume of the **Life Guards.** Single rose pattern rose bosses with non tapering chinchain, the headband of chamois. Together with a chamois helmet bag, and an earlier helmet tin with plaque engraved Major R. Evans. Illus. **A post 1953 pattern helmet in what appeared to be in VGC, apart from the plume socket which was turned sideways.**

1995 June Bosleys £2600.
Royal Horse Guards. A fine post 1902 example of an **officers** helmet. Skull of German silver, gilt rose pattern ear bosses, leather backed chinchain. Cut silver star, pierced garter on translucent enamel. Simulated red yak hair plume with rose boss. Original chamois lining. An EXC example. (some minor dulling). Gilt remains fresh. Illus. **The plume did not look to be of yak hair.** N.B. See Fig: 5. for an example of a similar helmet.

1997 Feb Bosleys £825.
The Life Guards. A good post 1953 **troopers** helmet. Silvered skull with brass and silvered Queen's crown helmet plate. Gilded rose bosses support chinchain. White horsehair plume with button boss. Original leather lining. With minor service wear, otherwise VGC.

1997 Nov Wallis & Wallis £1000.
The Life Guards. A good ERII **other ranks** white metal helmet. Brass mounts, leather backed chinchain and large ear rosettes. Brass and white metal helmet plate, white metal top mount with white hair plume with brass ball and white metal rosette, leather liner. VGC. (minor dents top right). Illus. **This helmet looked to be in almost 'new' condition.**

1999 Feb Military Antiques £1800.
The Life Guards. A good Post 1902 **officers** silvered helmet complete with white plume with gilt finial, KC helmet plate, leather liner, ear rosettes and chinchain. GC. **Skull, very minor dents, liner with service wear, otherwise in GC.**

1999 Feb Military Antiques £680.
Royal Horse Guards. A Victorian **troopers** white metal helmet complete with red plume with finial, QVC helmet plate, leather liner, ear rosettes and chinchain. GC. (with service wear). **Both ear rosettes present, one fitted with a hook. Minor skull dents, chinchain stitching as found, the ends of the wreath either side of 'The George' damaged, otherwise in near GC for age.**

Dragoon Guards 1847 Pattern

1970 Oct Wallis & Wallis £25.
1st (King's) Dragoon Guards. An **officers** helmet, gilt overall, white hair plume. GC. (ear bosses and chinstrap missing, some leaf spray on side of badge missing, no lining). **Poor cond. Incorrect colour plume.**

1970 Oct Wallis & Wallis £49.
6th Dragoon Guards (Carabiniers). An **officers** helmet with plume. Brass skull (no traces of gilt), black hair plume with large rosette, bosses to chinchain (no leather backing) GC. Tip of laurel leaf on helmet plate missing.

1971 Tradition Magazine £95.
7th (Princess Royal's) Dragoon Guards. An **other ranks** pattern helmet with plume, chinchain and rosettes. **Near GC. Some damage to base of plume socket, chinchain shortened.**

1973 Jan Wallis & Wallis £520.
5th (Princess Charlotte of Wales's) Dragoon Guards. An **officers** helmet, with ear rosettes and chinchain, no plume. This historic relic of the Charge of the Heavy Brigade at Balaclava on the 25th October 1854, was worn on that morning by Lieutenant Hay Swinfen. **The finials to the plume socket bent inwards, chinchain backing missing, otherwise in VGC considering age and <u>service wear.</u> Lt Swinfen (later Lieutenant Colonel) was born on the 15th January 1830 and died 22nd June 1914. He was the last surviving combatant officer of this most famous charge**. N.B. See Fig: 16. for an example of a similar helmet.

1975 May Wallis & Wallis £65.
3rd (Prince of Wales's) Dragoon Guards. A Victorian **other ranks** pattern helmet. Brass helmet plate and foliated mounts, plume holder. Quite GC, (most of lining, chinchain, plume and bosses missing, some dents and minor cracks).

1975 Dec Wallis & Wallis £200.
7th (Princess Royal's) Dragoon Guards. A Victorian brass **other ranks** helmet, black and white plume, large rococo pattern badge. Large Tudor rose bosses. GC. (brass rubbed with cleaning, lining as found). Illus. **GC. Chinchain absent.**

1980 Nov Wallis & Wallis £500.
4th (Royal Irish) Dragoon Guards. An 1847 pattern **officers** helmet with gilt skull, mounts. Badge with silvered cut star, velvet backed chinchain. White plume with rosette. GC. (minor dents and splits to skull, well restored overall, the gilt bright). Illus. **Below GC. The plume rosette was an other ranks pattern.** N.B. See Fig: 15. for an example of a similar helmet.

1982 April/May Geoff White Militaria £185.
7th (Princess Royal's) Dragoon Guards. <u>Helmet plate only.</u> A very fine silver and gilt **officers** 1847 pattern helmet plate. VGC. A fine and early badge. Illus. **EXC/VGC Cond. The gilt bright.**

1983 Feb Tradition (London) £385.
6th Dragoon Guards (Carabiniers). An **officers** helmet with red plume, helmet plate, chinchain and rosettes. **Below GC. The skull with many small dents, little trace of gilt. Solder repairs to inner skull seam, damage to helmet plate, the red plume a modern replacement.**

1991 Feb Blunderbuss £1750.
4th (Royal Irish) Dragoon Guards. An **officers** helmet with plume, chinchain

and ear rosettes. **EXC cond. The gilt on the skull, helmet plate, and fittings in very bright condition.**

1991 Oct Wallis & Wallis £1300.
1st (King's) Dragoon Guards. An **officers** 1847 pattern helmet, red hair plume, velvet backed chinchain and ear rosettes. Padded silk lining. VGC. (Beautifully restored and regilt overall). Illus. **VGC. Plume was a modern replacement item.** N.B. See Fig: 13. for an illustration of this helmet.

1991 Oct Wallis & Wallis £210.
4th (Royal Irish) Dragoon Guards. An **other ranks** helmet. Brass skull, leather backed chinchain and ear rosettes. Helmet plate with star behind centre device, white hair plume with rosette. QGC.

1994 Sept Blunderbuss £1650.
2nd Dragoon Guards (Queen's Bays). An **officers** helmet complete with chinchain, rosettes and plume. **GC. The gilt rubbed overall.**

1994 Oct Military Antiques £1250.
5th (Princess Charlotte of Wales's) Dragoon Guards. An **officers** helmet complete with plume, helmet plate, red leather head lining, chinchain and rosettes. Label attached to helmet stated '**worn at Balaclava**'. The proprietor stated this helmet came from the National Army Museum. **Skull dented at rear, the gilt rubbed, no backing to chinchain, plume possibly a modern copy, otherwise in GC for age.**

1995 Aug Bosleys £220.
3rd (Prince of Wales's) Dragoon Guards. Helmet Plate only. A fine 1847-71 **officers** helmet plate. A wreath, half laurel, half oak surrounding a shield. A cut silver star with gilt VR strap. Fresh condition with only minor service wear. Illus.

1995 Oct Bosleys £400.
6th Dragoon Guards (Carabiniers). A good 1849 pattern **troopers** helmet with plume. Helmet with graduated chinchain supported by two rose bosses. Helmet plate with entwined cypher, cut steel star (part of oak leaves absent). Leather lining, replacement red horsehair plume. Officially strengthened and signs of solder marks to skull, chinchain backing a replacement. **Near GC. Wrongly described in catalogue as a 3rd Dragoon Guards helmet.**

1995 Dec Bosleys £2200.
1st (King's) Dragoon Guards. A fine Albert pattern helmet, fire gilt helmet plate. Fire gilt plume holder with scarlet horsehair plume. Two gilt rose bosses support chinchain with red leather backing. Leather sweatband now absent. Accompanied by **rare foreign service quilted helmet cover with neck flap.** Contained in original japanned tin. VGC. Fire gilt remains fresh. **VGC. It is extremely rare to find a helmet complete with its carrying tin, let alone with the foreign service cover.**

1998 July Regimentals £1250.
5th (Princess Charlotte of Wales's) Dragoon Guards. A good example of an **other ranks** 1847 pattern helmet with plume. Complete with helmet plate, ear rosettes, chinchain, and leather liner. GC. Skull polished bright. **Plume age discoloured, small repair to laurel leaves on plate, otherwise in GC.**

Dragoon Guards 1871 Pattern

1960 Jan Wallis & Wallis £10.
4th (Royal Irish) Dragoon Guards. An **officers** pattern helmet. No plume, but fitted with inter-changeable ball and spike. With japanned tin case. VGC. (enamel on badge as found). **It is most unusual to find a helmet fitted with the ball and spike fitment. VGC/GC.**

1962 Nov Wallis & Wallis £35.
1st (King's) Dragoon Guards. An **officers** gilt helmet. George V cypher to centre of helmet plate. Complete with its scarlet plume and scaled chinstrap. A few slight dents, otherwise in VGC. Illus. **It is exceedingly rare for a post 1911 version of this regiments helmet to be offered for sale.**

1962 Nov Wallis & Wallis £20.
6th Dragoon Guards (Carabiniers). An **officers** gilt helmet with plume. White hair plume and scaled chinstrap (no backing). Fair Condition. (Gilt worn and a few dents). Illus. **The plume looked to be of the Life Guards pattern, and was therefore incorrect for this helmet.**

1963 March Wallis & Wallis £13.
2nd Dragoon Guards (Queen's Bays). A late Victorian **officers** helmet with silver, gilt and enamel badge. Complete with its black plume in japanned case. QGC (Badge slightly as found). N.B. See Fig: 22. for an example of a similar helmet.

1969 Sept Wallis & Wallis £10.
3rd (Prince of Wales's) Dragoon Guards. Helmet Plate only. An **officers** silver and enamel helmet plate. VGC. (tip of star missing), also an enamelled shako plate of R.M.A. (2).

1971 Nov Sothebys £110.
7th (Princess Royal's) Dragoon Guards. A Victorian **officers** helmet complete with plume, helmet plate, liner, ear rosettes and chinchain.

1972 March Wallis & Wallis £91.
5th (Princess Charlotte of Wales's) Dragoon Guards. An **officers** gilt helmet c. 1900. Silver star badge, silver numeral on gilt ground. Original lining, red & white hair plume. GC. (gilt worn, plume fastener not original). Illus. **Plume looked to be an other ranks pattern, otherwise a VGC helmet.** N.B. See Fig: 29. for an example of a similar helmet.

1975 May Christies £273.
7th (Princess Royal') Dragoon Guards. A 1901 pattern **officers** helmet with black & white plume. Illus. **ED VII Royal Cypher to centre device of the helmet plate. The plume looked to be an other ranks pattern, some links loose on chinchain, otherwise GC.**

1979 Sept Wallis & Wallis £900.
3rd (Prince of Wales's) Dragoon Guards. An **officers** helmet with gilt skull and mounts. Good silvered, gilt & enamel badge. Black & red plume with gilt rosette. Officers name in ink on lining "Davies". GC. (minor dents to skull and peak). Illus. **This helmet, even though fitted with an other ranks plume, realised an exceedingly high price for 1979.** N.B. See Fig: 24 for an example of a similar helmet.

1979 Sept Wallis & Wallis £700.
6th Dragoon Guards (Carabineers). An **officers** helmet. Gilt skull with gilt mounts, leather backed chinchain and ear rosettes. Silvered and gilt badge, white hair plume with gilt rose finial. GC. (minor dents to skull, head lining torn). **The centre device on the helmet plate was the pattern with the non voided crown arches.** N.B. See Fig: 31 for an example of a similar helmet.

1980 Dec Blunderbuss £370.
7th (Princess Royal's) Dragoon Guards. A **troopers** helmet complete with plume, helmet plate, liner, ear rosettes and chinchain. VGC. **An VGC helmet.**

1982 Feb Tradition £685.
4th (Royal Irish) Dragoon Guards. An **officers** pattern helmet complete with plume, helmet plate, leather head lining, ear rosettes and chinchain. GC. **Gilt on skull worn, some scratches, chinchain backing as found. GC.**

1984 Oct Wallis & Wallis £850.
7th (Princess Royal's) Dragoon Guards. A Victorian **officers** helmet complete with plume, helmet plate, liner, ear rosettes and chinchain. VGC. Illus. **Gilt bright, minor tears to lining, otherwise VGC.** N.B. See Fig: 35. for an example of a similar helmet.

1985 Sept Wallis & Wallis £55.
4th (Royal Irish) Dragoon Guards. <u>Helmet Plate only.</u> A **troopers** brass & white metal helmet plate. Near VGC. Illus.

1986 March Tradition £1150.
2nd Dragoon Guards (Queen's Bays). A post 1902 **officers** helmet complete with plume, helmet plate, silk lining, ear rosettes and chinchain. GC. **To the front of the skull a small hole, together with some creases. The skiver lining the inner front peak had been replaced, as had the head lining and the chinchain. N.B. The enamel backing the ER VII cypher was orange in colour. Below GC.**

1986 Sept Blunderbuss £1200.
4th (Royal Irish) Dragoon Guards. An **officers** helmet with plume, helmet plate, ear rosettes and chinchain. GC. **The head lining was missing, the gilt had been polished off, the enamel as found, incorrect pattern ear rosettes. GC/Poor cond.**

1989 Nov Wallis & Wallis £650.
4th (Royal Irish) Dragoon Guards. A **troopers** helmet, brass skull, leather backed chinchain & rosettes. Brass & white metal plate, white hair plume. Leather lining. Basically GC. (minor skull distressing, seam spilt, ear rosettes restored). Illus. **The chinchain appeared to have been shortened.**

1990 Jan Christies £528.
2nd Dragoon Guards (Queen's Bays). A gilt helmet with standard **other ranks** white metal and brass front plate bearing the regimental number. Black hair plume. GC. Illus. **The term 'gilt' as used to describe this helmet is unusual, possibly it was an officers pattern skull fitted with an other ranks helmet plate.**

1991 July Blunderbuss £1750.
3rd (Prince of Wales's) Dragoon Guards. An officers helmet with plume, helmet plate, ear rosettes and chinchain etc. EXC. **The gilt on the skull was unmarked, the helmet plate star and P.O.W.'s feathers being silver plated. The ear rosettes however appeared to be from a blue cloth helmet, with the plume and chinchain possibly being replacement items, otherwise EXC/VGC.**

1992 July Wallis & Wallis £40.
6th Dragoon Guards (Carabiniers). <u>Helmet Plate only.</u> An **other ranks** helmet plate. GC. (leather missing, two studs shortened).

1992 Sept Regimentals £1850.
4th (Royal Irish) Dragoon Guards. An **officers** helmet with plume, helmet plate, quilted cloth lining, ear rosettes and chinchain. EXC. **Possible minor damage to the enamel of the shamrock stalk on the helmet plate, otherwise EXC.**

1993 March Wallis & Wallis £195.
1st (King's) Dragoon Guards. <u>Helmet Plate only.</u> A Victorian **officers** silver, gilt and enamel helmet plate with separate silver and gilt scroll. Item nailed to an oak wall shield. GC. (one point of star missing). **The centre device was the 'V.R. cypher version. There were two nail holes in the star, with a similar hole at each end of the scroll.**

1993 May Regimentals £885.
2nd Dragoon Guards (Queen's Bays). An **other ranks** pattern helmet with horsehair plume, helmet plate, liner, ear rosettes and chinchain. VGC. **A very nice helmet, in need of light cleaning, otherwise VGC/GC.**

1993 July Regimentals £1850.
2nd Dragoon Guards (Queen's Bays). An **officers** helmet complete with plume, helmet plate, leather and silk lining, ear rosettes and velvet backed chinchain. VGC. **The ER VII cypher was backed with orange coloured enamel and had minor chips, the plume rosette was not the correct pattern for this regiment, otherwise a helmet in VGC.**

1993 July Wallis & Wallis £40.
2nd Dragoon Guards (Queen's Bays) <u>Helmet Plate only.</u> A good **other ranks** white metal and brass helmet plate. Leather backing to white metal "2". Four screw studs. Near VGC.

1993 July Wallis & Wallis £220.
3rd (Prince of Wales's) Dragoon Guards. <u>Helmet Plate only.</u> An **officers** gilt and silver plated helmet plate. Red & blue enamelled centre. GC. (enamel chipped at bottom, clasp fitting added to back).

1994 Sept Blunderbuss £2250.
1st (King's) Dragoon Guards. An **officers** helmet with plume. The skull and all fittings in VGC, the chinchain and ear rosettes in GC. **The centre device on this helmet was the 'Crest of England' version. This helmet came from the collection of a well respected collector.** N.B. See Fig: 21 for an example of a similar helmet.

1994 Sept Blunderbuss £2300.
3rd (Prince of Wales's) Dragoon Guards. An **officers** helmet, complete with plume, helmet plate, ear rosettes and chinchain. VGC. **Skull, plate, ear rosettes and chinchain in EXC cond, plume looked to be a modern replacement.**

1994 Sept Blunderbuss £2400.
4th (Royal Irish) Dragoon Guards. An **officers** pattern helmet, complete with plume, helmet plate, ear rosettes and chinchain. VGC. **Plume possibly a modern replacement.** N.B. See Fig: 28. for an example of a similar helmet.

1994 Sept Blunderbuss £2300.
5th (Princess Charlotte of Wales's) Dragoon Guards. An **officers** gilt helmet, complete with plume, helmet plate, beige quilted head lining, ear rosettes and chinchain. EXC. **The plume holder fitted to the helmet was the ball beneath the socket pattern, indicating that this was a rare post 1922 example. VGC.**

1995 March Wallis & Wallis £95.
4th (Royal Irish) Dragoon Guards. Helmet Plate only. A good **other ranks** brass & white metal helmet plate. GC.

1995 March Spinks £1400.
6th Dragoon Guards (Carabiniers). An **officers** gilt-brass full dress helmet, circa 1912. With rayed white metal star mounted with Royal Crest in white metal within a gilt strap. White plume, incorrect chinchain, (lining slightly defective). Label inside reads " 347 Annesley 18/6/12". Illus. **The plume was an other ranks pattern, and the ear rosettes were not the correct pattern for the helmet, otherwise in VGC/GC.** N.B. James Howard Adolphus Annesley joined the 18th Hussars in 1893. He saw action during the Boer War, and some time after the end of this war he transferred to the 3rd (Prince of Wales's) Dragoon Guards, then in 1905 to the 6th Dragoon Guards. He commanded the latter regiment 1913-14 and became a C.M.G.

1995 Aug Bosleys £75.
3rd (Prince of Wales's) Dragoon Guards. Helmet Plate only. A good **other ranks** post 1871 helmet plate. VGC.

1995 Oct Wallis & Wallis £950.
6th Dragoon Guards (Carabiniers). A very late Victorian **officers** gilt helmet with plume. **The centre device of the helmet plate was the pattern with non voided arches to the crown. The ear rosettes looked to be the other ranks pattern, also the plume rosette was not the correct pattern for this helmet, otherwise VGC.**

1995 Nov Regimentals £785.
3rd (Prince of Wales's) Dragoon Guards. A good **other ranks** brass helmet with undented skull, troopers leather liner, complete with red & black plume. VGC. N.B. See Fig: 38. for an example of a similar helmet.

1995 Nov Regimentals £825.
4th (Royal Irish) Dragoon Guards. A good **troopers** 1871 pattern, all brass skull, white horsehair plume, leather liner and chinstrap, complete. Undented. VGC.

1995 Nov Regimentals £765.
5th (Princess Charlotte of Wales's) Dragoon Guards. A good **other ranks** example having nickel plated skull with all brass fittings. Red horsehair plume, **other ranks** leather liner, complete with chinstrap. GC. **The red plume indicates that possibly this was a musicians helmet.**

1995 Nov Spinks £1600.
4th (Royal Irish) Dragoon Guards. An **officers** fine full dress helmet with white horsehair plume, helmet plate, head lining, ear rosettes and chinchain. (minor repairs to star plate, lining and chinchain replaced). **GC.**

1996 Feb Bosleys £60.
5th (Princess Charlotte of Wales's) Dragoon Guards. Helmet Plate only. A post 1871 **other ranks** helmet plate. Centre re-affixed, two ray tips slightly as found, otherwise GC. **QGC.**

1996 March Wallis & Wallis £125.
2nd Dragoon Guards (Queen's Bays). Helmet Plate only. An ER VII **officers** gilt and silver plated helmet plate of the 1st Dragoon Guards. Red and blue enamel backing, four short studs. GC. A generally crisp example (red and blue enamel chipped at top left). Illus. **Having closely examined the plate the author is confident that this was in fact a 2nd D/Gds plate, and not a 1st D/Gds version as listed in the catalogue.**

1996 April Bosleys £150.
2nd Dragoon Guards (Queen's Bays). Helmet Plate only. A fine example of an **other ranks** 1871 pattern helmet plate. White metal star with gilt metal garter. To the centre a silvered "2" on a black leather ground. VGC.

1996 July Spinks £1900.
7th (Princess Royal's) Dragoon Guards. An **officers** fine gilt helmet with helmet plate bearing "VR" in white metal. Original lining, good black and white plume. Illus.

1998 Feb Bosleys £900.
7th (Princess Royal's) Dragoon Guards. A good 1871 brass **troopers** helmet. Helmet plate, black over white plume with rose boss. Rose head bosses with leather backed chinchain, replaced leather lining. With minor service and age wear, otherwise GC. Illus. **N.B. For some unknown reason this regiments other ranks pattern helmets, and helmet plates, usually sell for more than those of the other six regiments.**

1998 Oct Bosleys £650.
1st (King's) Dragoon Guards. A good Boer War example of the 1871 pattern **other ranks** helmet. Brass skull with helmet plate, regimental pattern horsehair plume. Rose head bosses with replaced chinchain, leather lining to interior. Internal back peak edging stamped "1 DG 6.99". Some service wear otherwise generally VGC. Illus. **The front peak appeared to be marked, overwise in GC.**

1998 Oct Bosleys £1800.
5th (Princess Charlotte of Wales's) Dragoon Guards. A fine scarce 1871 **officers** helmet. Fire gilt skull, silvered star with gilt strap. White over red plume, leather sweatband with silk edging, gilt ear rosettes and velvet backed chinchain. Exterior of helmet professionally refurbished, the gilt bright and fresh. VGC.

Minor service wear. **The plume appeared to be a modern replacement. Near VGC.**

1998 Oct Bosleys £620.
6th Dragoon Guards (Carabiniers). A good 1871 pattern **other ranks** helmet. Brass skull, to the front a white metal star bearing gilt metal garter which encircles the numeral "6". White hair plume, brass rose head bosses with leather backed chinchain, leather liner to interior. With minor service wear, one or two stitching faults to chinchain, otherwise VGC.

1999 Jan Blunderbuss £1040.
3rd (Prince of Wales's) Dragoon Guards. A **troopers** helmet complete with plume, helmet plate, liner, ear rosettes & chinchain. VGC. **The skull had been lacquered, otherwise a nice example. VGC/GC.**

1999 Jan Blunderbuss £2200.
1st (King's) Dragoon Guards. An **officers** gilt metal helmet complete with red horsehair plume, helmet plate, cloth lining, ear rosettes and chinchain. GC. **The plume was an other ranks pattern, there was some damage to the lettering on the scroll, the skull with minor dents, otherwise GC.**

1999 Jan Blunderbuss £2250.
2nd Dragoon Guards (Queen's Bays). An **officers** post 1902 gilt metal helmet complete with black plume, ER VII helmet plate, silk and leather head lining, ear rosettes and velvet backed chinchain. EXC. **The ear rosettes were not the correct pattern for this helmet, otherwise helmet in VGC.**

Dragoons 1847 Pattern

1966 July Wallis & Wallis £36.
6th (Inniskilling) Dragoons. An **officers** helmet with plume. A fine Albert helmet with silver plated skull. VGC. (plume rosette missing). **Silver plated skull indicates post 1855.**

1984 Oct Wallis & Wallis £280.
6th (Inniskilling) Dragoons. A Victorian **other ranks** Albert pattern helmet. White metal skull, brass mounts, ear rosettes and helmet plate, white hair plume. QGC. (worn overall, no chinchain, lining as found). **Poor cond. Small crack to skull, one plume socket finial missing, damage to helmet plate, very little of liner remaining.**

1987 May Blunderbuss 1350.
1st (Royal) Dragoons. An **officers** 'Albert' pattern helmet with plume. Silver coloured skull, gilt plate with gilt beaded star with silver strap/VR to centre. Silk lining, rosettes and chinchain. VGC. (small piece of acanthus leaf missing on plate). **VGC/GC. Plume and chinchain replaced, the silver die-struck centre device was extremely rare, possibly indicating that this was a senior N.C.O.'s helmet.**

1992 May Wallis & Wallis £600.
1st (Royal) Dragoons. A Victorian **other ranks** white metal helmet. Leather backed chinchain and large rosettes, brass helmet plate, black hair plume with brass rosette, leather liner. Basically GC. (several cracks to skull, minor wear overall). Illus.

1994 Sept Blunderbuss £2300.
1st (Royal) Dragoons. A silver coloured **officers** helmet with plume, chinchain and rosettes. VGC. **In need of light cleaning, the plume a modern replacement, otherwise EXC/VGC cond. Known to have come from the collection of a respected collector.** N.B. See Fig: 43. for an example of a similar helmet.

1996 Oct Bosleys £450.
6th (Inniskilling) Dragoons. Helmet Plate only. A very fine 1847 -71 pattern **officer**s helmet plate, gilt wreath, star, strap and VR. Three screw posts to rear (one slightly shortened). VGC. Retains most of its original fire gilt finish. Illus.

1996 Dec Bosleys £850.
1st (Royal) Dragoons. A good example of an **other ranks** 1847 pattern helmet. Brass skull, brass helmet plate with silvered star and brass strap. Rose head bosses, leather backed chinchain, leather lining, black hair plume with brass rosette. Minor service wear, otherwise GC. (backing to chinchain replaced). **The brass skull would indicate that this was a pre 1855 pattern helmet.**

1997 Dec Regimentals £1250.
6th (Inniskilling) Dragoons. An 1855 pattern **other ranks** helmet complete with plume and rosette, helmet plate, ear rosettes and chinchain, leather liner. **One plume socket finial missing, otherwise in GC.**

1st and 6th Dragoons 1871 Pattern

1962 Nov Wallis & Wallis £22.
1st (Royal) Dragoons. A post 1902 **officers** white metal helmet, complete with purple plume and scaled chinstrap. VGC. **Plume should be black, the purple plume probably from a Westminster Dragoons helmet.**

1972 Jan Wallis & Wallis £69.
1st (Royal) Dragoons. A Victorian **officers** helmet. Silver plated skull with gilt star plate & fittings, complete with chinchain. GC. (Minor dents to skull, rosettes painted gold, chinchain lining worn). Illus. **This helmet was fitted with a ball and spike, in place of the more usual plume socket.**

1982 May Blunderbuss £370.
1st (Royal) Dragoons. A **troopers** helmet complete with plume, helmet plate, ear rosettes and chinchain etc. GC. **The chinchain backing had possibly been replaced, otherwise GC.**

1982 June Regimentals £500.
1st (Royal) Dragoons. An Victorian **officers** pattern helmet. Silvered skull, chinchain. VGC. **No head lining, backing to chinchain absent, otherwise VGC/GC.**

1985 Sept Christies £2200.
6th (Inniskilling) Dragoons. The helmet of Captain L.E.G. Oates, with plume, helmet plate, ear rosettes and chinchain. Contained in a helmet case with name plate of E.G.B. Oates (nephew of Capt Oates). Sold with a letter from him to the present owner confirming provenance. **Captain L.E.G. Oates was a member of Captain Scott's ill fated Antarctic expedition of 1910. The hel-**

met was sold to the 5th Royal Inniskilling Dragoon Guards Regiment. N.B. See Fig: 49 for an late version example of this pattern of helmet.

1991 Feb Blunderbuss £1750.
6th (Inniskilling) Dragoons. An **officers** helmet complete with plume, helmet plate, cloth lining, ear rosettes and chinchain. EXC. **The gilt bright, the plume a modern replacement, otherwise EXC.**

1992 May Wallis & Wallis £1200.
1st (Royal) Dragoons. A Victorian **officers** silver plated helmet. Gilt ball & spike, red leather backed chinchain & rosettes, gilt cut star with silver plated garter, padded silk lining. In its tin case with name plate "Mr M.R. Burrell Esq, Royal Dragoons". GC. Illus. **Sir Merrik Raymond Burrell C.B.E., Lt 24/Feb/1900. Saw service in the Boer War, High Sheriff of Sussex 1918. Near VGC.** N.B. See Fig: 46. for an example of a similar helmet.

1993 Nov Wallis & Wallis £560.
6th (Inniskilling) Dragoons. An **other ranks** white metal helmet with brass mounts, leather backed chinchain & rosettes. Brass & white metal helmet plate, white hair plume with rosette, leather lining. GC. (restored & polished bright overall). Illus. **Incorrectly described in catalogue as being 6th Dragoon Guards.**

1995 Oct Regimentals £1850.
6th (Inniskilling) Dragoons. A superb untouched example of the 1871 pattern **officers** helmet with white horsehair plume. Silvered skull, gilt & silver helmet plate, silk head lining, ear rosettes and chinchain EXC. **A rare pre 1880 helmet with the 'VR' centre device to the helmet plate, the gilt very crisp. EXC.** N.B. See Fig: 48. for an example of a similar helmet.

1997 May Blunderbuss £1040.
1st (Royal) Dragoons. A **troopers** helmet with black plume, helmet plate, liner, ear rosettes and chinchain. GC. **The leather loose on the chinchain, otherwise GC.** N.B. See Fig: 50. for an example of a similar helmet.

1998 Aug Bosleys £1300.
1st (Royal) Dragoons. A very fine 1871 pattern **officers** helmet with silvered skull, gilt & silvered helmet plate. Ear rosettes & red morocco backed chinchain, soft quilted silk head lining. With carrying case bearing nameplate "E.G. Troyte-Bullock Esq, The Royal Dragoons". The gilt polished to brass, one minor ripple not affecting appearance, otherwise VGC. **Even allowing for the condition of the gilt, and the slight ripple, a very low price for such a good helmet.**

1999 Jan Regimentals £885.
1st (Royal) Dragoons. An **other ranks** 1871 pattern helmet complete with plume, helmet plate, liner, ear rosettes & chinchain. GC. (with service wear). **Some dents to rear of skull, liner loose.**

Finally, before moving on to provide details of various yeomanry cavalry helmets, sold both through militaria shops and at auction salesrooms, I list below information relating to a 'mystery' helmet that realised £2100 at a London salesroom in 1997.

The description that follows is reproduced as it was printed in the salesroom catalogue, and includes some additional text from within the catalogue relating to the helmet. As I was unable to examine the actual helmet, I am unable to express a considered opinion on this item of head-dress. I did however observe from the catalogue illustration that the plume holder appeared to be of Type: J., and that the crown surmounting the helmet plate, (described below as being 'non-standard') was of Type: P., both of which were of the type to be seen on the helmets of the Staffordshire Yeomanry of the period c. 1850 to c. 1893/94, as was the white metal peak binding, and the white metal ornamentation, which may, or may not be significant.

A Victorian Heavy Cavalry style Helmet, possibly for a General Officer
A Good and extremely unusual and interesting metal helmet, generally of 1847 "Albert" pattern but with a concave front peak, the skull lacquered black, the peak binding and ornamentation similar to that of standard Heavy Cavalry helmets but of white metal (now heavily tarnished). The plate of Albert style but surmounted by a non-standard version of the crown, the white metal hobnailed star struck rather than cut, and mounted with a domed gilt centre bearing white metal *VR* cypher within a plain (uninscribed) strap. Black horsehair plume in white metal socket, narrow white metal chinchain with red leather backing, good internal headband of tan Morocco leather with silk element above, the peaks lined with green Morocco leather. See illustration.

This helmet may be of considerable importance. It has been well used, suggesting that it is not merely an experimental pattern. The absence of any regimental title in the centre of the plate indicates that it probably does not belong, as one might expect, to a Volunteer or Yeomanry unit. Furthermore, the unusual concave front peak makes it conceivable that it was worn by a General Officer of Heavy Cavalry on active service. Significantly, the only other known example of an Albert helmet with a concave peak was that worn by Sir James Scarlett when commanding the Heavy Brigade in the Crimean War, although Scarlett's helmet is not identical to this one.

Yeomanry Cavalry Helmets

For many years the selling price of either an officers, or an other ranks helmet of a yeomanry regiment has always been far lower than that of a regular cavalry regiments helmet. However quite recently this situation has changed, and these days the difference between the cost of a regular, and a yeomanry helmet has narrowed considerably.

Below is given a recorded selling price for a helmet of most the yeomanry helmets covered in this book, these prices having been collated from either auction salesroom catalogues, or from helmets offered for sale in various reputable London militaria shops. Once again, where the word 'Illus' is included within the text, this indicates that the helmet concerned was illustrated in the relevant salesroom catalogue. N.B. For easy reference, the helmets have been listed in alphabetical regiment order, rather than in date order.

Berkshire Yeomanry

1980 Sept Wallis & Wallis £550.
A scarce **officers** silvered helmet c. 1875. Gilt mounts, hobnailed star, silver and gilt device. Ear rosettes and velvet backed chinchain. White hair plume with white hair brush with gilt finial, quilted cloth lining. GC. (few very minor dents to skull). Illus. **Plume may have been a modern replacement.**

1998 April Bosleys £180.
Helmet Plate only. A fine **other ranks** helmet plate c. 1897 comprising a brass eight pointed star with silvered strap bearing regimental title, with star and crescent to centre. Three screw post to reverse. VGC. Illus.

1999 Jan Blunderbuss £2600.
A fine **officers** silvered helmet complete with gilt and silvered helmet plate, ear rosettes and chinchain, white horsehair plume with rosette. VGC. **A very nice condition c. 1875 pattern helmet.**

Derbyshire Yeomanry

1972 Oct Wallis & Wallis £190.
A fine George V **officers** Albert pattern helmet. Silver plated skull, gilt mounts, large gilt "GRV" cypher helmet plate. With a red and white whalebone plume with finial, ear rosettes and chinchain. In its original tin carrying case bearing name 'Sir Philip Brocklehurst Derbyshire Yeomanry', with tin for plume. Illus. **The plume socket finials bent inwards, the plume dirty, otherwise in VGC.** Two conflicting prices were given for this helmet, these being £190 and £235.

1984 May Wallis & Wallis £450.
A fine, late Victorian **other ranks** silvered helmet. Leather backed chinchain & rose bosses, white over red plume with rose finial. Large badge bearing crowned 'V.R.' cypher. Leather lining with old label "Harry Lyons Contractor, 12 Ritter St, Woolwich 21.1/2" (in ink). VGC. Illus. **A rare helmet, minor scratches to upper front of skull, otherwise in VGC.**

1991 Nov Wallis & Wallis £570.
A Victorian **officers** Albert pattern helmet. Silver plated skull, large crowned 'V.R.' cypher badge, ear rosettes and chinchain. Red brush, with white over red plume with rosette. Leather lining. Basically GC. (Few skull dents, lining silk, and chinchain backing missing, some rubbing to gilt). Needs careful cleaning. Illus.

1993 Jan Wallis & Wallis £75.
Helmet Plate only. A good **other ranks** gilding metal, crowned royal cypher helmet plate. Near VGC.

Duke of Lancaster's Own Yeomanry

1979 Sept Wallis & Wallis £600.
A Victorian **officers** 1871 pattern helmet. Silvered skull with gilt wreath, crowned badge bearing three lions. Red leather backed chinchain & ear rosettes. White horsehair plume with **white metal** finial. Tailors label inside with name "Thurles". GC. Illus. **the plume looked to be an other ranks pattern, otherwise in VGC/GC.**

1980 Sept Wallis & Wallis £450.
A rare Victorian **officers** black japanned helmet c. 1865. Fine gilt badge bearing three lions, ear rosettes and chinchain. Silk lining. White hair upright hair plume, with falling white hair plume and gilt rosette. VGC. (interior painted green). Illus. **The tall inner plume socket was absent from the plume holder, otherwise looked to be near VGC.**

1982 March Blunderbuss £26.
Helmet Plate only. A Victorian **troopers** brass helmet plate. GC. **This was a Post 1871 example retaining all its original screw studs to reverse. GC.**

1998 May Blunderbuss £2600.
A Victorian **officers** silvered helmet complete with white hair plume, gilt helmet plate, liner, ear rosettes and chinchain. EXC. **The gilt in bright condition, the plume however looked as if it might be a modern replacement, otherwise in EXC overall.**

1998 Feb Bosleys £400.
Helmet Plate only. A fine example c. 1863-78. Large gilt wreath with ornate shield bearing three lions, surmounted by a crown. All three screw posts to reverse. Two small pinholes professionally plugged. Generally VGC. Illus. **Although not mentioned in the catalogues description, I would suggest that this was an officers pattern plate as it was evident that the three lions were a separate fitment superimposed upon the shield. This was an exceedingly high price for such an example.**

Essex Yeomanry

1972 Jan Wallis & Wallis £87.
A good brass helmet, red shredded whalebone plume, with chinchain & ear bosses. GC. (in above average condition). Illus. **Catalogue description did not list if officers or other ranks, although the plume was certainly of the latter pattern.**

1981 Feb Blunderbuss £400.
A **troopers** brass helmet complete with red hair plume, helmet plate and scroll, leather liner, ear rosettes and chinchain. GC. **One tip of rayed star as found, chinchain loose on backing. Near GC.** N.B. See Fig:52. for an illustration of this helmet.

1995 Sept Military Antiques £2000.
An **officers** gilt helmet complete with red hair plume & rosette. gilt and silvered helmet plate, gilt scroll, ear rosettes and chinchain, beige quilted liner. With its metal carrying case. EXC. **An untouched example in EXC condition.**

1997 Feb Bosleys £690.
A good scarce Post 1908 **troopers** brass helmet, with brass and white metal plate bearing "Decus Et Tutamen" to strap, silvered scroll. Scarlet hair plume, rose head bosses & leather backed chinchain, leather head lining. Minor service wear, otherwise VGC. Illus. **Although not listed in catalogue description, the chinchain backing was very much in as 'found condition'.**

Fife Mounted Rifles

1980 Dec Wallis & Wallis £350.
A Victorian **officers** leather helmet with white metal and gilt mounts. Velvet backed chinchain, white horsehair plume GC. Illus.

1996 Dec Bosleys £1000.
A good late 19th century **officer** example. Skull & peaks of black leather, regimental pattern helmet plate. Gilt metal plume holder with white horsehair plume. Two bosses support a silvered chinchain with brown velvet backing. Quilted cotton sweatband with silk edging. To the interior the name "Proudfoot". Minor age wear and congealing to the leather, otherwise GC. Illus.

Fife Light Horse

1979 Dec Wallis & Wallis £410.
A Victorian **officers** white metal helmet, silvered & gilt badge and motto scroll. Ear rosette & leather backed chinchain, white horsehair plume with **gilt** rosette. GC. (minor faults to inside, lining as found). Illus. **The sword held by the knight on the helmet plate was missing its blade, and the plume rosette was the incorrect colour for this regiment, otherwise near GC.**

1980 July Sothebys £300.
A post 1871 pattern helmet. white metal skull with regimental badge and leaves, leather liner, original chinstrap, retaining original plume. c. 1896. In tin box with initials WSP on side. GC. **Not stated if officers or other ranks pattern.**

1981 Feb Blunderbuss £420.
An **officers** helmet complete with white plume with silvered rosette. White metal skull, silvered & gilt regimental helmet plate, ear rosettes and chinchain, quilted cloth lining. VGC/GC. **Burnt onto the rear peak the name 'Palm', with the same name scratched on inside of skull. The head lining as found, otherwise VGC/GC. Note. W. Stuart Palm held the post of Surgeon Captain 11th July 1894.** N.B. See Fig: 53. for an illustration of this helmet with the plume removed.

1994 Dec Bosleys £950.
A rare 1871 pattern **other ranks** helmet. White metal body with regimental device to centre, white horsehair plume. Retains original leather sweatband, white metal ear rosettes and chinchain (leather missing). With minor dents, otherwise VGC. Illus.

Glasgow Yeomanry

1972 Jan Wallis & Wallis £125.
A fine Victorian **officers** helmet c. 1860. Profusely decorated with gilt foliage, large crowned badge. Rosettes & chinchain, green cock's feather plume. GC. Illus.

1983 Sept Wallis & Wallis £750.
A fine Victorian **officers** helmet. Silvered skull, velvet backed chinchain & large ear rosettes. Silver and gilt crowned helmet plate. With its scarce undress top-spike. Silk lining. In its chamois leather bag and tin case with nameplate to "W.D. Campbell Esq". EXC condition. (minor lining wear). Illus. **This extremely fine helmet was purchased by the National Army Museum. N.B. Walter Douglas Campbell (1850-1914) commissioned 24th April 1876.**

1984 Oct Wallis & Wallis £950.
An **officers** helmet with green cock's feather plume. Complete with helmet plate, ear rosettes and velvet backed chinchain. VGC. Illus. **This helmet was fitted with the 1871 pattern plume holder, and the cock's feather plume did not sit correctly upon the plume socket. Otherwise VGC.**

1990 Jan Christies £605.
A Victorian white metal helmet with brass fittings, and brass and white metal helmet plate. Lining of stitched fabric, ear rosettes and chinchain, together with a large dark green feather plume (probably from a Royal Company of Archers cocked hat). Chinchain lining defective. **No mention given in the catalogues description as to the overall condition of this helmet. N.B. With regard to the feather plume mentioned above, the officers of this regiment did wear such a plume in their helmets when in full dress, and therefore the plume mentioned was probably the correct one.**

1997 Jan Aldershot Militaria Fair £225.
Helmet Plate only. An **officers** gilt and white metal helmet plate, complete with all screw studs to reverse. Very minor staining, the gilt bright. VGC.

Hampshire Yeomanry

1980 July Blunderbuss £380.
A white metal **troopers** pattern helmet, with white horsehair plume having a white metal rosette. White metal skull with all fittings in white metal. White metal star with brass strap inscribed "Hampshire Yeomanry", with brass rose. White metal ear rosettes & chinchain. GC. **Front and rear peak skiver age worn, otherwise in GC.**

1992 Aug Wallis & Wallis £210.
A Victorian **other ranks** helmet. White metal mounts, graduated link chinchain and ear rosettes. Brass and white metal helmet plate with black leather centre backing. Red hair plume with plain white metal rosette, leather lining. Basically GC. (some dents, chinchain backing missing, tip of spike damaged, plume replaced). **The red plume might possibly indicate that this was either a musicians, or a trumpeters helmet. Helmet in less than GC.**

Hampshire Carabiniers

1972 Sept Wallis & Wallis £102.
A fine Victorian **officers** silvered helmet. Silver & gilt badge of the 'Hampshire Carabiniers', ear rosettes & chinchain. GC. (refinished overall, plume missing). Illus.

1979 June Wallis & Wallis £310.
A Post 1902 **officers** white metal helmet. Gilt mounts, gilt and silvered badge. Head lining, with a leather backed chinchain. GC. (no plume, slight gilt rubbing, minor abrasion marks).

1984 July Military Antiques £525.
A Victorian **officers** helmet. Gilt mounts, gilt and silvered helmet plate, gilt ear rosettes & gilt leather backed chinchain. Silk lining with name inside "Best". GC. (gilt rubbed overall, plume missing). **T.G. Best. Captain: 4th May 1892, previously served with the Royal Horse Artillery. Helmet in GC.** N.B. See Fig: 54A. for an illustration of helmet.

1998 April Bosleys £800.
A rare example of the 1871 pattern **officers** helmet. Silvered skull with gilt fittings. Gilt star, silvered strap inscribed "Hampshire Carabiniers", with gilt rose. Gilt ear rosettes with leather backed chinchain. Quilted silk lining, scarlet horsehair plume. Overall age wear, some dulling, lining part shot, otherwise GC. Illus. **The plume looked to be an other ranks pattern, and possibly in view of its colour from a musicians or trumpeters helmet.**

Hertfordshire Yeomanry

1985 Oct Wallis & Wallis £50.
Helmet Plate only. A good Victorian **troopers** helmet plate. White metal hart on a brass crowned ornamental shield. Near VGC. Illus. **One screw stud to reverse re-soldered, otherwise VGC.**

1988 May Blunderbuss £1150.
An Victorian **officers** silver plated helmet. Gilt and silvered QVC helmet plate, gilt fittings, gilt ear rosettes and leather backed chinchain, beige quilted head lining. Black horsehair plume with gilt rosette. EXC. **The gilt in bright condition, the skull unmarked except for a small contemporary hole repair which did not effect the helmet's appearance. Overall condition: EXC.** N.B. See Fig: 55. for an illustration of helmet.

1989 June Phillips Auctioneers £950.
An **officers** helmet. Silvered skull with gilt fittings, including crowned front plate with silver stag. Gilt spike, rosettes & chinchain, silk lining. c. 1870. GC. (backing to chinchain lacking). **An extremely rare Pre 1880 version, predating the use of a plume holder on this regiments helmet.**

1992 May Wallis & Wallis £1000.
A good Victorian **officers** silver plated helmet. Gilt ornaments, top mount spike, velvet backed chinchain and large rosettes. Gilt crowned shield helmet plate bearing silver plated hart. Padded silk lining, in its tin case with nameplate "S. Gurney Sheppard". VGC. (plume missing, chinchain stitching loose). Illus. **Samuel Guerney Sheppard: 2nd Lieutenant 13.1.1900. Awarded D.S.O. for services during the Boer War. Killed in action at Gallipoli in 1915 whilst leading regiment (as temporary Lt Colonel) into action.**

Lancashire Mounted Rifle Volunteers

1990 Jan Christies £1540.
A rare 'Albert' pattern helmet of white metal with white metal ornament and plate, the latter incorporating the shield of Lancaster and regimental title. Red leather lining to helmet and chinchain. Red and white plume with large brass rose finial. With a metal helmet case. Illus. **The catalogue did not state if an officers or an other ranks pattern helmet. The author has no record of another example of this extremely rare helmet being offered for sale.**

Lothians & Berwickshire Yeomanry

1980 Nov Wallis & Wallis £450.
A Victorian **officers** helmet. White metal skull, gilt mounts and badge with silvered garter & title scrolls. Ear rosettes & chinchain, liner, hair plume. Basically GC. (Gilt rubbed, top right hand corner of wreath missing, lining & chinchain as found, plume rosette missing). Illus. **Helmet fitted with an incorrect colour plume. Below GC.**

1988 May Wallis & Wallis £1000.
A Victorian **troopers** helmet with plume, helmet plate, chinchain & ear rosettes. GC (chinchain backing as found) Illus. **This looked to be a nice helmet GC.**

1990 Oct Wallis & Wallis £65.
Helmet Plate only. A Victorian **other ranks** thin, die-struck two part helmet plate. Basically GC. (junction of crown repaired). Illus.

1998 Dec Bosleys £600.
A good scarce 1871 pattern **troopers** helmet. Silvered skull decorated with brass thistles. Helmet plate of crowned garter, thistle wreath & Order of The Thistle Star. Brass rose head bosses with replacement chinchain. Brown leather lining bearing in ink **"L & BYC 68" and "No 102"**. White hair plume with rose boss. Minor service wear, one or two points on wreath as found, otherwise GC. Illus.

Lothians & Border Horse

1986 July Blunderbuss £1150.
An **officers** silvered helmet complete with gilt & silvered helmet plate together with silvered scrolls. Gilt ear rosettes and chinchain, quilted cloth lining, white horsehair plume with gilt rosette. VGC. **The gilt bright, one very minor crack to lower wreath of helmet plate, otherwise in VGC. Name on label attached to lining "Linlithgow".** See Chapter: 5. Endnote No.9. for service details. N.B. See Fig: 56. for an illustration of the helmet.

Montgomeryshire Yeomanry

1979 Sept Wallis & Wallis £1025.
A fine **officers** black metal helmet c. 1860. Large bulbous mount supports red hair plume with gilt finial. Rayed silver backplate bearing dragon & strap. Silvered lion head bosses, rope ringed velvet backed chinchain, padded lining. VGC. (refinished overall). Illus. **The price realised obviously reflected the rarity of this pattern of helmet.**

1982 May Blunderbuss £420.
An **officers** white metal helmet, complete with helmet plate, white hair plume with gilt rosette, chinchain and ear rosettes, quilted cloth lining. EXC. **An untouched example with all original fittings, and in EXC condition.** N.B. See Fig: 57. for an illustration of the helmet.

1983 Aug Wallis & Wallis £425.
An **officers** spiked helmet of the pattern worn 1882-96. White metal skull, helmet plate, mounts, ear rosettes & chinchain. Leather lining. GC. (minor skull dents, chinchain stitching as found). Illus. **This rare pattern helmet was fitted with a rayed star plate, and therefore was probably an other ranks, and not an officers pattern as described in the catalogue.**

1995 Nov Spinks' £600.
A **troopers** fine helmet, similar in style to regular Dragoon helmets, but white metal throughout. Star plate bearing the dragon with regimental title, white horsehair plume. GC. Illus. **Whilst not mentioned in the description given in the catalogue, the helmet was complete with ear rosettes, chinchain, and plume rosette.**

1999 April Bosley's £1900.
A very fine officers example. Red morocco leather backed chinchain, quilted silk lining, white hair plume. Original Japanned tin named to J.D. Frost, esq. V.GC.

Norfolk Imperial Yeomanry

1984 Sept Wallis & Wallis £170.
Helmet Plate only. An Ed VII **officers** gilt and silvered helmet plate. GC. (lower end of wreath detached). Illus. **Near GC.**

1988 Oct Wallis & Wallis £150.
An **other ranks** black leather helmet, brass binding to peaks, ear to ear wreath, top mount and one ear rosette. Yellow hair plume & rosette. Leather lining. QGC. (peak binding dented and loose, chinchain missing, brass tarnished).

1997 Feb Bosleys £803.
A fine Ed VII **troopers** helmet. Black patent leather skull, regimental pattern plate. A fluted socket with saffron yellow plume with rose head boss. Two rose head bosses with brass chinchain, leather liner to interior. A good example. Illus.

Northamptonshire Yeomanry

1982 May Wallis & Wallis £700.
A very fine **officers** silvered helmet c. 1907. Plume mount, leather backed chinchain, large silvered star badge, the centre device in gilt. Complete with its pale blue over white horsehair plume. VGC. Illus. **Helmet in EXC condition.**

1995 Oct Military Antiques £1900.
An **officers** silvered helmet complete with silver and gilt helmet plate, gilt ear rosettes and gilt chinchain. Blue over white horsehair plume with gilt rosette, quilted cloth liner, GC. **There appeared to be some damage to the ball/socket of the plume holder, plume may have been a modern replacement.**

1996 May Wallis & Wallis £1600.
An **officers** helmet complete with gilt and silvered helmet plate, ear rosettes, chinchain, and plume. GC. **The plume socket was turned sideways indicating possible damage to the fitment. Near GC.**

North Somerset Yeomanry

1970 July Wallis & Wallis £95.
A fine Victorian **officers** silvered helmet c. 1850. Complete with gilt badge and fittings, white hair plume, chinchain. VGC. (small repair crack to rear of skull). Illus. **Although not mentioned in the catalogue description, large 'Albert' pattern ear rosettes were fitted to this helmet.**

1984 May Wallis & Wallis £500.
A fine Victorian **officers** silvered helmet c. 1880. Crowned badge with centre device and title of regiment. White horsehair plume, red leather backed chinchain and gilt lion head ear bosses. VGC. (plume rosette missing, minor wear to gilt on chinchain). Illus. **This was an extremely attractive helmet.**

1996 July Spinks £1500.
An extremely fine 'Albert' pattern helmet. Massive white metal skull with gilt fittings. Original lining, white horsehair plume. VGC. (rose at top of plume possibly a replacement). Illus. **Helmet from the Power-Hynes collection.**

1996 Aug Bosleys £270.
Helmet Plate only. A good **other ranks** example. Large gilt wreath, silvered star, gilt metal strap inscribed "The North Somerset". One or two points absent on star, otherwise toned, but in VGC. Illus. **This was an extremely high price realised for a slightly damaged other ranks plate.**

Shropshire Yeomanry

1983 April London Arms Fair £78.
Helmet Plate only. A Post 1908 **officers** gilt metal helmet plate. Gilt shield surmounted by KC, with silver diamond-cut star and gilt centre device bearing title "Shropshire Yeomanry". VGC. **All screw studs, washers and nuts present to reverse, gilt in VGC.**

1995 Nov Spinks £2600.
An **officers** magnificent white metal helmet. Gilt fittings, rococo shield surmounted by a KC, white metal hobnailed star and gilt oval with regimental title. Red and white horsehair plume, gilt chinchain and gilt ear rosettes. Red leather lining. In its tin case with plaque inscribed "R.C. Donaldson-Hudson Esq, Shropshire Yeomanry". VGC. Illus. **The plume may have been an other ranks pattern, otherwise VGC overall.**

1996 Dec Bosleys £750.
A good Post 1871 **other ranks** pattern helmet with silvered skull. Brass helmet plate with Post 1902 KC mounted with silvered cut star with brass title strap bearing "Shropshire Imperial Yeomanry". White over red horsehair plume, rose head ear bosses with leather backed chinchain. Leather lining to interior. GC. (with minor service wear). Illus.

South Salopian Yeomanry Cavalry

1984 May Wallis & Wallis £230.
An **officers** 'Albert' pattern helmet. Silvered skull, gilt and silvered badge. Chinchain, black horsehair plume with large gilt rosette. GC. (minor skull dents, some restoration overall).

1989 Oct Tradition £465.
'Albert' pattern helmet with white plume and rosette. Crowned helmet plate with white metal hobnailed star with brass strap with regimental title. Ear rosettes and velvet backed chinchain, leather head lining. GC. **Not identified as**

either other ranks or officers pattern, and fitted with incorrect colour plume. As traces of gilt remaining on helmet plate, possibly a N.C.O.'s helmet. N.B. See Fig: 57A. for an illustration of helmet.

1995 May Wallis & Wallis £750.
An **other ranks** pattern helmet. Brass ornaments and mounts, leather backed graduated chinchain with ear rosettes. Crowned, brass and white metal helmet plate, white hair plume with brass rosette, leather lining. GC. (minor dents, lower wreath of helmet plate split, lining and ear rosettes restored). Illus. **Incorrect colour plume fitted to helmet.**

1997 Oct Bosleys £120.
<u>Helmet Plate only</u>. A good example. Brass wreath, ornate shield surmounted by a crown. White metal hobnailed star with strap bearing "South Salopian Yeomanry" with three loggerheads to centre. Three short screw posts to reverse (one a contemporary replacement, old strengthening repair to crown and orb), otherwise GC. Illus. **From the description given, I would suggest that this was an other ranks pattern plate.**

Staffordshire Yeomanry

1976 Dec Wallis & Wallis £700.
A fine **officers** <u>black leather</u> helmet c. 1850. Large silvered badge with gilt garter and knot. Silvered chinchain with ear rosettes, black hair plume with <u>acorn finial</u>. Makers label 'Andrews, Helmet maker to Her Majesty, Pall Mall'. In its tin case with label bearing "Major Hon W. Bagot, Q.O.R.Y.". **The Hon William Bagot (later 3rd Lord Bagot) was Lt Colonel (Commandant) of the regiment 1854.**

1984 May Regimentals £400.
An **officers** black metal helmet with white plume and rosette. Silvered helmet plate with gilt strap and knot to centre device. Silvered ear rosettes and velvet backed chinchain, leather and silk lining. Near GC (with service wear). **Japanning worn in places, lining as found, the plume a modern replacement.** N.B. See Fig: 58. for an illustration of helmet.

1990 Jan Christies £825.
An **officers** black japanned metal helmet ornamented with white metal fittings (now finished with metallic paint), and a very fine gilt and white metal star centre to the plate. Red leather lining to chinchain, black hair plume with gilt rose finial. Illus. **No indication given in the catalogue as to the condition of helmet. The plume holder fitted to the helmet was the late version Post 1871 pattern, the plume rosette however should have been silvered/white metal.**

1995 Feb Bosleys £1600.
A scarce 1850 pattern **officers** <u>leather helmet</u>. Silvered plume holder, boss and chinchain, white horsehair plume. German silver helmet plate with gilt fretted garter, and gilt knot. Original cotton lining with small ink label of "C.M.W.". VGC. (helmet attributed to Sir Charles Michael Wolseley Bt, born 4/7/1846, served 1874-1885).

1995 Oct Bosleys £850.
An **other ranks** helmet having black finished skull, with all fittings in contrasting silver. Troopers liner, fitted with white hair plume, undented skull. GC.

Suffolk Yeomanry

1979 Nov Wallis & Wallis £290.
A Victorian **officers** helmet. Gilt skull and mounts, gilt and silvered badge, white horsehair plume with rosette. GC. (one or two minor dents, chinchain backing as found). Illus.

1982 Sept Wallis & Wallis £190.
A Victorian **troopers** helmet. Brass skull and mounts, large badge with beaded white metal star, brass title strap. White hair plume. Basically GC. (no chinchain, ear rosettes or plume rosette, small crack in skull).

1988 Jubilee Sale Wallis & Wallis £1350.
An **officers** gilt metal helmet, with hair plume and also with <u>feather plume</u>. With tin carrying case. The helmet named to officer, the gilt very bright. VGC.

1997 Dec Bosleys £600.
A scarce **troopers** example having brass skull, helmet plate of half oak, half laurel with a shield surmounted by a crown and silvered hobnailed star with brass title strap. Rose head bosses and chinchain (with replacement leather backing). White hair plume with replacement rose boss. Leather liner. Minor restoration overwise GC.

Sussex Yeomanry

1984 May Wallis & Wallis £1275.
A very fine **officers** silvered helmet with gilt fittings. Leather backed gilt chinchain and rose bosses. <u>Yellow over purple</u> horsehair plume supported by a bulbous gilt mount with fluted terminal. Large gilt rayed star badge with silver Arms of Sussex within a gilt oval band. Brown cloth lining. EXC. Illus. **This was a record auction price for a Post-1902 yeomanry helmet at that period of time. However that said, the chinchain did not look to be original to the helmet, and the ball beneath a socket pattern of plume holder was of a type unknown to the author, differing considerably from the plume holder fitted to other known examples of this regiments helmet.**

Westminster Dragoons

1980 July Sothebys £180.
An **other ranks** helmet with white metal skull and brass decoration. Brass star with white metal regimental badge, brass chinchain, purple hair plume, original lining. Illus. **Some service wear to chinchain, otherwise looked to be in GC.** N.B. See Fig: 60. for an illustration of a similar helmet.

1984 May Wallis & Wallis £290.
A Post 1902 **other ranks** silvered helmet, brass fittings with leather backed chinchain and rose bosses, original purple plume with rose finial. Brass rayed star with crowned white metal badge and "I.Y." in brass at base. Leather lining. VGC. (very minor dents to skull, chinchain leather replaced, lining worn). Illus.

This helmet, having very minor dents, the c/chain leather replaced and the lining worn, was I would suggest in GC only.

1986 April London Arms Fair £725.
An **officers** silver plated helmet with gilt metal fittings. Gilt and silvered helmet plate, gilt metal ear rosettes and gilt metal, leather backed chinchain. Beige quilted head lining. White horsehair plume with rosette. VGC. **The plume was an associated other ranks pattern, the peak skiver age worn, otherwise in VGC.**

1989 Nov Wallis & Wallis £130.
Helmet Plate only. A good scarce **other ranks helmet** plate. Near VGC. Illus. **Brass rayed star, white metal crowned garter with brass numeral '2', two labels and the letters "I.Y." in brass.**

1st West Yorkshire Yeomanry

1991 April Wallis & Wallis £85.
Helmet Plate only A Victorian **officers** helmet plate of the 1st West Yorkshire Yeomanry Cavalry. GC. (lugs resoldered). Illus.

2nd West Yorkshire Yeomanry

1960 Jan Wallis & Wallis £15.
An **officers** silver plated helmet with white plume. VGC. In japanned case.

1970 June Wallis & Wallis £120.
A fine Victorian **officers** silvered helmet. 'Albert' pattern c. 1850 complete with gilt fittings and badge. White hair plume, and lion head bosses. VGC. Illus. **Although not mentioned in the catalogue description, the chinchain was present and the silvered skull had a nice patina. The plume however looked to be an other ranks pattern, otherwise in EXC condition.**

1981 June Sothebys £340.
An **officers** helmet. Plated skull with brass rim and decorative bands. The front with wreath encircling a white metal sunburst with brass centre bearing white metal rose and regimental title, the whole surmounted by a crown. Brass chinchain with bosses in form of lions head. White horsehair plume, original lining. Illus. **Although not mention in the catalogue description, the plume was complete with a large rosette, the chinchain stitching being slightly as found, otherwise looked to be in GC.**

1989 June Phillips £580.
A Victorian **other ranks** helmet. Steel skull with brass fitting, black hair plume. Liner and backing to chinchain lacking. Illus. **Plume rosette present, apart from the missing head lining and chinchain backing the helmet looked to be in GC.**

Yorkshire Dragoons

1976 Dec Wallis & Wallis £150.
A Victorian **other ranks** white metal helmet with white plume and chinchain (both non-original). GC. (some restoration overall). Illus.

1989 Nov Wallis & Wallis £130.
Helmet Plate only. A good quality Victorian **officers** cast silver and gilt helmet plate. Near VGC and generally crisp. Illus. **All screw studs present to reverse. This helmet plate previously sold at W & W in September 1984 for £110.**

1997 Aug Regimentals £1250.
A Victorian **officers** silver plated helmet complete with silvered and gilt helmet plate. Silvered ear rosettes and chinchain, quilted cloth lining, white horsehair plume with silvered rosette. VGC. **This was a late version Victorian helmet being fitted with the Post 1871 pattern plume holder. Apart from a very minute crack to reverse of skull, the helmet was in VGC.** N.B. See Fig: 61. for an illustration of helmet.

1998 Aug Bosleys £130.
Helmet Plate only. A fine and scarce **other ranks** example worn c. 1900. Rose leaf wreath surmounted by a crown, with a star mounted with a gilt strap enclosing a white rose. Three screw posts to reverse. VGC. Illus.

1998 Dec Bosleys £1300.
An **officers** scarce and fine example c. 1876-1904. Silvered skull decorated with floral leaf decoration. Helmet plate comprises wreath surmounted by a crown, eight pointed silvered hobnailed star with brass strap and brass Yorkshire rose. Rose head bosses, silvered chinchain (with stitching faults to backing). Acanthus plume holder, white hair plume with rose head boss. Quilted cotton and silk lining. The helmet is toned, otherwise near VGC. **Both the plume holder and the plume were of the 'Albert' pattern, the crown surmounting the helmet plate was the QVC version, and the 'floral leaf design' referred to was in fact the regimental rose-leaf pattern. I doubt that the 'Yorkshire rose' was in brass as described above, as it should always be silver in colour.**

Collecting in The Future

As will be seen from the above price guide, it is quite apparent the British cavalry helmets of both regular and yeomanry regiments have appreciated in price at a very respectable rate over the past forty years, and there is no known reason why they should not continue to do so. Whilst this is very good news for collectors with a well established collection, it is not so for those just starting a collection, or those with a one or two helmets who wish to increase their collection. Additionally over the past ten years or so, fewer items of military headdress have been offered for sale at the specialist militaria shops and at the salesrooms of those auction houses that hold specialised militaria sales. This may well have had an effect on the value of those helmets that have been offered for sale during the period concerned, which again is not good news for all collectors of British cavalry helmets.

Finally with regard to the helmets of the Household Cavalry Regiment, should the trial pattern polymer based skulls as mentioned in Chapter: 4. under the heading *'Towards 2000 and Onwards'* eventually be adopted, this may result in those helmets having a metal skull being gradually phased out when the condition of those helmets eventually reaches a state that makes them beyond economical repair. This might eventually also have an impact on the full dress uniform worn by the musicians in the band of the 1st The Queen's Dragoon Guards, and in the band of The Royal Dragoon Guards whose members currently wear helmets having metal skulls.

Should in the course of time the day come when helmets when metal skulls are phased out, this may well have the effect of making these helmets rarer and therefore more desirable to collectors, which will almost certainly increase their value considerably. Looking even further ahead, should in the future cavalry helmets with polymer based skulls ever come onto the 'open market', I would suggest that initially they may be treated with suspicion as was the case with the fibre glass lance caps adopted by the 16/5th Lancers. Eventually however, the time may come when there have been sufficient numbers of these helmets having the polymer based skull sold at either auction, or at militaria shops, when they will no doubt become accepted as collectable militaria items.

Replacement Plumes for the Helmet

To me, a helmet without its plume is incomplete, for surely the plume is the 'crowning glory' of a cavalry helmet.

I can recall visiting a military tailor and outfitters premises located just off of Savile Row in the West End of London some years ago, were I was permitted to examine two cavalry officers 1871 pattern helmets on display in the window of the shop. Upon speaking to the Sales Assistant, I enquired why both the helmets lacked their plumes, only to be informed that, 'they had paid the refuse collectors to take them away when they had had a clear out of the premises some years ago'. Readers can, I am sure imagine my feelings when being informed of this wanton destruction of these most collectable and rare items.

Whilst genuine examples of either officers, or other ranks pattern plumes for helmets of British regular cavalry regiments, are on rare occasions offered for sale, at either auction salesrooms or at specialist militaria shops, the plumes for yeomanry helmets appear never to be offered for sale. On the infrequent occasions that a regular cavalry regiments plume is offered for sale by auction, it is often accompanied by other sundry items of militaria such as belt buckles, cap lines, waist belts etc., and is therefore sold as 'a lot'. The price realised for such a 'lot' obviously encompasses all the items included which therefore makes it difficult to estimate the actual value of the plume itself.

Not withstanding the above, before concluding this particular chapter, I have assembled below a short selection of officers and other ranks pattern horsehair plumes that have sold over the past seventeen years at the salesroom of Wallis and Wallis (W & W), together with two examples from Bosleys salesroom. N.B. The descriptions below are reproduced approximately as they appeared in the relevant sales catalogue.

The Life Guards

1982 March W & W £44.
A good special pattern white horsehair plume for Life Guards **troopers** helmet. Brass rod and nut, with ball top, plain white metal rosette. VGC.

1987 Nov W & W £30.
A Victorian Life Guards O.R.'s white horsehair plume in japanned tin case. GC. (cup missing), and a khaki cover for tropical helmet. GC.

1997 July W & W £115.
A good white hair plume for Life Guards **officers** helmet, with spike, screw on ball and plain rosette. Near VGC.

Royal Horse Guards

1983 Sept W & W £16.
A good red hair plume for RHG troopers helmet. VGC. (no rosette).

1986 Oct W & W £60.
A red helmet plume of **Field Marshal Earl Haig,** in its shaped tin case with brass plate engraved "Field Marshal, Earl Haig K.T. Royal Horse Guards". GC. (tin paint worn).

1993 Oct W & W £100.
A good RHG **officers** scarlet plume with gilt ball and large rosette. In its tin case with nameplate "Captain Burns, Royal Horse Guards". GC. The gilt good. N.B. **This named plume sold at Wallis & Wallis in September 1984 for £30., and again in October 1991 for £140. It is most unusual that on the last occasion the price realised was lower than the previous sale price.**

Dragoon Guards

1st Dragoon Guards

1984 May W & W £55.
A black hair plume with brass rosette for **Albert** pattern helmet, plus white plume & 12th Lancers plume. Average GC.

1986 Nov W & W £60.
A red horsehair plume for KDG troopers helmet with small brass rosette. GC.

1997 July W & W £130.
2 scarce hair plumes for 1st Dragoon Guards helmets with spikes and brass rosettes. In tin case with approx. 30 rolls of lace. GC.

2nd Dragoon Guards & 1st Dragoons

1989 May W & W £90.
A black hair plume for **Albert** pattern helmet (rosette missing). Cap lines, a gilt buckle, waistbelt & slings. Average GC. N.B. **This plume could have belonged to a helmet of any of the Dragoon Guards regiments and the 1st & 6th Dragoons Pre 1855.**

1991 Nov W & W £60.
2 Dragoon Guards O.R.'s black plumes with brass rosettes, 2 green hair plumes, and other fittings.

3rd Dragoon Guards

1986 Sept W & W £60.
A black over red horsehair plume for troopers helmet with brass rosette. VGC.

1995 Oct Bosleys £25.
A troopers black over red horsehair, complete with screw and bolt. GC.

4th & 6th Dragoon Guards and also the 6th Dragoons

1984 June W & W £75.
A good white horsehair plume for **officers 'Albert'** pattern helmet with gilt rosette. GC.

1996 March W & W £70.
A good white hair plume with gilt rosette for officers 'Albert' pattern helmet, original looped nut. Near VGC.

5th Dragoon Guards

1982 Dec W & W £25.
A white & red horsehair plume with brass rosette for 5th Dragoon Guards troopers helmet. VGC.

1986 Nov W & W £55.
A white over red plume for 5th Dragoon Guards troopers **'Albert'** pattern helmet with brass rosette. GC.

1993 June W & W £80.
A red & white hair plume with brass rosette for 5th Dragoon Guards O.R.'s helmet. GC. And a relic white metal helmet FC.

1997 June W & W £60.
2 good Dragoon Guards O.R.'s hair plumes. Black and red for 3rd Dragoon Guards, white and red for **5th DG.** In makers wrapping, both with small brass rosettes. GC to VGC.

7th Dragoon Guards

1989 May W & W £90.
An **officers** black over white hair plume of the 7th Dragoon Guards with large rosette. In its tin case. GC.

1998 Dec Bosleys £70.
A scarce example. Black over white regimental pattern horsehair plume with gilt rose boss. Complete with locking nut to the thread. Contained in original tin. Near VGC.

Appendix II

Past and Present Titles of the Household Cavalry, Dragoon Guards, and Dragoon Regiments

The Household Cavalry

1st and 2nd Life Guards

1660 His Majesty's 1st, 2nd, and 3rd Troop of Horse Guards.
1661 The Scottish (or 4th) Troop of Horse Guards was raised in Edinburgh, Scotland.
1678 1st, 2nd, and 3rd Troops of Horse Grenadier Guards raised.
1686 4th (Scottish) Troop of Horse Grenadier Guards are raised.
1709 The 1st, 2nd, and 3rd Troops of Horse Grenadier Guards are retitled the 1st Troop of Horse Grenadier Guards, with the 4th(Scottish) Troop being retitled the 2nd Troop of Horse Grenadier Guards.
1746 3rd and 4th Troops of Horse Guards are disbanded.
1788 The 1st Troop of Horse Guards and the 1st Troop of Horse Grenadier Guards amalgamated to become the 1st Regiment of Life Guards, with the 2nd Troop of Horse Guards, and the 2nd Troop of Horse Grenadier Guards combining, and being retitled the 2nd Regiment of Life Guards.
1922 The 1st and 2nd Regiment of Life Guards merged to form The Life Guards (1st and 2nd).
1928 Retitled: The Life Guards. (June 1928).
1992 **The Household Cavalry Regiment** (19th October 92) (96).

Royal Horse Guards

1661 The Royal Regiment of Horse (also known as *Earl of Oxford's Regiment of Horse*).
1685 Royal Regiment of Horse (Guards).
1714 Royal Regiment of Horse Guards.
1875 Royal Horse Guards
1891 Royal Horse Guards (The Blues).
1969 Merged with The Royal Dragoons (1st Dragoons) to become The Blues & Royals (Royal Horse Guards & 1st Dragoons). (29th March 1969).
1992 **The Household Cavalry Regiment** (19th October 1992) (97).

The Dragoon Guards

1st Dragoon Guards

1685 The Queen's Regiment of Horse (2nd Horse).
1714 The King's Own Regiment of Horse.

1746 1st (or The King's) Regiment of Dragoon Guards.
1856 1st (King's) Dragoon Guards.
1920 1st King's Dragoon Guards.
1959 Merged with the 2nd Dragoon Guards (1st January 1959).
1st The Queen's Dragoon Guards.

2nd Dragoon Guards

1685 *The Earl of Peterborough's Regiment of Horse*.
1715 The Princess of Wales's Own Regiment of Horse.
1727 The Queen's Own Royal Regiment of Horse.
1746 2nd or Queen's Regiment of Dragoon Guards.
1870 2nd Dragoon Guards (Queen's Bays).
1921 The Queen's Bays (2nd Dragoon Guards).
1959 **1st The Queen's Dragoon Guards** (1st January 1959).

3rd Dragoon Guards

1685 *The Earl of Plymouth's Regiment of Horse* (ranked as 4th Horse).
1746 3rd Regiment of Dragoon Guards.
1765 3rd (The Prince of Wales's) Dragoon Guards.
1921 3rd Dragoon Guards (Prince of Wales's).
1922 Merged with the 6th Dragoon Guards
3rd Carabiniers (The Prince of Wales's Dragoon Guards).
1971 Merged with the Royal Scots Greys (2nd Dragoons). (2nd July 1971).
The Royal Scots Dragoon Guards (Carabiniers and Greys)**.**

4th Dragoon Guards

1685 *Arran's Horse* (or Cuirassiers).
1687 re-ranked as 5th horse.
1715 The Prince of Wales's Own Regiment of Horse.
1746 1st Horse (Irish Establishment).
1788 4th (Royal Irish) Dragoon Guards.
1921 4th Royal Irish Dragoon Guards.
1922 Merged with the 7th Dragoon Guards (April 1922).
4th/7th Dragoon Guards.
1936 4th/7th Royal Dragoon Guards (October 1936).
1992 Merged with the 5th Royal Inniskilling Dragoon Guards (1st August 1992).
The Royal Dragoon Guards

5th Dragoon Guards

1685 The *Earl of Shrewsbury's Horse* (ranked as 7th Horse).
1698 Re-ranked as 6th Horse.
1746 2nd Horse (Irish Establishment).
1788 5th Dragoon Guards.
1804 5th (Princess Charlotte of Wales's) Dragoon Guards.
1920 5th Dragoon Guards (Princess Charlotte of Wales's).
1922 Merged with 6th Dragoons (April 1922). 5th/6th Dragoons.
1927 5th Inniskilling Dragoon Guards (May 1927).

1935 5th Royal Inniskilling Dragoon Guards (June 1935).
1992 Merged with the 4th/7th Dragoon Guards (1st August 1992).
The Royal Dragoon Guards.

6th Dragoon Guards

1685 *The Queen Dowager's Regiment of Horse* (also known as *Lumley's Horse)*.
1691 The Carabineers, also 1st Carabineers (now ranked as 8th Horse).
1746 3rd Regiment of Horse (Irish Establishment).
1756 3rd Horse or Carabineers.
1788 6th Dragoon Guards.
1826 6th Dragoon Guards (Carabineers).
1855 6th Dragoon Guards (Carabiniers). (Spelling changed).
1920 The Carabiniers (6th Dragoon Guards).
1922 Merged with the 3rd Dragoon Guards.
3rd Carabiniers (the Prince of Wales's Dragoon Guards).
1971 Merged with the Royal Scots Greys (2nd Dragoons). (2nd July 1971).
The Royal Scots Dragoon Guards (Carabiniers and Greys).

7th Dragoon Guards

1688 The *Earl of Devonshire's Horse* (also known as *Cavendish's Horse)*.
1692 Re-ranked as 8th Horse.
1746 4th Horse (Irish Establishment).
1788 7th (Princess Royal's) Dragoon Guards.
1921 7th Dragoon Guards (Princess Royal's)
1922 Merged with the 4th Dragoon Guards
4th/7th Dragoon Guards (April 1922).
1936 4th/7th Royal Dragoon Guards (October 1936).
1992 Merged with the 5th Royal Inniskilling Dragoon Guards (1st August 1992).
The Royal Dragoon Guards (98).

The Dragoons

1st Dragoons

1661 Tangier Horse.
1684 The King's Own Royal Regiment of Dragoons.
1690 The Royal Regiment of Dragoons.
1751 1st (Royal) Dragoons.
1920 1st The Royal Dragoons.
1961 The Royal Dragoons (1st Dragoons).
1969 Merged with the Royal Horse Guards (The Blues) to become The Blues and Royals (Royal Horse Guards & 1st Dragoons) (29 March 1969).
1992 **The Household Cavalry Regiment** (19th October 1992).

2nd Dragoons

1681 Royal Regiment of Scots Dragoons.
1688 Ranked as 2nd Dragoons.
1707 Royal Regiment of North British Dragoons, also known as *The Scots Regiment of White Horses*.

1751 2nd (or Royal North British) Regiment of Dragoons.
1866 2nd (Royal North British) Dragoons (Royal Scots Greys).
1921 The Royal Scots Greys (2nd Dragoons).
1971 Merged with the 3rd Carabiniers (Prince of Wales's Dragoon Guards) (2nd July 1971).
Royal Scots Dragoon Guards (Carabiniers and Greys).

6th Dragoons

1690 *Conynham's Dragoons* or 6th Dragoons.
1751 6th (Inniskilling) Dragoons.
1921 The Inniskillings (6th Dragoons).
1922 Merged with the 5th (Princess Charlotte of Wales's) Dragoon Guards (April 1922).
5th/6th Dragoons.
1927 5th Inniskilling Dragoon Guards (May 1927).
1935 5th Royal Inniskilling Dragoon Guards (June 1935).
1992 Merged with the 4th/7th Royal Dragoon Guards (1st August 1992).
The Royal Dragoon Guards (98).

Appendix III

Explanation of Abbreviations

Below is listed an explanation for each of the abbreviations used in the text. N.B. All explanations including those relating to honours and awards are listed alphabetically and not by order of precedence.

Bt	Baronet.
C.B.	Companion of the Bath.
C.M.G.	Companion of St. Michael and St. George.
D.C.L.	Doctor of Civil Law.
Dns	Dragoons.
D.S.O.	Companion of the Distinguished Service Order.
D.L.	Deputy-Lieutenant.
ERII	Elizabeth Regina the Second.
ER VII	Edward Regina the Seventh.
F.R.G.S.	Fellow of the Royal Geographical Society
F.R.Hist S.	Fellow of the Royal Historical Society.
F.S.A.	Fellow of the Society of Antiquaries.
G.C.B.	Knight Grand Cross of the Bath.
G.C.H.	Knight Grand Cross of Hanover.
G.C.M.G.	Knight Grand Cross of St. Michael and St. George.
G.C.I.E.	Knight Grand Commander of the Indian Empire.
G.C.S.I.	Knight Grand Commander of the Star of India.
G.C.V.O.	Knight Grand Cross the Royal Victorian Order.
G.R.	George Rex.
GRV	George Rex the Fifth.
GRVI	George Rex the Sixth.
H.I.M.	His/Her Imperial Majesty.
H.R.H.	His/Her Royal Highness.
H.S.H.	His/Her Serene Highness.
J.P.	Justice of the Peace.
K.D.G.	King's Dragoon Guards.
K.B.E.	Knight Commander Order of the British Empire.
K.C.B.	Knight Commander of the Bath.
K.G.	Knight of the Garter.
K.P.	Knight of St. Patrick.
Kt.	Knight.
K.T.	Knight of the Order of The Thistle.
L.G.	Life Guards.
LL.D	Doctor of Laws.
O.B.E.	Officer of the Order of the British Empire.
O.M.	Order of Merit.
O.R.'s	Other Ranks.
P.C.	Privy Councillor.
R.S.M.	Regimental Sergeant Major.
R.E.M.E.	Royal Electrical and Mechanical Engineers.
R.H.G./D.	Royal Horse Guards/Dragoons.
R.Q.M.C.	Regimental Quartermaster Corporal.
Rtd	Retired.
S.F.A.H.R.	Society for Army Historical Research.
S.S.M.	Squadron Sergeant Major.
T.D.	Territorial Decoration.
V.C.	Victoria Cross.
V.R.	Victoria Regina.

Appendix IV

Regimental Plume Colours at a Glance

Household Cavalry	**Plume Colour**
1st Life Guards	White
2nd Life Guards	White
Royal Horse Guards	Red
Cavalry of the Line	
1st Dragoon Guards	Red
2nd Dragoon Guards	Black
3rd Dragoon Guards	Black over red
4th Dragoon Guards	White
5th Dragoon Guards	White over red
6th Dragoon Guards	White
7th Dragoon Guards	Black over white
1st (Royal) Dragoons	Black
2nd (R.S.G.)Dragoons	White
6th (Innisk)Dragoons	White
Yeomanry Regiments	
Berkshire Yeomanry	White
Derbyshire Yeomanry	White over red
Duke of Lancaster's Own Yeomanry	White
Essex Yeomanry	Red
Fife Light Horse	White
Glasgow Yeomanry	Black horsehair or
Glasgow Yeomanry	Green cocks feathers
Hampshire Yeomanry	White
Hertfordshire Yeomanry	Black
Herts Light Horse	Red
Imperial Yeomanry	White
Lancashire Mounted Rifles	White over red
Lothians and Berwickshire Yeomanry	White
Lothians and Border Horse Yeomanry	White
Montgomeryshire Yeomanry	White
Norfolk Imperial Yeomanry	Yellow
Northampton Yeomanry	Blue over white
North Somerset Yeomanry	Black
Shropshire Yeomanry	White over red
South Salopian Yeomanry	Black
Staffordshire Yeomanry	Black, later White
Suffolk Yeomanry	White
Sussex Light Horse Volunteers	None
Sussex Yeomanry	Yellow over blue
Westminster Dragoons	Purple c. 1902
Westminster Dragoons	White c. 1911
1st West Yorkshire Yeomanry	White
2nd West Yorkshire Yeomanry	Black
Yorkshire Dragoons	White

Source References

(1) *The Monthly Army List for October 1897*. Published by the War Office 30 September 1897.

(2) Army Museums Ogilby Trust.

(3) *Head Dresses of the British Army - Cavalry*. W.Y. Carman.

(4) The Household Cavalry Museum, Windsor.

(4A) *General Abbreviated History of Present Day Household Cavalry Full Dress*.

(4B) *The Life Guards, Dress and Appointments*. C. Stadden.

(5) *The Journal of The Society for Army Historical Research*, Volume 18. Published 1939.

(6) 'Royal Personages and Regimental Uniforms 1840-1939'. R.G, Harris. Published in *Journal of the Society for Army Historical Research*. Vol LX1V Number 257.

(7) *Good-bye to Boot and Saddle*. Lieutenant-Colonel The Hon E.G. French D.S.O.

(8) Written correspondence between the National Army Museum, Chelsea, London, and the author 1975.

(9) *Wide Eyed in Babylon* by Ray Milland. Published by Bodley Head.

(10) *Through Fifteen Reigns*.

(11) *The Cavalry Journal* October 1933. Page 586.

(12) *The Household Cavalry Regiment*. R.Manser.

(13) *The King's Guard - Horse and Foot*. H. Legge-Bourke.

(14) Ministry of Supply, Directorate of Equipment and Store. 'A Comprehensive Literary and Photographic Record of Full Dress Clothing.' August 1955.

(15) *Dress Regulations for Officers of The Army*, Pamphlet No 2. 'Household Division'. Published by H.M.S.O, 1973.

(16) *History of the Dress of the British Soldier*. Lieutenant Colonel J. Luard. Published c. 1852. Page 163.

(17) *A History of the British Cavalry 1816-1919*, Volume 2. (1851-1871) . The Marquess of Angelsey. 1975.

(18) *The Journal of the Society for Army Historical Research*. Volume 56. Number 225. Published 1978.

(19) *A History of the 4th/7th Royal Dragoon Guards and their predecessors 1685-1980*. Published by the regiment 1982. J.M. Brereton. Page 232.

(20) *Into the Valley of Death*. John and Boris Mollo. Published 1991 by Windrow & Greene, London.

(21) *The Cavalry Journal,* Volume XXXI.

(22) *Who Was Who 1941-1950*. Published 1951. Adam & Charles Black, London.

(22A) *Burke's Peerage,* 1949.

(23) *In the Finest Tradition*. Stephen Wood. Published 1988 by Mainstream Publishing Co (Edinburgh) Ltd.

(24) *Who Was Who 1951-1960*. Published 1961. Adam & Charles Black, London.

(25) *The Army List December 1901*. War Office.

(26) Wallis And Wallis (Sussex) . Spring Special Sale 1984.

(27) Spink's (London) . Auction Sale held 28th March 1995.

(28) *Head-Dress Badges of the British Army*. Volume One. Hugh King & Arthur Kipling.

(29) *Journal of the Crown Imperial Society*, March 1983. Letter written by W. Lambert Esq.

(30) Sealed pattern helmet plate. 3rd Carabiniers 1929. National Army Museum. Accession No.56414.

(31) A photograph of a mounted troop of the 3rd Carabiniers (Prince of Wales's Dragoon Guards). c. 1930. National Army Museum. Accession No. 4120.

(32) *Soldier Magazine*. Article entitled 'History of the Button' by Philip Wilcox.

(33) *Leopard, The Story of my Horse*. Colonel M. Ansell.

(34) *Soldier On*. Colonel M. Ansell.

(35) Photograph of a mounted officer of the 5th/6th Dragoons (5th Inniskilling Dragoon Guards) c. 1925. National Army Museum. Accession No. 4095.

(36) Photograph of the officers of the 5th Inniskilling Dragoon Guards c. 1929. National Army Museum. Accession No.17595.

(37) *Journal of the Queen's Dragoon Guards*. Volume One. Number 4. 1962.

(38) *4th/7th Dragoon Guards Magazine*. April 1986.

(39) Information given to the author verbally by the late John Collins, a former Regimental Sergeant Major in the 5th Royal Inniskilling Dragoon Guards.

(40) *Royal Scots Greys*. Charles Grant.

(41) *British Military Uniforms from Contemporary Pictures*. W.Y. Carman.

(42) *The Inniskilling Dragoons*. Major E.S. Jackson. 1909.

(43) *The Army List 1839*.

(44) *The Monthly Army List for October 1880*.

(45) *The Gallant Six Hundred*. John Harris. 1973.

(46) *The History of the 2nd Dragoons 'Royal Scots Greys'*. Edward Almack F.S.A. 1908.

(47) The Army List 1882.

(48) The Monthly Army List for July 1881.

(49) *Regiment Magazine*. Issue One.: 'The Life Guards.' Page 37: Field Marshall, The Marquis of Angelsey. Page 13: Kettle-drummer.

(50) *Regiment Magazine*. Issue Two. 'The Blues and Royals'. Page 39.

(51) Photograph of the helmet worn by the Duke of Connaught. National Army Museum. Accession No. 4927.

(52) An article entitled 'The Royal Dragoon 1895' by A.H. Bowling published in *Modelworld Magazine*.

(53) A series of articles by Major Roy Wilson entitled 'The Yeomanry Cavalry' Published in *Military Modelling Magazine,* 1985.

(54) *The Uniforms of the British Yeomanry Force 1794-1914* (*T.U.O.T.B.Y.F.*) Volume: 7. The Yorkshire Dragoons.

(55) *T.U.O.T.B.Y.F.* Volume: 13. 'The East Kent Mounted Rifles'.

(56) *T.U.O.T.B.Y.F.* Volume: 12. 'The Yeomanry Cavalry of Norfolk'.

(57) *T.U.O.T.B.Y.F.* Volume: 2. 'North Somerset Yeomanry'.

(58) *T.U.O.T.B.Y.F.* Volume: 6. 'The Duke of Lancaster's Own Yeomanry'.

(59) *T.U.O.T.B.Y.F.* Volume: 15. 'Staffordshire Yeomanry'.

(60) *T.U.O.T.B.Y.F.* Volume: 5. '3rd County of London (Sharpshooters)'.

(61) *British Military Uniforms*. W.Y. Carman F.S.A. 1962.

(62) *T.U.O.T.B.Y.F.* No: 14. 'Yeomanry Drum Banners and Mounted Bands'.

(63) *Headdresses of the British Army - Yeomanry*. W.Y. Carman 1970.

(64) *The Volunteer Cavalry of Derbyshire*. M.D. Brittain. 1983.

(65) *The Royal Scots Greys*. Michael Blacklock.1971.

(66) A letter in the National Army Museum's bin-book A-G: Yeomanry

(67) *The Yeomanry Regiments, A Pictorial History*. P.J.R. Mileham.

(68) 'British Cavalry Regiments: Fife and Forfar Yeomanry'. Christopher Rothero. *Military Modelling,* Sept 1976.

(69) *T.U.O.T.B.Y.F.* Volume: 10. 'The Yeomanry Force at The 1911 Coronation'.

(70) 'The Hampshire Yeomanry in 1897.' R.G. Harris. *Military Modelling,* July 1978.

(71) Information provided by Bill Mortimer of the Aldershot Militaria Society. October 1992.

(72) *Fifty Years of Yeomanry Uniforms*. R.G. Harris. 1972.

(73) *Hertfordshire Yeomanry and Artillery Uniforms, Arms and Equipment*. J.D. Sainsbury.

(74) *Boutell's Heraldry*. J.P. Brooke-Little. 1950.

(75) *Basic Heraldry*. Stephen Friar and John Ferguson. 1993.

(76) *Sabres to Scout Cars, The Lothians and Border Horse*. A.S. Gardiner c. 1985.

(77) *The Montgomeryshire Yeomanry 1856-1866*. Philip J. Haythornthwaite.

(78) *The Historical Records of the Yeomanry and Volunteers of Montgomeryshire 1803-1908*. Lt Colonel R.W. Williams Wynn, D.S.O. and Benson Freeman Esq. 1909.

(79) Correspondence written by F. Mitchell of Manchester, England, to the author. August 1991.

(80) Description based on a helmet sold at a Buckinghamshire auction saleroom 1996.

(81) Photograph of an other ranks helmet of the Shropshire Yeomanry Cavalry. National Army Museum. Accession No 67008.

(82) *The Monthly Army List for January 1890.*

(83) *The Lyles Arms & Armour Review* 1981. Page 247.

(84) *The Lyles Arms & Armour Review* 1982. Page 225.

(85) *T.U.O.T.B.Y.F.* Volume: 1. 'The Sussex Yeomanry Cavalry'.

(86) An article entitled '2nd County of London (Westminster Dragoons)' by Christopher Rothero published in *Military Modelling Magazine,* May 1977.

(87) *2nd County of London (Westminster Dragoons) Yeomanry - The First Twenty Years*. Major E. Rowe. 1962.

(88) A photograph in the archives of the National Army Museum illustrating an officers Post 1902 helmet plate of the Yorkshire Dragoons disassembled for cleaning, in which the former 1st West Yorkshire Yeomanry titles can be seen.

(89) *Yeomanry Wars, The History of the Yeomanry Volunteers and Volunteer Associated Cavalry*. Peter D. Athawes.

(90) *Cavalry and Yeomanry Badges 1914*. F. Wilkinson. Arms and Armour Press 1973.

(91) *The Shropshire Yeomanry (6th) (Dragoons),* R.A.C. (T.A.) G. Archer Parfitt. Pub by the Regiment 1965.

(92) *Band International Magazine*. Volume 5. 1983.

(93) 'Headdresses of the Yorkshire Yeomanry'. An article by W.Y. Carman. *Antique Arms & Militaria Magazine*. Volume No 1. Issue No 7. April 1979.

(94) *Dictionary of National Biography 1941-1950.*

(95) Written correspondence by F. Mitchell of Manchester to the author 1991.

(96) *A Handbook of British Regiments*. Christopher Chant.

(97) *A Guide to the Regiments and Corps of the British Army on the Regular Establishment*. J.M. Brereton.

(98) *Captain Oates - Soldier and Explorer*. S. Limb & P. Cordingley 1982.

(99) *The Regiment Magazine*. No.8 Vol. 1. May 23rd 1896.

(100) Written correspondence from W.Y. Carman to the author. December 1998.

(101) Written correspondence from W.Y. Carman to the author January 1999.

Selected Bibliography

Suggestions for Further Reading

Angelsey The Marquess of: *A History of the British Cavalry 1816-1919. Volume Two (1851-1871)*: London: Leo Cooper., c. 1975.

Ansell, Michael. Colonel, Sir: *Leopard, The Story of My Horse.* Coggeshall, Essex: Quartilles International Limited., 1980.

Ansell, Michael. Colonel, Sir: *Soldier On.* London: Peter Davies Limited., 1973.

Athawes, Peter D.: *The History of the Yeomanry Volunteers and Volunteer Associated Cavalry.* Aberdeen: The Scottish Cultural Press., 1994.

Barlow L. & Smith R.J.: *The Uniforms of the British Yeomanry Force 1794-1914. Volume: 1. The Sussex Yeomanry Cavalry c. 1981. Volume: 2. North Somerset Yeomanry c. 1981/82. Volume: 6. The Duke of Lancaster's Own Yeomanry 1983. Volume: 7. The Yorkshire Dragoons 1984.* Aldershot, Hampshire: Robert Ogilby Trust.

Brereton, J.A.M.: *A Guide to the Regiments and Corps of the British Army on the Regular Establishment*. London: Bodley Head., 1985.

Brereton, J.M.: *A History of the 4th/7th Royal Dragoon Guards and their predecessors 1685-1980*. Published by the Regiment., 1982.

Carman, William. Y.: *British Military Uniforms From Contemporary Pictures, Henry VII to the Present Day.* London: Leonard Hill (Books) Limited., 1957.

Carman, William. Y.: *Head Dresses of the British Army - Cavalry.* Surrey, England: Carman., 1968.

Carman, William. Y.: *Head Dresses of the British Army - Yeomanry.* Surrey, England: Carman., 1970.

Carman. William. Y.: *Richard Simkin's Uniforms of the British Army - The Cavalry Regiments.* Exeter, Devon: Webb & Bower., 1982.

Chant, Christopher: *A Handbook of British Regiments.* London & New York: Routledge., 1988.

French The Hon E.G.: *Good-Bye to Boot and Saddle.* London: Hutchinson & Co (Publishers) Ltd., 1951.

Harris R.G.: *Yeomanry Drum Banners and Mounted Bands.* Aldershot, Hampshire: Robert Ogilby Trust., 1991.

King, Hugh & Kipling, Arthur: *Head-Dress Badges of the British Army Volume One.* Originally published in 1979, and republished Farnham, Surrey, England: Hugh King., 1995.

Limb, Sue & Cordingley, Patrick: *Captain Oates - Soldier and Explorer.* Batsford Books., 1982.

Manser, Roy: *The Household Cavalry Regiment.* London: Almark Publishing Co Limited., 1975.

Mileham, P.J.R.: *The Yeomanry Regiments - A Pictorial History.* Tunbridge Wells, Kent: Spellmount Limited., 1985.

Rankin, Robert.H. Colonel: *A Pictorial History of Military Head-Dress 1660-1914.* London: Arms & Armour Press., 1976.

Sainsbury, J.D.: *Hertfordshire Yeomanry and Artillery Uniforms, Arms and Equipment*. Welwyn, Herts: Hertfordshire Yeomanry and Artillery Historical Trust., 1980.

Smith, R.J. & Coogan, C.R.: *The Uniforms of the British Yeomanry Force 1794-1914. Volume: 15. Staffordshire Yeomanry.* Aldershot, Hampshire: Robert Ogilby Trust., 1993.

Smith, R.J. & Harris, R.G.: *The Uniforms of the British Yeomanry force 1794-1914. Volume: 10. The Yeomanry Force at the 1911 Coronation. 1998, and Volume: 12. The Yeomanry Cavalry of Norfolk.* Aldershot, Hampshire: Robert Ogilby Trust., 1991.

Stadden, Charles: *The Life Guards, Dress and Appointments 1660-1914.* London: Almark Publishing Co Limited., 1971.

Walton, P.S. Lieutenant Colonel: *Simkin's Soldiers, The British Army in 1900, Volume One.* Dorking, Surrey: The Victorian Military Society., 1981.

Watson, J.N.P: *Through Fifteen Reigns, A Complete History of the Household Cavalry.* Staplehurst, Kent: Spellmount Limited., 1997.

Wilkinson, Frederick: *Militaria.* London and Sydney: Ward Lock & Company., 1969.

Wilkinson-Latham, Robert & Christopher: *Cavalry Uniforms of Britain and the Commonwealth including other Mounted Troops.* London: Blandford Press., 1969.

Williams Wynn, Lt Colonel & Freeman, Benson: *The Historical Records of the Yeomanry and Volunteers of Montgomeryshire* 1803-1908. England: Woodall, Minshall, Thomas & Co., 1909.

Nexus: Regiment Magazine. Issue No. 1. The Life Guards 1660-1994. March 1994. Issue No. 2. The Blues and Royals 1660-1994. May 1994. Issue No. 5. The Yeomanry 1794-1994. November 1994. Issue No. 25. British Line Heavy Cavalry Regiments 1660-1914. Nov 1997. Hemel Hempstead, Hertfordshire: Specialist Interest Limited.

War Office: *Dress Regulations for The Officers of the Army (Including Militia) 1900.* H.M.S.O. Reprinted by David & Charles (Publishers) Ltd., 1970.

War Office: *Dress Regulations for The Officers of the Army 1934.* H.M.S.O. Wembley, Middlesex: Reprinted by Ray Westlake Books., 1986.

The Fond Farewell

The regiment is on parade, ready and eager for the march past, the trooper's easing the stiffness in their joints by adjusting their position in the saddle, and by stretching their legs in the stirrups. The horses are snorting, their tails twitching, their hooves stamping on the parade ground, eager for the off.

Upon the saluting dais, representing his Majesty King George VI, stands H.R.H. The Duke of Gloucester, resplendent in the uniform of the Colonel-in-Chief of the 10th Royal Hussars.

A trumpet sounds, the regiment moves off, led by the Commanding Officer, in his review order uniform of gilt helmet with red and white plume, scarlet tunic decorated with gold braid and lace, blue breeches with a central gold stripe, and black knee boots complete with spurs. His charger attired with regimental pattern harness, and a blue and gold shabraque decorated with the distinctive devices and battle honours of the regiment. Accompanying this officer is his trumpeter, wearing his distinguishing scarlet plume atop of his brass helmet, his uniform immaculate, his trumpet at the ready.

A short distance behind the Colonel is the officer commanding the escort, his plume blowing in the wind, the sun glinting on his helmet, with his sword at the carry position. Following closely behind is a mounted, squadron sergeant major, also in review order, bearing the unfurled regimental standard, and being flanked either side by a mounted sergeant with sword at the carry.

The salute is taken by the Duke of Gloucester, who is obviously moved by this spectacular sight, for was he not once himself, a serving officer in a cavalry regiment, who would well appreciate the time and effort spent in preparing for this ceremony, by both officer's and men alike, not of course forgetting the horses.

Following shortly behind the Escort to the Standard, comes the regimental band led by the kettle-drummer mounted upon the drumhorse, a magnificent example of a piebald. The mounted bandsmen follow closely behind, trotting slowly passed the saluting dais, playing a regimental march, the bass horn, bassoon, clarinet, cymbals, euphonium, trombone, and trumpets, each with its individually distinctive sound.

Finally there comes the regiment itself, the officers in khaki service dress, leading their squadrons, the rank and file dressed in a similar manner. For the rank and file the full dress uniform is never likely be worn again, their magnificent brass helmets, and scarlet tunics have all been returned to the clothing stores, never to be re-issued. Their swords glisten in the sun, and as they pass we hear the sound of creaking saddles, jangling curb chains, the clatter of sword scabbards, and the clomp of many hooves. Amongst this splendour there is great sadness, with tears in the eyes of many a veteran and seasoned trooper, a great many of whom fought in the First World War. For this is the last mounted parade of the regiment, and its **'Goodbye old Friend'** to the faithful horses of the troopers and officers, for tomorrow comes mechanization, and with it the horses replacement - **The Tank.**

Index